Narcissism And Family Law

A Practitioner's Guide

Dr Supriya McKenna (MBBS)

Karin Walker (LLB MCIArb)

 BATH PUBLISHING

Published February 2021

ISBN 978-1-9163023-3-4

Bath Publishing Limited
27 Charmouth Road
Bath
BA1 3LJ
Tel: 01225 577810
email: info@bathpublishing.co.uk
www.bathpublishing.co.uk

Bath Publishing is a company registered in England: 5209173

Registered Office: As above

Dedications

Supriya

For my children, India and Theo.

And for you, our readers, participating with open minds and curiosity.
Let's turn on the light.

"The acknowledgement of a single possibility can change everything."
(*Aberjhani*)

Karin

For my family and friends.

"There is no greater joy, nor greater reward than to make a fundamental
difference in someone's life."
(*Mary Rose McGeady*)

"One person can make a difference, and everyone should try."
(*John F. Kennedy*)

About the authors

Dr Supriya McKenna

Supriya started her career as a family doctor (GP) and magazine health writer in the UK. Having developed an interest in the field of narcissism, she now works as an educator, writer, coach and mentor in this area. She advises professionals dealing with clients who have been affected by narcissistic individuals, and also works directly with those who have fallen victim to narcissistic abuse, including in the area of separation and divorce. She has hands-on experience of the UK Family Court system, and is committed to raising awareness of personality disordered individuals in society at large, in order to minimise the adverse impact they can have on those around them, and to empower victims to break the generational chains of narcissistic abuse.

Supriya is a moderately accomplished singer, an amateur poet, a dog lover and proud mother. She adores the great British countryside, beautiful landscapes and excellent architecture.

Karin Walker

Karin is a solicitor, mediator, arbitrator (finance and children) and a collaborative practitioner. She founded KGW Family Law, based in Woking, UK, in 2012, where her objective remains to guide clients towards the best possible solution that places family first.

Karin is recognised by both the Legal 500 and Chambers and Partners as a leader in her field. She regularly writes on the subject of family law, speaks nationally and internationally on all aspects of family law and has made appearances in the national press and on television. She was an elected member of the Resolution National Committee and chair of the Resolution DR committee from 2014 to 2017.

Karin is married with two children and two grandchildren. She is a Liveryman of the Worshipful Company of Arbitrators and a Trustee of Guildford Shakespeare Company. She enjoys gardening, running, walking her dog and spending time with her family and friends.

Supriya and Karin have also co-written a companion book for clients: *Divorcing a Narcissist: The lure, the loss and the law.*

Contents

Chapter 3: Representing a client with NPD   95

Chapter 4: Representing a client whose spouse has NPD

Chapter 5: Issues regarding children

Chapter 6: Well-being

The Last Word

Glossary

Further reading

Index

Introduction

The law is a profession which characteristically, yet unexpectedly, trails behind others. Lawyers were first permitted to advertise in 1986. In 2019 it was first properly recognised that lawyers, particularly family lawyers, should take some time to focus on their own well-being. This book is written with that need very much in mind.

Family practitioners are empathic by nature. Some might say that empathy is essential to properly equip the family lawyer for their professional role, helping separating couples to resolve their disputes either by agreement or adjudication.

The family lawyer is not only skilled in legal practice; they will also have some insight into psychology and patterns of behaviour, i.e. what makes someone 'tick'. They will spend much of their working life interacting with people, most particularly their own client but also 'the other side' and their legal representative.

Just as UK lawyers have a tendency to fall behind other professionals in terms of marketing and self-help, we are also led by the US in terms of concept recognition. Narcissistic Personality Disorder (NPD) is only now properly becoming recognised in the UK as a personality disorder. People who suffer from this personality trait are highly likely to suffer from relationship breakdown.

Commonly our clients will tell us of the behaviours demonstrated by their spouse, which may cause us to conclude that they have been subjected to abuse at the hands of a spouse suffering from narcissistic personality disorder. But what if that person is your own client? And what if you are subjected to that same abusive behaviour in the role of their legal representative?

The purpose of this book is to help provide you with the tools to recognise and deal with such individuals; protecting the welfare and well-being of your client, and, even as importantly, yourself.

1

A narcissist will be charming, flattering, endearing; keen to win you over into their camp. They may appear confident, self-centred and even arrogant. At some point however, usually in the very early years of their life, they will have suffered some trauma which severely damaged their own self-esteem and ability to empathise with others. The result is an inherent sense of self-loathing and a desperate need to manipulate others to make them feel better about themselves, while at the same time being too emotionally stunted to be able to form any kind of close bond with a partner, children or indeed anyone whom they may encounter.

Such people are often successful in their chosen sphere, and very practiced at drawing those who cross their path into the fictional world which they build around themselves, in which to drown their feelings of self-hatred. The result is a dangerous game of manipulation and deceit.

A very special set of skills is required to support your client in having the strength and resilience to extricate themselves from such a relationship; perhaps at the same time supporting children, who remain in an ongoing relationship with that parent.

Recognising that it is your own client who suffers from this personality disorder is even more important, to ensure that you are not unwittingly lured into a situation which may subject you to abuse, in your role as a professional. Our intention is to help you recognise, at an early stage, individuals who suffer from this disorder, support your clients and protect yourselves.

Of course, as a consequence of the very nature of the disorder, those who suffer from NPD are likely to be involved in a relationship which breaks down, and be in need of legal support. The purpose of this book is not to dissuade you from acting on behalf of the narcissistic client. We hope to empower you to recognise the sort of person this is, enabling you to make choices. Our aim, if your decision is to act, is to endeavour to ensure that you have the skills to provide the service which will be required.

To conclude this introduction, we must briefly address the view that many lawyers also, in fact, suffer from NPD. That may, of course, be correct, but it must be remembered that a lawyer is simply a mouthpiece and scribe for their client, trained to enable the public at large to have their case presented in the best possible way. Although the lawyer will provide advice, they are always acting upon instructions and therefore, although their own personality traits may influence their correspondence and style, it is not the purpose of this book to consider this as an issue.

What is a narcissist?

1

A simple manual to the mis-wired narcissistic brain

The term 'narcissist' conjures up a variety of images. Some think of the selfie-taking social media addict, expertly pouting at the camera. Others may suspect the mirror watcher, staring dreamily at their own reflection. You might guess that it is the combination of selfishness and vanity that makes up the essence of a narcissist. Power crazy politicians may spring to mind, or difficult bosses. You could be forgiven for thinking of drivers of flashy sports cars, or compulsive wearers of designer labels. Mildly irritating. Occasionally infuriating. Difficult at times, even. But relatively benign. Others may think of megalomaniacs or dictators; genocidal generals or crazed murderous lunatics. Cult leaders. Evil villains. People most of us are never likely to meet. Many more may think of 'narcissism' as simply a buzzword, trendy and overused; bandied about, here in the UK, for conversational effect. And a few will believe that, as everyone is a little bit narcissistic (this is correct, by the way), they should discard the term entirely.

The fact is this: in the main, on this side of the pond, Narcissistic Personality Disorder isn't properly understood or even fully recognised. Sadly, we lag behind our American counterparts in this area, both in the medical profession and in the law, and the stereotypes above are not always helpful or accurate. We, the authors, feel it is time for this to change.

Why is NPD not well recognised in the UK?

The International Classification of Diseases and Related Health Problems, Tenth Edition (ICD-10) is used as the gold standard for medical diagnoses here in the UK. At this point in time, what the Americans separately categorise as 'Narcissistic Personality Disorder (NPD)' only gets a brief mention in ICD-10. It falls into the "Other Specific Personality Disorders" section, stated as "including eccentric, 'haltlose' type, immature, narcissistic, passive-aggressive, and psycho-neurotic personality disorders." So it's there, named, and nodded to for completeness, but without any detail. NPD is potentially further lost in translation in the upcoming new edition, ICD-11 (which comes into force in 2022). Here, *all* personality disorders are re-classified into a single diagnosis of 'Personality Disorder' which may be mild, moderate or severe. In other words, NPD is not specifically defined in ICD-11, although it fits the criteria as a personality disorder. The real world impact of this remains to be seen.

However, over in the USA, the DSM-5 (the American Psychiatric Association's Diagnostic and Statistical Manual of Mental Disorders, Fifth Edition) is the authoritative guide to the diagnosis of mental disorders. In this manual, Narcissistic Personality Disorder is described in some detail as one of ten distinct diagnosable personality disorders.

It is clear that 'narcissists' (correctly meaning those exhibiting behaviours consistent with Narcissistic Personality Disorder) exist on our shores as well as in the USA – and recognising their well-defined patterns of behaviour will be empowering to you both as the lawyer who has found themselves representing a narcissistic client, and as the lawyer representing the spouse of a narcissist.

Marriage breakdown is very common in those with NPD, because of the difficult and abusive behaviours that the family is subjected to as a direct result of the personality disorder. No age group and no length of marriage is spared; even (and some might say, especially) the so called 'Silver Separators' are affected.

Understanding the mindset of the narcissistic individual enables the lawyer to predict challenging behaviours, and therefore pre-empt them with effective strategies.

Most importantly, a good percentage of cases which may be seen as simply 'high conflict' actually involve a narcissistically disordered person. Understanding the mindset of the narcissistic individual enables the lawyer to predict challenging behaviours, and therefore pre-empt them with effective strategies.

"Chance favours the prepared mind" (Louis Pasteur)

Of course, as a lawyer, it is not your job to 'diagnose' Narcissistic Personality Disorder, either in a client, or in the spouse of your client, and nor should it be. Many people, understandably, also feel uncomfortable with the concept of 'labelling' when it comes to situations such as these. However, those with NPD exhibit exact, clear, repeatable, defined behaviours which are consistent and predictable. These behaviours, particularly through divorce proceedings and child arrangements issues, cause mayhem. By their adversarial nature, family courts are a playground for those with NPD, providing fuel for such behaviours.

Whether one feels comfortable using a label of NPD or not, the behaviours are occurring regardless. It is not necessary to acknowledge the label of NPD, if you feel it is unhelpful. But we do suggest that by acknowledging the patterns of behaviour, you will be able to approach resulting issues with helpful targeted precision. We also respectfully request that you accept that we will be using the medical terminology of 'Narcissistic Personality Disorder' as well as the terms 'narcissist', 'narcissistic adaptation' and 'narcissism' throughout this book as shorthand for the behaviours which we ask you to recognise. For us, there is no judgement implied in using these terms.

Put another way, in spite of the shorthand, we are not confining people to a label. Individuals are as richly infinite in personality as the number of ways musical notes can be combined to form a symphony; we are simply pointing out recurring behaviours, in much the same way as a musician would recognise repeating themes that occur within different musical works. Every person is a symphony, uniquely original, narcissistic or not.

It's also worth being aware that as only humans, lawyers who encounter these types will invariably find them infuriating. We are all guilty of labelling people in these circumstances; it is easy in our minds to label them as 'difficult', 'mad', 'nasty' or worse. We suggest that rather than reflexly making these unflattering judgements, it would be fairer, more accurate and infinitely more helpful to all involved to use the correct terminology.

How common is NPD?

The lifetime incidence of NPD in the USA is quoted as being between 0.5%[1] and 6.2%,[2] depending on the study and methods used. Clearly more standardised studies need to be carried out on this. What seems to be consistent, though, is that NPD is more common in males, men overall accounting for around 75% of those diagnosed.

> **NPD is more common in males, men overall accounting for around 75% of those diagnosed.**

The figures are also higher in forensic and military populations, and in psychiatric and psychological clinical populations.

We will delve more deeply into the behaviours exhibited by those with NPD after a brief look at the textbook definition, below.

DSM-5 definition of NPD

In the American Psychiatric Association's Diagnostic and Statistical Manual of Mental Disorders, Fifth Edition (DSM-5), NPD is defined in two different ways.

The first is as follows:

- A pervasive pattern of grandiosity (in fantasy or behaviour)

- A constant need for admiration

- A lack of empathy

beginning by early adulthood and present in a variety of contexts.

---

[1] *Torgersen, S. Epidemiology. Oldham JM, Skodol AE, Bender DS. The American Psychiatric Publishing Textbook of Personality Disorders. Washington, DC: American Psychiatric Publishing; 2005. 129-141.*

[2] *Stinson F, Dawson D, Goldstein R, et al. Prevalence, correlates, disability, and comorbidity of DSM-IV narcissistic personality disorder: Results from the Wave 2 National Epidemiologic Survey on Alcohol and Related Conditions. J Clin Psychol. 2008;69(7):1033–1045.*

A person with NPD will have at least five of the following nine criteria:

- A grandiose sense of self-importance

- A preoccupation with fantasies of unlimited success, power, brilliance, beauty or ideal love

- A belief that he or she is special and unique and can only be understood by, or should associate with, other special or high-status people or institutions

- A need for excessive admiration

- A sense of entitlement

- Interpersonally exploitive behaviour

- A lack of empathy

- Envy of others or a belief that others are envious of him or her

- A demonstration of arrogant and haughty behaviours or attitudes

The second, more modern, alternative model for diagnosing NPD is described in a new section of DSM-5 (Section III); the *'Emerging Measures and Models'* section.

In this new model, paraphrased below, NPD is characterised by difficulties in two or more of the following four areas:

- **Identity**. Those with NPD excessively refer to others for their own self-definition and self-esteem regulation. In other words, their own self-esteem and how they see themselves is overly dependent on how others view them. Their appraisal of themselves is either overly inflated or overly deflated, and they may vacillate between the two extremes. These fluctuations in self-esteem directly affect their emotions at any time.

- **Self-direction**. Those with NPD set goals in order to gain approval from others. They have personal standards that are either unreasonably high (in order to see oneself as exceptional) or too low (from a sense of entitlement from others). They are frequently unaware of their own motivations in relation to this. Because of this, they can be high achievers, or the exact opposite, expecting others to provide for them.

- **Empathy**. Those with NPD have impaired ability to recognise or identify with the feelings and needs of others. However, they are excessively attuned to the reactions of others, but only if these are perceived as relevant to the self. They over or under estimate their own effect on others.

- **Intimacy**. Those with NPD have relationships that are largely superficial. Relationships exist to regulate their own self-esteem. Relationships are not fully mutual, as those with NPD have little genuine interest in others' experiences and are driven by a need for personal gain.

In addition to the areas above, NPD is characterised by the presence of both of the following pathological personality traits:

- **Grandiosity**. Feelings of entitlement, either overt or covert; self-centeredness; firm attachment to the belief that one is better than others; condescension toward others.

- **Attention seeking**. Excessive attempts to attract and be the focus of the attention of others; admiration seeking.

Narcissists are therefore neither 'evil' nor 'bad'. Nor are they 'mentally ill' (unless they have some co-existing mental illness, such as depression). NPD is what is known as an adaptation. In other words, this particular personality type has become hardwired into their brains as a result of how they adapted to their adverse environment and upbringing in their formative years.

Those with NPD cannot appreciate (other than intellectually) that others are distinct from themselves, and have needs, wishes, thoughts and feelings separate from their own. It is as if they are stuck in the toddler stage or adolescent stage of emotional development, in which the world revolves around them. You may be struck by this if you take another look at the listed DSM features of NPD.

But whilst those with NPD cannot be considered intrinsically 'bad', some of the behaviours which they exhibit and the traumatic effect these have on those around them are certainly not 'nice' or 'desirable'. They may be acceptable in a three year old, and understandable in a 15 year old, but in adulthood they are abusive. Little wonder, then, that divorce is rife in this group.

NPD cannot be treated with medication. The only treatment is specialist psychotherapy, which can take between five and ten years to have an effect. The vast majority of people with NPD will not wish to be formally diagnosed, as they either will have no insight into their personality disorder, or if they do, they will not see it as a problem. This is a personality adaptation which serves most narcissists well in life as they are able to exploit others without a guilty conscience (due to the combination of a fundamental lack of empathy and a need to see themselves as superior). Only a very very tiny minority (usually the highly intelligent, high functioning variety) will be motivated enough to undergo specialist psychotherapy. Of those that do present to professionals, it is often family members at their wits' end who instigated the process of diagnosis, often as an ultimatum ("Either you go to therapy or we get a divorce"). Of these, most will drop out of treatment as it involves a deeply honest look within, which is often too hard to bear.

The vast majority of narcissists will therefore never be 'cured' or 'changed'.

Interestingly, a study conducted at Queen's University, Belfast, showed that the more obvious type of narcissist, the 'Exhibitionist Narcissist' is actually happier in life than most people. They are mentally tougher, and perceive less stress. For them, there is nothing to fix as the exploitative nature of the disorder largely works to their benefit. It's not hard to see how this could have an effect on the numbers that present for diagnosis and treatment.[3]

Is narcissism on the increase?

Many speak of an epidemic in NPD, with cases on the rise. This may or may not be true, but it seems that many of the traits associated with NPD are increasingly seen as positive attributes to be aspired to such as the ruthless pursuit of wealth, power, status and fame. It may be that narcissistic traits are being culturally embedded in our societies and being normalised as a result. Some psychologists postulate that the modern way in which we build our children's self-esteem may be contributing to a rise in narcissism, with educators and parents telling their children how special and unique they are to make them feel more confident, rather than encouraging them to achieve self-esteem through hard work ("My clever little princess …").

---

[3] *Kostas A. Papageorgiou, Foteini-Maria Gianniou, Paul Wilson, Giovanni B. Moneta, Delfina Bilello, Peter J. Clough. The bright side of dark: Exploring the positive effect of narcissism on perceived stress through mental toughness. Personality and Individual Differences, 2019; 139: 116 DOI: 10.1016/j.paid.2018.11.004.*
Kostas A. Papageorgiou, Andrew Denovan, Neil Dagnall. The positive effect of narcissism on depressive symptoms through mental toughness: Narcissism may be a dark trait but it does help with seeing the world less grey. European Psychiatry, 2019; 55: 74 DOI: 10.1016/j.eurpsy.2018.10.002.

Many believe that social media has a part to play, with numbers of 'friends' and 'likes' conferring an addictive and misplaced sense of self-worth to those with narcissistic tendencies. Carefully curated, photo-shopped and filtered images posted with idealised stories give a sense of the perfect life, none of which bears any resemblance to the messy truth that goes along with being human. People can construct whole new identities, glittering online personas for the world to comment on and to be jealous of. Being an 'influencer' is an actual job, and real life relationships and connections may be waning as superficiality increases.

Even online dating results in people being seen as commodities, not humans with real feelings. Empathy in this arena seems to be on the decline, with ghosting and breadcrumbing being the norm, and hook-ups are easy to find in this new digital age. All of this is fuel to a narcissistically disordered person; an excellent way to distract oneself from the chronic boredom and emptiness that lie at the core of this condition, and to bolster one's fragile ego with approval and validation from multiple sources. Perhaps these environmental factors are also making more people narcissistic, or perhaps they are simply just new ways for those who already have narcissistic personality adaptations to outwardly express their narcissistic behaviours. Only time will tell.

How does someone 'get' Narcissistic Personality Disorder?

> **Even though NPD can be handed down through the generations, the consensus is that narcissists are made, not born – it is not genetic.**

In order to get to grips with the confusing and abusive behaviours displayed by the narcissist, it helps to consider what led to this personality adaptation in the first place. Even though NPD can be handed down through the generations, the consensus is that narcissists are made, not born – it is not genetic.

As a result of how they adapted to their upbringing, the narcissist is deeply lacking in self-esteem and has little sense of a true identity. It's crucial to understand that this is the core wound which leads them to behave in the abusive ways that they do. Almost everything that the narcissist does is done to avoid feeling the emptiness and low self-worth within them.

There are a variety of parenting styles that can lead to NPD. Many are as a result of being brought up by narcissistic parents, but this is not always the case. These styles can also overlap.

1. Conditional love

Children in these households may be brought up to believe that they are only worthy of love and attention when they achieve greatly. When they come first in the music competition or get into the national swimming team, they are showered with praise. When they get 99% in an exam, their parents may still ask if anyone else did better than them. They are not valued by their parents unless they are perfect and the very best in many arenas – the scholarship winner, the most polite child in the room and also the prettiest. Status and specialness is everything, and they are a huge disappointment if they fail.

They are not seen or heard for who they truly are by their parents, and are forced to have hobbies and interests that only their parents see as worthy, rather than being encouraged to explore their own likes and interests. Any attempt to show their real selves is met with humiliation, derision, withdrawal or disapproval. These children work incredibly hard to please their parents, desperate to win their approval and love, caught in a never-ending upward spiral of achievement. They develop a sense of self based on external validation, and a sense of emptiness within. The child comes to believe that they are only lovable if they are flawless, and become deeply ashamed of any areas where they are less than perfect. They have an important role to play for their parents, whether they like it or not. Parental approval and, later, the approval of the outside world become pillars essential for propping up their low intrinsic self-esteem and the image of themselves that they present to the world. Interestingly, as adults, they may describe their childhood as having been ideal and loving, and their parents as good.

2. The belittling parent

This parent, often a narcissist, may be explosive and easily angered. They ridicule and humiliate their children and partner, put them down and invalidate their feelings. They devalue and demean their family and others as a way of inflating their own shaky sense of self-worth, but of course, no child could possibly know this. They may alternate victims within the family unit, so no one is sure where they stand at any time. These children tiptoe around the parent's moods, and may try to avoid them or placate them where possible. "You are useless" may be a common refrain, and the child may internalise this message but outwardly have the need to prove to the world and themselves that they are special, and that the parent was wrong. These children may grow up feeling driven to be wealthy, powerful or famous as a way of justifying their own exist-ences and finding external validation. They may learn that power is an effective tool to use in their own relationships. Alternatively, as adults, they may become afraid of seeking the spotlight, and seek to affirm their sense of specialness by basking in the glow of another. It's easy to see how NPD can be passed down the generations in this way.

3. The narcissistic parent who uses their children as admirers

In these households an exhibitionist narcissistic parent uses their children as their fan club. The children are brought up to idealise the parent, placing them on a pedestal and worshipping them. They are taught not to out-do the parent or seek admiration for themselves, and they are demeaned, criticised and devalued if they do. In return for this adoration, the narcissistic parent rewards them with attention, praise and conditional love. These children can grow up to become so called 'Closet Narcissists'. They have been unwittingly taught narcissistic values and beliefs (and the associated abuse tactics), but tend to shy away from the spotlight, achieving their own sense of specialness or importance by associat-ing with those who they admire. They find may themselves re-enacting their childhood role in their adult life as the supporting actress or actor in another Exhibitionist Narcissist's show, possibly with their boss or partner.

4. The overvaluing parent

These parents, possibly in a misguided attempt to raise their child's healthy self-esteem (possibly as a result of the so-called 'self-esteem movement'), see their child as unique and extraordinary. These parents idealise the child, inflat-ing their achievements and bragging about them, holding up the child as being flawless. They overestimate the child's qualities, and over-praise them, lavishing them with applause even when the child doesn't perform well. They believe their child to be cleverer than they actually are. It may be that the child internalises their parents inflated view of them and comes to believe that they are unique, extraordinary, superior to others and entitled to privileges.

Narcissistic supply and the False Self

Those with NPD do not look as if they have low self-esteem – in fact, in most types, quite the reverse is true. They outwardly project a 'False Self', which they cannot maintain without attention from others (which comes in the form of drama, conflict and adoration). This False Self often appears grandiose or self-assured, and is so convincing and so at odds with the underlying emptiness that a casual onlooker would find it difficult to see what lies beneath. Many refer to this outward image as a 'mask', which can temporarily drop when the narcissist feels threatened or abandoned.

The False Self has an important job to do. It shields the narcissistic individual from facing the truth about themselves – that they are vulnerable, afraid and unhappy – and it defends them against anxiety, depression, panic and emptiness.

Essentially, narcissists require validation from external sources, and this validation must be constant. Think of their False Self as a suit of armour which, although impressive, is constantly rusting in lots of different places. It needs continual repair, patching up and polishing from the outside, from multiple sources. No one source (or person) will ever be enough to keep the narcissist's armour intact.

In other words, narcissists need 'feeding' attention, in some form or other, to maintain the fragile image that they present to the world. This, in turn, props up their lack of sense of worthiness and self-esteem which are otherwise lacking. They need to see themselves reflected positively in the eyes of others, and if that is not available, conflict, drama or attention in any other form will do.

This external validation is what is termed 'Narcissistic Supply'. Without narcissistic supply those with NPD are forced to feel their own sense of unworthiness and shame – this feels like an existential crisis to a narcissist, to be avoided at all costs. Narcissistic supply is the narcissist's oxygen. To a narcissist, the words of Oscar Wilde may ring true: "There is only one thing in life worse than being talked about, and that is not being talked about".

This plays out in the divorce process, a feeding ground for narcissistic supply, where the narcissist obtains it from his or her own lawyer as well as from the spouse, and, often through sympathy, from those around them.

What does a narcissist look like in daily life?

It is commonly accepted that there are four major ways that those with NPD present themselves to the outside world; as the Exhibitionist Narcissist, the Closet Narcissist, the Devaluing Narcissist and the Communal Narcissist. Whilst those with NPD will present predominantly in one of these ways, some overlap is possible, depending on the situation the narcissist finds themselves in, and what works well for them in that situation. There are also subtypes, which reveal themselves in the narcissist's behaviour. Some use sexuality and looks as their means of getting attention (the somatic subtype). Others use their intellect

"There is only one thing in life

worse than being talked about, and

that is not being talked about".

Oscar Wilde

(the cerebral subtype). And some use all of these at various times, in varying proportions.

It's also important to realise that those with narcissistic adaptations, like all people, have a range of individual personality traits. They can be nice at times. They come in many different shapes and sizes. There are as many different outward appearances as there are narcissists. What is consistent between types, however, is their desperate need to cling to feeling special. It's just how they do this that differs.

It is widely quoted that NPD is more common in men (the ratio of males to females is estimated to be around 3:1), but this is actually only true in the Exhibitionist Narcissist category. This might be because brashness, loudness and being overtly competitive are traits which society finds more acceptable in men, whereas female narcissists tend to express their narcissism in different ways, falling into one of the other categories. Closet Narcissists and Communal Narcissists are thought to be equally represented by both genders.

What follows below are descriptions of each of the four major types of narcissist, with case studies to illustrate.

Some of these, if you have not seen such cases first hand, may seem implausible to you; bizarre and over the top, even. However all of the characters are drawn from real life examples, and they are not caricatures; they are not exaggerated for effect. The behaviours in these case histories occur commonly in actual cases of narcissistic personality disorder, unbelievable though they may at first seem. Behaviours such as these surreptitiously go on to become the victim's normal, as their expectations of how they should be treated adjust, little by little, in response to their ongoing abuse. Add in shame that they are tolerating such abuse, worry that they will not be believed by others, the ever present hope that things will go back to how they were when all was perfect and 'trauma bonding' (described in the next chapter), and you have a victim who feels very stuck in their toxic homelife indeed. Leaving the narcissist is a momentous act of courage, and it can take months or years of separation from the narcissist for the victim be able to see things clearly, and to appreciate the full extent of what they were subjected to.

The Exhibitionist Narcissist

Dennis

The Exhibitionist Narcissist (also known as the 'Grandiose' or 'Overt' Narcissist) is the typically extroverted type. They are superficially charming in whatever way works best for them, and on the surface there are unlimited different outward appearances. They may present themselves as the affable buffoon, or the magnanimous entrepreneur. The altruistic pastor, with a dedicated following. The hardworking doctor, the dentist, or the strong, powerful CEO. The housewife, with over-achieving children and the perfect home. The childless housewife engaging in Twitter rants. The failed actress, or the famous actor. Many are financially successful in their chosen fields, but many are not, preferring instead to exploit others financially, as a result of the sense of entitlement which is part and parcel of the disorder.

What is common to all narcissists of this type, though, is their ability to deploy devastating charisma at the drop of a hat. At first they are very likeable indeed, with big personalities and winning smiles.

The Exhibitionist Narcissist

► superficially charming

► the affable buffoon

► magnanimous entrepreneur

► big personalities

► winning smiles

► sense of entitlement

The recipient of their charms often feels flattered that such a person could be shining their light on them. The high functioning narcissists might be able to keep up the charm offensive for years, but lower functioning types will often let other behaviours come to the fore more quickly.

Traits of the Exhibitionist Narcissist tend to stand out less in younger narcissists (think of the arrogance of youth, for example), but as the narcissist ages, they can seem more pronounced and incongruent with reality. (Note that there are cases in which narcissistic traits become less pronounced with age too – it seems very much to be an individual outcome).

Dennis

Sixty year old Dennis is larger than life. Gregarious. Charismatic. Funny, even. He describes himself as a 'property magnate', although he is actually an estate agent, employed by a small local firm.

If you'd ever met him, even in his younger days, you would probably have found it difficult to get a word in edgeways. He has a tendency to shout people down if they try to speak, and he interrupts constantly. Dennis's conversation is purely based upon stories about his life, which he tells in minute detail, holding court for hours around a dinner table. He will talk about people you have never met, and about his job, which he explains in grand terms. And, if he is unfortunate enough to lose control of the conversation at the table, he will start quoting limericks and one liners in a voice so loud that he will actually be shouting, until everyone has to stop their conversations and listen.

Dennis will brag throughout his anecdotes what an excellent memory he has for detail. In fact, one of his favourite phrases, delivered as he taps his forehead with his forefinger, is: "I'm as sharp as they come – absolutely *nothing* passes me by. I'm one clever cookie." He's always been vain too – his locks are the result of expensive anti-balding treatments, and he'll regularly catch sight of himself in the mirror and say: "God Dennis, you're one handsome fella." It's all done with a big smile though, as if he's being ironic. It's disarming. At first.

Dennis might, at some stage, ask you a token question about your life, if you happened to be at one of these soirees. But

Dennis

if your answer lasted more than a sentence, he would start jiggling his hands and legs impatiently, and even humming tunelessly over you, before finally cutting you off. He would not listen to your answer, and certainly would not be able to talk to you further about it. Dennis doesn't do real two-way conversation. He talks at you, not with you.

At these events, his long-suffering wife, Jane, is silent, until asked to confirm something in his stories, which she will jump to immediately with the girly giggle that is expected of her, and which has become automatic over 30 years of marriage. The rest of the time she looks bored, empty, and utterly disengaged. A once vivacious woman, she hasn't felt as if she has been heard or seen for decades. Even her hair is styled the way Dennis likes – long and blonde, when she prefers a short bob. She loves red roses, but Dennis has never bought her flowers, often quoting 'a Chinese proverb' if she ever hints: "The man who truly loves a woman *never* buys her flowers", he would say grandly, making her feel that she should be grateful for this romantic non-gesture.

When she first met Dennis she was in her late twenties, paralysed with grief at the early death of her fiancé. He told her that he'd been sent to her by God to cure her of her grief. That their love was special, unique, perfect. He was dashing, clever and full of life, and her parents were charmed, and happily gave them their blessing to marry. At long last her pain was taken away and she felt lucky as he whisked her away from her parents. But she barely saw them again after that – Dennis made her feel guilty when she went to visit (he would never accompany her) and would punish her with silent treatments that lasted for days, until she came to learn that it just wasn't worth it. He was so lovely to her most of the rest of the time, after all. The same went for her friends – one by one she lost touch with them, and her circle contracted to just Dennis. "It's just you and me against the world", he would tell her. The ultimate romance.

These days, in restaurants, Dennis orders for his wife, without consulting with her, in an upper class accent that bears no resemblance whatsoever to his normal voice. He'll always customise his order somehow – a special side order that's not on

Dennis

the menu, a separate plate of basil leaves perhaps. He's slightly cold and aloof to the waiting staff, but not openly rude, not like you hear narcissists are supposed to be, although Jane cringes at his aggression and impatience when he orders a takeaway over the phone. Dennis always manages to look unimpressed with the food when it arrives, and if there happens to be an overweight person in the restaurant, Dennis will be sure to mention it later, and say how the sight of them eating put him off his food. No one would dare point out that Dennis is rather on the rotund side himself, of course.

When it comes to control, Dennis has taken over most of Jane's roles in the house, except for the most menial tasks, and is also in charge of all the finances and bills. Any changes to the house are decided by him, and all interior design and furniture buying decisions are exclusively his realm. He took control so gradually that she barely noticed, and when she did, she felt she should be grateful to him for trying to reduce the burden on her. A few years ago, Jane was disappointed that when he re-did the kitchen he did not install a new dishwasher in place of the old one, but she did not make a fuss. She just got on with the washing-up as expected, quietly resentful. She doesn't know how she'd cope without him, although she has fantasised about leaving for many years. But she knows that Dennis would try to destroy her if she left, both financially and emotionally – he has made that abundantly clear, with threats to burn down the house if she so much as thought about it. It's too late to leave. Besides, Dennis has convinced her in no uncertain terms that "no one else could ever love her".

Dennis has even stopped Jane, who once loved to cook, from planning and cooking the meals, wearing her down with years of 'good humoured' critiques of her offerings, and she's been downgraded to just cleaning up the mess he makes whilst cooking. She feels she should be grateful, but can't quite artic-ulate why she just feels angry. Dennis's meals are pretty poor, but delivered with such great fanfare that no one would ever dare tell him. He's convinced that he is a superior chef.

Dennis sold Jane's car many years ago, and insists that he does all the driving. Every car journey with him is a white knuckle ride, with blind corners being taken at breakneck speed, and

Dennis

terrifyingly risky overtaking. Dennis accelerates past horses, saying they should not be on the road, and ploughs through puddles, soaking any unfortunate pedestrian who might happen to be nearby, completely unremorseful.

Jane has learned to zone out and dissociate from the experience, closing her eyes and trying to accept that Dennis is an expert driver. He's only written off a few cars, after all. She tries not to remember the time he drove the car through a three foot deep river, and got stuck in it, nor his seeming confusion at not getting to the other side. It was as if he thought he could defy the rules of nature – as if the water should have parted for him. But then again, the rules never do seem to apply to Dennis.

The painful neck she experiences from her head being repeatedly thrown back into the headrest after every journey with him is now something she has simply chosen to accept, as are the points that she has had put on her driving licence for speeding when Dennis had, in fact, been the driver. It would seem exploitation, risk taking, lack of empathy and a belief that the law does not apply to him are particularly prominent when Dennis gets behind the wheel.

Jane's world now revolves exclusively around Dennis's plans and wants. Her only family, her parents, are now dead, but Dennis's family, who have never approved of his wife, have always been in the picture. She had enjoyed working before and, briefly, during her marriage, but Dennis made it clear that he wanted her to be at home, so she gave up a job she loved, even though they desperately needed the money. When Dennis or any of her children are out of earshot and so free to speak, she will tell you, as the outsider, wistful stories of her days at work in hushed tones so that the family does not hear. But as soon as they reappear, you'll be struck by how abruptly and guiltily she changes the subject, and reverts back to her default subservience.

Jane has been accused of having affairs more times that she can remember, with almost any male that comes to the house. Plumbers, electricians, postmen, neighbours – Dennis believes she's been with them all, and if she can convince him

Dennis

that she hasn't had a physical affair, then he will accuse her of being emotionally involved. It's got to the point where she actually feels guilty when he rages at her, and finds herself apologising, reflexly. She's even questioned herself at times, unsure whether she's got it wrong, and she is, in fact, the one behaving badly. Even though she knows about Dennis's propensity for watching pornography on his computer late at night, she still believes that he has higher moral standards than her, because he tells her so. It doesn't even occur to her that he is projecting. That he is the one having serial affairs with younger women he's met at work or online.

When the children were little, money had been extremely tight, but Dennis had insisted upon buying a large house on the very best estate in the area, because image is important to Dennis. He justified it in financial terms, in his usual overbearing, know-it-all way. It seemed to make sense to his wife at the time, and she bowed to his superior intellect.

But the house was a wreck, needing years of work doing on it, and Dennis put his young family to work on it with him, as they could not afford tradesmen. All the work done on the house had to be absolutely perfect – not even the slightest bump in the walls. It was extremely slow going, and the young children would spend endless hours sanding down woodwork to get it ready for Dennis's painting. It took decades for the house to be finished, and the children spent their entire childhoods living in a building site. And when the lounge was finally finished to perfection, with a flawless white carpet and a glittering chandelier, the room was locked by Dennis, and opened only occasionally for visitors, his own children having to occupy even less of the house than before.

The family struggled financially as the mortgage payments were huge – they actually went hungry at times and were poorly clothed. But, as the breadwinner, Dennis would always find enough for a couple of pints of beer in the pub, and would sometimes tantalise his young children by returning to the house with an Indian takeaway for just himself. His wife, his enabler, never said a word about her rising resentment.

Dennis

Many years later, upon the death of her parents, Jane's inheritance got them out of the financial hole they had been in. There was no question what it would be used for – paying off some of the mortgage and an eye-wateringly expensive holiday to the Seychelles. It wasn't her cup of tea at all, but Dennis insisted. He spent the fortnight asking her to cover up and leaving her alone in the room at night whilst he 'talked property' with the wealthy holiday makers whose approval he secretly sought.

In the early days, Dennis was prone to terrifying rages, and would smash things up. He would throw their wedding dinner china at the wall, jump up and down on the glass coffee table that used to be Jane's beloved grandmother's, and slash furniture with a knife, threatening suicide as he did so. The children would huddle with their mother as he raged violently, and they never knew what kind of mood he would be in. They did notice, however, that during these uncontrollable outbursts he was able to avoid damaging the antique harpsichord that he had managed to procure. Dennis knew better then to damage such a status symbol, and no one was allowed to touch it, let alone play it. Dennis himself can't play a note but he will tell you that he has a fine singing voice and is a natural musician.

In spite of it all, Dennis's two sons grew up desperate for his approval. At times he would cut all contact with them if they did not succumb to his will – sometimes for years. But in spite of this, their desperate need for his approval and conditional love continued into their adulthoods, even when they became parents themselves. With Dennis, even now, there is always a golden child, although who that is at any one time varies, depending on who aligns with him in the latest invented family drama. For his sons, their wives and their own children, one minute you are flavour of the month; the next, a huge disappointment, or someone who is 'too big for their boots'. There is no in between. His family's successes are either over-celebrated or resentfully downplayed by Dennis and backstabbing and badmouthing is the norm in this family. Under the surface, someone is always getting the silent treatment although, in public, it is always hugs, giant smiles and over the top professions of love. The image of a perfect happy family, to be

Dennis

maintained at all costs. Notably, no one ever dares criticise Dennis though, not even behind closed doors.

And in spite of all of this, Dennis genuinely sees himself as the ultimate family man – a loving father and husband, and his eyes will suddenly well up as he tells you this, for just a second or two. Still moved by and believing these shallow displays of emotion, his adult sons orbit around him to this day, unaware of their roles as mere bit parts in his show. They probably even agree with his own assessment of his fine, upstanding character, so enmeshed are they in his world and in their own dysfunctional upbringing.

Although he might sound like a fictional cartoon villain, there are many real versions of Dennis in homes everywhere. Of course, not all narcissists are as clichéd as Dennis, and most are nowhere near as easy to spot. But even those overt narcissists like Dennis seem to go unnoticed. They simply wreak havoc on the lives of those around them, with controlling abuse, until the day, if it ever arrives, when someone finally plucks up the courage to break free.

And when that happens, the so-called 'narcissistic injury' experienced by the abandoned narcissist leads to even more rage, wrath and abuse. "Hell has no fury like a narcissist scorned", to misquote the proverb. These are the divorces that go well beyond simple acrimony.

The Closet Narcissist

Susan

T he Closet Narcissist (also called the 'Vulnerable', 'Introverted' or 'Covert' Narcissist) is very much harder to spot than the exhibitionist type. The difficulty lies in the outward appearance that the Closet Narcissist projects to the world, which is not immediately recognisable as arising from NPD. They generally appear, on the surface, mild mannered and meek, a little insecure but warm.[1]

The Closet Narcissist looks very different from the exhibitionist type of narcissist because, deep down, although they need to feel special, have a sense of entitlement, are preoccupied with status and have all the other features associated with NPD, they are *afraid to be the centre of attention because they fear being exposed as being inadequate and false.*

Closet Narcissists were taught in childhood that they were not allowed to act as if they were special or seek attention, and they were punished harshly for doing so, often by a narcissistic parent, who wanted them to admire them and cater to their needs instead. Like the exhibitionists, they desperately need external validation to crush their core feelings of low self-esteem and inadequacy, but they have to go about getting this feeling of specialness using covert tactics.

Most often they try to feel special *by association*, by attaching themselves to a person, cause or object that they hold up as being special. Then, rather than

---

[1] *The Emerging Self (1993), James F Masterson.*

asking people to admire them directly, they divert attention away to this third party, asking people to admire it instead, whilst basking in the reflected glory, soaking up its perfection, wonderfulness, uniqueness and entitlement to special treatment. They often consider themselves as 'the wind beneath the wings' of another.

The problem with this is that they have made an emotional investment in whatever it is they have idealised, so when that person, cause or object falls off its pedestal, there is no more glory in which to bask. This is when they find their true feelings of inadequacy are exposed, and depression hits. Depression is more common than in the Exhibitionist Narcissists, who are not emotionally invested in people and objects in the same way as the Closets, as they use them merely as mirrors to reflect back their own perceived greatness rather than as the *source* of their own importance.

Closet Narcissists can be manipulative, talking behind others people's backs, and resentful and envious of others who do get noticed. They tend to play the victim in order to secure attention, and may work hard at their jobs to covertly get noticed. Compared to their exhibitionist cousins, they can be more defensive and might view others as being more hostile.

The Closet Narcissist

- ► mild mannered and meek

- ► insecure but warm

- ► plays the victim

- ► need to feel special by association

- ► preoccupied with status

- ► afraid to be the centre of attention

- ► sense of entitlement

Susan is 55. She's quietly spoken, with a gentle manner. Susan comes across as articulate and thoughtful, and she dresses her plumpish figure in tasteful, reasonable quality clothes.

She goes through cycles – at times you won't find Susan out of doors without full, expertly applied makeup, even just for a trip to the supermarket, and her hair will be nicely styled any time she leaves the house. But at other times she will make no effort at all, hoping to just slip by unnoticed. She's just a perfectly decent woman, who listens to Radio 4, never misses her favourite soap opera, reads every Booker prize nominated novel, and enjoys following people on Facebook. Even though she's in her fifties, she still talks about all the games she played with her perfect baby son when she was a stay at home mum. She seems kind. Giving. A little shy. A little put upon perhaps. But otherwise the very image of a devoted mother, step-grandmother and wife.

Susan came from a working class background. Her father was a brutish man who undermined her confidence at every turn, telling her that she was "no bloody good" and yet expecting her to idolise him. Secretly she knew she wanted greater things, and decided from an early age to escape into a better social class.

Susan can't remember ever having spoken like the rest of her family, and her voice never bore a trace of the Yorkshire accent she was surrounded by. In fact, so different was her accent to all those her around her, including her three siblings, that her nickname was 'Duchess'.

Susan left school at 16 with a few basic qualifications, but she wanted more for her life than just to stay in the town where she grew up. She applied herself to diligently learning typing and secretarial skills and, a few years later, secured a job as a secretary in a small solicitor's firm in the South of England, miles away from her family.

Within weeks, Susan had become enthralled with her boss, Roger. To her Roger was perfect. A high earning lawyer, who was clever, sophisticated and debonair. She stayed late at the

Susan

office and worked as hard as she could to get his attention. She would live for the occasions that Roger would buy her lunch as a thank you for all her hard work, and eventually her adoration paid off. Within a year Roger had left his wife and children to be with Susan, twenty years his junior. It was a whirlwind romance, and Susan made sure she was to Roger everything his wife was not, throwing herself 100% into her role as the perfect partner for him. The fact that he was special, and had chosen her, made her feel special too, and she believed she was the envy of her peers and family.

She delighted in buying Wedgewood china for their new flat and made sure Roger's wardrobe had all the accoutrements befitting of such a high status man. Designer silk ties, expensive cufflinks, handmade shoes – all the things his wife hadn't deemed him important enough to have.

She didn't object when Roger bought her a new top-of-the-range car, but she would quietly tell other people that she was embarrassed about driving it as it felt like she was showing off. This became a pattern, Susan always managing to subtly find fault with things, albeit in her gentle, self-effacing, 'I'm not good enough' sort of way. He should have given the flowers he bought her to his mother as they were her favourite blooms; she felt too self-conscious to wear the stunning diamond necklace he'd bought (although she casually dropped it into conversation with others); the surprise pamper day at the spa was a lovely treat but not her sort of thing, and so on.

Susan's cooking skills quickly made her the 'hostess with the mostest', initially winning favour with Roger's friends, but she never seemed to make any meaningful friendships of her own. When one of his friends' wives, who was much older than her, did not invite her to her daughter's hen party, Susan took it personally and cried for hours on end about how humiliated she felt at her insensitivity. "That's the last time I invite *her* for dinner," she fumed to herself, once her tears had subsided, and she resolved to give the wife in question the cold shoulder from that day on. She couldn't help but spread a little malicious gossip amongst the wives about the woman in question too, suggesting that she was worried about her mental health.

After a year or so, Roger started trying to encourage Susan to take up a hobby in order to make some friends, but Susan resisted, making up excuse after excuse. Unknown to him, Susan would moan to her family about how desperate she was to take an evening art class and join a book club, but how she felt that Roger would be upset with her if she went out, especially as he worked such long hours. Susan was an expert at playing the victim, telling others how she was missing out under the guise of putting someone else's needs above her own. This was a pattern that continued throughout her life and interactions with others.

The reality was that it was Susan who didn't like Roger going out in the evenings or weekends. Whilst initially she supported his interests, telling him how much she admired him for them, and cheering at the finish lines of his running and cycling races, once she felt secure in their relationship, she grew tired of them. She would go quiet when it was time for him to go out, and would barely speak to him for 24 hours afterwards, although she would tell him, monosyllabically that it was fine, and that nothing was wrong. Susan hated being left on her own.

Roger, a sensitive soul, couldn't stand these silent treatments, and slowly gave up his hobbies, including his longstanding poker night with pals. Susan was delighted, and rewarded him with wonderful romantic dinners and passionate nights on the evenings when he would have previously been out. Roger's young partner had him hooked, and he ignored his gut instinct that something was wrong. He even found himself cutting himself off from any of his friends who tried to broach the subject of Susan's isolating behaviour. In time, Roger became drawn into Susan's romantic notion that they didn't need anyone else in their lives.

The wedding was a tiny affair – just a few close family members were invited, as Susan said she didn't want to be in the spotlight. She fell pregnant very quickly, and the birth itself was long and traumatic. Susan still revels in telling stories about it, referring to it as the best day of her life. She carries the baby's hospital wristband around with her in her handbag

Susan

to this day, even though Sebastian is now grown up – a clear token of her commitment to her family and motherhood.

Roger and Susan decided to take it in turns to bottle feed the baby at night, but when it was Roger's turn, she would stay awake anyway, not really trusting him to do it right. On her nights she would become cross with Roger if he fell asleep, expecting him to be on standby for her if she needed anything, even though by this time Roger was back at work. Contrary to her version of events, Susan did not cope well with motherhood, and Roger wondered whether she had postnatal depression. He felt that he couldn't do anything right, from the way he cooked, to the vacuuming, to even the way he made her coffee. She told her family, behind his back, that Roger was never home and was unsupportive, in spite of his hard work in the home and the increasing number of chores that she considered to be 'blue jobs'. By the time Sebastian was a year old she was out of control – she would start arguments in the car about Roger's driving and would regularly pull at the wheel or try to stop the car by pulling on the handbrake.

Roger and her mother encouraged her to visit her GP at this point, but Roger was confused when she came back from the surgery with a note for him, telling him that the doctor had signed *him* off work for two weeks, on the grounds that *he* was behaving oddly, and that he needed to see the doctor to be assessed for depression.

Susan was sure from the day that Sebastian was born that he was destined for great things and would one day follow in his father's footsteps as a great lawyer. Even as a baby she dressed him up in little suits. But when Sebastian had been at school for a few years, it became clear to his teachers that he was behind on his reading, and they asked Susan and Roger if they would consider having him tested for dyslexia. Susan was disgusted at the suggestion, and felt that the school were shaming Sebastian, and her. She moved him to a fee-paying school, on the understanding that dyslexia was never brought up again by the teachers. Roger just went along with it, as he now often found himself doing, bowing to her wisdom in such matters.

Susan, for all her quiet proclamations of Sebastian's brilliance to others, would put Sebastian down in private, criticising the way he spoke, stood and interacted with others, and telling him that he was slower than all the other children. When he didn't get the lead in the nativity play she was be deeply resentful of the mother of the child who did, and quietly suggested to the biggest gossip amongst the other mums that she had heard someone say that bribery had been involved.

Susan was to be disappointed at every turn by Sebastian's academic difficulties, but she insisted that if he worked harder he would still be able to become a lawyer. Sebastian grew up resenting his mother more and more and, aged 16, begged her to allow him to have a test for dyslexia. She refused, saying that it was unnecessary.

It became clear to Sebastian over time that his mother could not accept him as being anything less than perfect, as it reflected badly on her. He never did achieve academically and left school to start an apprenticeship as a builder, much to Susan's disdain and embarrassment, especially as Roger's children from his previous marriage had gone on to have high flying careers. Sebastian felt like his 'failures' were seen as a deliberate and personal affront to his mother, something others might criticise *her* for.

Susan was outraged by other people's immoral behaviour, judging them harshly for anything that didn't measure up to her high moral standards, even though she herself had met Roger when he was married.

If Roger was even mildly friendly to a waitress or any other woman, Susan's jealousy would surface, and her mood would spiral downwards. Feeling abandoned and rejected she would accuse Roger of not loving her, with much quiet sobbing. She would move into the spare room for days on these occasions, whilst licking her wounds. Her double standards were never noticed by Roger, and Susan would tell him that as he had been unfaithful to his wife with her, he couldn't be trusted. She would sink into depressions at these times, and many others too.

Susan

From her thirties onwards, poor Susan suffered from a variety of ailments. Her sore fingers, which she was sure was arthritis, were due to her mother teaching her to type when she was young. Her chronic back pain was due to the hours she would spend in her childhood, bent over an ironing board. Her knee pain was caused by her mother neglecting the injury she sustained whilst playing hockey aged 15. When Roger actually required an operation on his knee, Susan, exaggerating wildly, posted on Facebook that she had been told that he might need an amputation. Flurries of sympathetic comments came flooding in, and Roger, who valued his privacy at the best of times, was quietly embarrassed. Roger was dismayed to find her cold and unhelpful after his knee replacement operation, and dismissive of his pain, focusing instead on how miserable she felt about a perceived slight from some superficial acquaintance or other.

In the early days, when Roger's older children from his first marriage visited, Susan would perfectly play her role of caring, friendly stepmother, whilst digging for details of their home, holidays and lives.

Once they had left Susan would quietly express her concerns and worries about how their mother was bringing them up and spoiling them, whilst making a big show of clearing up the house after them, scrubbing every surface excessively, huffing and puffing. She was particularly aggrieved if they kept any of their belongings at her house, making little comments about the 'inconvenience' every now and then. When Roger came upon a notebook in which Susan had detailed all the things that his children had left at the house, and for how long, he realised just how much Susan felt that everyone was taking advantage of her hospitality and generous nature.

When her step-children had their own partners and children, Susan would beg them to allow her to babysit, and would send numerous lonely sounding text messages saying how much she missed them. But when the day came for her to babysit her step-grandchildren, she would always complain to anyone else who would listen about how put upon, used and unappreciated she was.

She would make comments about her step daughter-in-laws' child-rearing methods to Roger, always under the guise of concern, and she took great delight in 'worrying' about the grandchildren's diet and her daughter-in-law's post-baby weight. She would be perturbed about the size of their houses, and would constantly be asking when they would be moving, to give the step-grandchildren more space.

It seemed to Susan that she had the weight of the world on her shoulders with all her worry. If you talk to her now, after serving you tea and cake, she will sigh and admit to you how difficult her life is, having to look after her ailing elderly parents (who live many miles away, and are actually being cared for by her sister), her babysitting duties regarding her grandchildren (who she only actually now sees once a month, and now never to babysit) and looking after Roger (who although he is now nearly 75, is very physically fit).

Susan quietly complains that Roger doesn't like to drive as much as he used to, and seems resentful of the fact that she is now married to an old man. Susan doesn't like to drive in the dark, on unfamiliar roads, at rush hour or on the motorway. She even plans all her drives so that she doesn't have make any right turns, and avoids roundabouts if at all possible. She insists that Roger continues to do most of the driving, even though his eyesight is failing, he is worried that he might crash, and despite the fact that even his children won't let him drive the grandchildren.

Roger has been miserable for years, but cannot put his finger on exactly why he feels so emotionally disconnected from Susan. Susan continues to go silent when hurt, to play the victim, and to make comments about him and his children behind his back. When his children do visit, she will always start an argument at the dinner table, by expertly pressing somebody's buttons, and then leaving the table to go to bed, whilst a heated argument ensues. No one has noticed the pattern yet.

Softly spoken, but passive aggressive, controlling and manipulative. Superficially self-effacing. Playing one person off another, and being quietly judgemental. Creating tension, stealthily. Offering only conditional love and unable to empathise with

Susan

another's pain. The long-suffering daughter, mother, grandmother and wife, who puts the best interests of others above all else. Believing in the fantasy of perfect romantic love with Roger, and being painfully wounded when he fails to deliver. Projecting an image of the perfect happy family to the outside world, but secretly jealous of others. Easily offended and highly sensitive to criticism. Prone to bouts of depression, shame and worthlessness. Secretly needing to believe she is morally and intellectually superior to others, although with no real evidence. And all the while, presenting a quietly charming exterior to the world, contradicted by the fact that she has hardly any real friendships at all.

The Devaluing Narcissist

Anton

T he Devaluing Narcissist is also called the 'Toxic' or 'Malignant' Narcissist.

These narcissists use grandiosity as a defence (e.g. claiming they are the best at something), but when this grandiosity is punctured, and their defences are brought down, they turn on others to bring them down. They exhibit many of the other more general narcissistic behaviours too, but what is more prominent in this type of narcissist is that they devalue, criticise, and demean others in order to inflate themselves. In reality, they are jealous and envious of others but, rather than express this, they put down the other party. They can be sadistic and have a strong sense of schadenfreude. Donald Trump, US President at the time of writing, demonstrates devaluation beautifully, putting down anyone who does not agree with him with public name calling, criticisms, badmouthing and ridiculing.

Those with higher intellect do this more stealthily. They either devalue the person behind their back to someone else: "He thinks his job is so difficult, but really a monkey could do it ..." or they tell the person they are devaluing that someone else has made the comments about them, for example, "My sister is worried that you are pregnant because of your weight gain ..." (meaning "you are fat").

Some believe that these Devaluing Narcissists are actually Exhibitionist Narcissists who aren't clever, talented, funny or charming enough to maintain their image of outer grandiosity, and so turn to devaluing others to maintain their false sense of superiority.

Some narcissists flit between the two types. On good days they are Exhibitionist Narcissists, on bad days, Devaluing. As the lawyer, you may find them magnanimous and charming on one day and corrosive on another (when they will coldly or angrily point out your flaws and refuse to pay your bill). They will always know better than you.

Anton

Anton is 49, and bisexual.

He used to be married to Michelle, with whom he had a child, but after ten years of marriage he left her for Peter, a successful IT architect who works at a big firm in London. Michelle will tell you that, in his wedding speech, the only thing Anton said about her was: "As you can all see, Michelle scrubs up well." She thought it was just his quirky sense of humour at the time, and smiled along with the wedding guests; but this was a pattern that was to continue throughout their marriage.

Anton is a dapper looking chap, always well presented in expensive jeans and perfectly ironed shirts. He has pearly-white teeth, and will flash you a huge winning smile when you see him; initially you cannot help but be drawn in by his friendliness.

Anton will tell you that he's had a variety of successful careers over his lifetime, and explain to you that he has many areas of expertise. You'd be forgiven for thinking that he was the primary earner, if you didn't know better. Most recently he described himself as a designer, but really he had just dabbled in designing expensive things for the large house he shared with Peter. Just two years ago he designed a metal and glass staircase for the house (a bit of a monstrosity, in Peter's view) but Peter had spent thousands on having it made just to keep Anton happy. Anton had seen something similar at a rich American friend's house, and decided that he needed to outdo it.

One thing is for sure; Anton is an excellent blagger. When married to his former wife, he lied on his CV about his qualifications, and was able to get two mediocre sales positions. But Anton lost both jobs after the six month probation periods, for reasons he could not convincingly explain away; but it was clear that his cocky arrogance would have been apparent to his bosses. Amongst other things, his CV tells you that he has been an entrepreneur, a web designer, a copywriter and, in his youth, a surfing instructor. (The truth is that he can barely surf at all, although his brother had been a big name in this sport). In reality, he spent most of the marriage as a house husband, but not a terribly effective one.

On meeting Anton, particularly if you are reasonably presentable, he might look you up and down and suggest alternative looks for you, even if he doesn't know you very well. "Why do you wear so much grey? It's depressing, darling. Try injecting some colour here and there." Or, "Have you thought about going blonde? You look like everybody else with your hair that way. It's so hard to tell people apart these days ..." You might just think he's a bit opinionated, at first. Or you might think he's genuinely trying to help. But over time you'll get used to that sinking feeling at his subtle (and not so subtle) put downs.

Anton is a bit of a show-off. He'll drop impressive things into conversations, and name drop where possible. He enjoys occasions where he can lean back expansively in his chair, his hands behind his head, and talk knowledgeably to an audience about things he considers himself to be an expert in, which is most things. He loves to play 'devil's advocate' when anyone expresses an opinion, but this is now wearing thin, and he has driven away most of their friends. If you want to send your child to private school,

The Devaluing Narcissist

► devalues, criticises, and demeans others in order to inflate themselves

► jealous and envious of others

► puts down the other party

► name calling, criticisms, badmouthing and ridiculing

Anton

Anton will tell you why they should be state educated, or vice versa. If you want to buy a Mercedes, Anton will tell you that what you need is a BMW. If you want to get a dog, Anton will give reasons why a cat would be better. It took Peter years to realise that Anton had no *real* opinions, other than when he felt slighted by another, when his low opinions of them were very real indeed.

In the absence of many deep friendships, Anton began to thrive on Twitter, creating full blown arguments about politics with anyone who would engage, and propagating conspiracy theories as if they were fact. He ranted and raged in the digital space about anyone who disagreed with him, alternately calling them 'hotshots' or 'stupid'. He did have a few people who thought he was great though, mostly younger gay men who he met through the internet, who were impressed with his worldly ways, maturity and wealth. Peter didn't like this at all, but Anton happily took him to their parties, to show him that he was being silly, and they were nothing more than friends. Peter wasn't sure, but knew that he would just have to trust him.

Whenever Anton met someone impressive or new, he would tell Peter how marvellous they were, ad nauseum, dropping them into any conversation that he could with the slightest excuse. He'd text them late into the night, whilst sitting next to Peter on the sofa, and chuckle loudly at their messages, especially when he knew that Peter was feeling a little insecure about them, or they were supposed to be sharing quality time together. If Peter said anything, Anton would accuse him of being paranoid and jealous, although it was Anton who would regularly go through Peter's phone messages and emails.

It was also Anton who would ring Peter constantly if he was at an evening work do, or had a late work finish, and then accuse him of having affairs when he got home. Again, it was Anton who would take Peter's pulse, comment on his breathing pattern, and snarl at him that he could read his mind, whilst accusing him of these affairs. And sadly, it was also Anton who would then refuse to speak to Peter for weeks after these late working nights, coldly blanking him, but he was still able to laugh at whatever sitcom he was watching on the TV. On one

Anton

level Peter knew this was abuse, but when Anton turned on the charm a few weeks later, acting loving and warm, he would forgive it all, grateful to be loved once more, and anxious to do whatever it took to stop these jealous episodes from recurring.

Anton had made a bit of money on a couple of flats in the early days at the start of the property boom, more by luck than design, but he still believes this qualifies him as an expert in all things property related.

After a few years together Peter learned to avoid taking him to friends' and colleagues' homes, finding his know-it-all attitude cringeworthy. And the more lovely the home, the more critical Anton would be. "But why did you buy a house with a north facing garden?" "I know you've finished doing up the house, but have you thought of knocking down this wall and this wall, and going for something more open plan?" "I'm surprised you have so much bedroom space, when you only have one reception room." "What you need is to dig out the floor and build a conversation pit." "You haven't put in a wine cellar?" "Oh, such a shame it's grade 2 listed – you can't replace the whole of the back of it with glass, and it's so very dark inside." "You don't have a larder?" he once said to the owner of a modest house on an estate, whose friendship was very important to Peter. "But where do you store your food?"

These visits would be followed by a journey home during which Anton would launch into an angry tirade about how Peter obviously preferred the other person's house to their own and that if he earned as much as he should, they'd also be able to buy a much better house themselves. He'd then spend days planning another modification to their own home – a bar, a cinema, remote controlled garden fountains. The building work was never ending, but no builder would ever stay for long after dealing with Anton's indecision, rudeness, perfectionism and know-it-all attitude. Peter kept haemorrhaging money on builder after builder, for years, just to try to steer clear of Anton's wrath. He didn't know for a long time that Anton had for years also been viewing houses for sale that were well out of their price range, nor that he'd put down so many false offers that the local estate agents had blacklisted him.

Anton

When Peter and Anton first met, Anton lavished attention upon Peter. He insisted that they spent almost every waking moment together, and they were barely out of each other's sight. He proclaimed his love for Peter within days, and spoke of their soulmate connection. Peter fell head over heels in love, and although he felt guilty about breaking up Anton's marriage, he also felt that he had finally found 'The One'. Anton had all the same interests as him, was a great listener and validated his deepest darkest fears and vulnerabilities. He felt heard, understood and adored like never before, but more than this, he felt valued and respected. Anton would take him out for him lovely meals, insist upon pressing his shirts for him, and would gaze adoringly at him as Peter serenaded him on his classical guitar. Peter felt lucky. Appreciated.

But over the years, Anton's criticisms of Peter grew and grew, and Peter found himself walking on eggshells. It got to the point where he never knew what kind of mood Anton would be in when he returned home from work, and he got used to walking through the door to be met with chaos and mess. It often took him 15 minutes to steel himself to get out of the car, once parked on the driveway. Dirty dishes and bowls were left around the house, chest hair shavings were clinging to the bathroom floor, and wet towels would be thrown on to Peter's side of the bed, leaving it damp. Boxer shorts and clothes would be all over the bedroom floor – Anton would empty drawers on to the floor whilst searching for an item, and then just walk away, expecting Peter to sort it all out. Even the cleaner they had twice a week could not keep on top of the mess, and Peter would find himself launching into the housework as soon as he got home, often having stopped en-route at the supermarket to buy food to cook, as he knew Anton would have been 'too busy' to do it. Most days he had to vacuum the cat hair from the sofa just for somewhere to sit. He tried for years explaining to Anton how this made him feel, but Anton would just look coldly at him and suggest he pay for a full time housekeeper if he didn't like it.

Peter was a keen gardener in his spare time when they met, so Anton developed an interest in this area too. Peter thought this was lovely, as it would be something they could do together, and he was thrilled when Anton decided to commence a gardening course which would lead to an impressive gardening qualification. Although Anton never got around to taking the exams, he started to consider himself to be the expert, and would return from the garden centre with a boot full of plants which he would place and leave in position for Peter to plant, whilst he reclined on the decking, barking orders, and complaining about how long the digging was taking Peter. If it wasn't fun, he didn't feel he should have to do it, although he was happy to reap the rewards of, and take the credit for, someone else's hard work.

Over the years, everything became either a power struggle or a competition. Peter was an accomplished amateur classical guitarist, and so Anton took lessons. When he realised he would never be as good at playing classical guitar as Peter, he began to openly wince at Peter's playing, or try to drown out the sound by turning the TV on to its loudest volume. Once, at a dinner party they had thrown, he even stuck his fingers in his ears and walked out of the room to go to bed, saying he had a migraine, when their guests had asked Peter to play something. And dinner parties became a bone of contention for other reasons too. Anton would leave most of the cooking and house tidying to Peter and then apologise to their guests about the food: "Oh dear, so sorry that Peter's chicken is dry." Peter even caught him stealthily turning up the stove and oven on one occasion, and when confronted he actually smirked. He'd always make a point of leaving the house just before the guests were due to arrive too, under the guise of picking up more wine, and then make his grand smiling entrance once they were there, seemingly oblivious to Peter's stress at being left in the lurch. And then he'd present his own offering, usually a dessert, with such feigned coy modesty, that his guests felt obliged to ooh and ahh in delight.

Anton also seemed to love being late. He was late to everything he could be. He'd arrive at weddings as the bride was walking down the aisle. He would prevaricate for so long about what to pack for holidays, leaving it all until the last minute so that they would miss flights, or end up not seated next to each other on the plane due to late check-ins. He would never manage to make it on time to work, even when he had had a paying job. And they would always miss the first ten minutes

Anton

of the show any time they went to the theatre, as he would insist upon taking his time getting ready, or having a last minute shower beforehand. He would even make Peter late for work on occasions, forcing him to apologise to his boss, and when Peter tried to discuss it, he showed no remorse, instead making a big show of looking bemused as to what all the fuss was about, calling Peter 'square' and 'boring' for wanting to be on time.

In the last year of their relationship, after a frazzled Peter told Anton that he would have to go to therapy if they were to stay together, Anton openly signed up to hook-up websites. He told Peter that he had never been sexually satisfied by him, but that as Peter would never be able to find another partner, he would continue to live with him. Peter was in pieces; an emotional wreck, driven to despair by Anton's cruelty. To Anton, this was just more proof that Peter was mentally unstable, and he'd regularly tell him that he was 'crazy'. Anton calmly and logically explained that he did not see why it should be a problem him having other partners whilst living with Peter, as it was 'just sex'. He even began to taunt Peter, telling him that he had 250 men interested in him, and messaged them openly. But when Peter stayed out one night at a friend's house, just to clear his head and get out of the house, Anton was livid, demanding to know where he had been and what he had been doing. The hypocrisy of this did not seem to register with him, and Peter, increasingly worried about his behaviour, spoke to his doctor, genuinely wondering whether Anton might have early dementia or a brain tumour.

Another day, during another taunting about his sexual partners, a distraught Peter grabbed Anton by the shoulders in desperation, shaking him to get his attention, tears flooding down his face. Anton threw him off violently. Later he calmly told Peter that he had called the police about the 'assault' and that they had told Anton that Peter would have to leave the house immediately or be arrested. Even through his agony, Peter knew that this was another fabrication.

Several months later, after many failed attempts during which Peter would always end up taking Anton back, Peter finally plucked up the courage to throw Anton out of the house

Anton

forever. Anton badmouthed Peter to everyone they knew, including his work colleagues, telling them that he was an abusive, violent, drug addict.

Thankfully, they had never married. Anton moved straight into another relationship, whilst Peter was left to mourn. He was not only grieving the loss of the relationship but coming to terms with the realisation that the relationship had never been about love; not as he understood it, anyway. The whole relationship had been a shallow lie.

Devaluing Narcissists are the narcissists who gain a sense of importance and superiority by putting others down, either subtly and behind their backs (if they are intelligent) or harshly and to their face if less so. They cannot bear others' successes, they see everyone as competition and are constantly comparing themselves to others.

They are particularly prone to vengeful behaviour in divorce and will stop at nothing to bring the other party down. They must win, at all costs, and compromise is not an option.

The Communal Narcissist

Jill

The Communal Narcissist (or 'Altruistic' Narcissist) might, at first glance, appear to be a contradiction in terms. These are the narcissists who prop up their self-esteem and sense of specialness by giving to others. They obtain admiration, attention and a sense of specialness ('narcissistic supply') from good works and deeds, seeing themselves as the *most* generous, the *most* caring, the *most* kind.[1]

They may start off in this vein with their significant others, but eventually their narcissism comes at the expense of those closest to them. They pride themselves on being 'nice', but quite often they give themselves away by becoming overly territorial in whatever arena they are practising their altruism. Whether they are intentionally deceiving others is unclear – it may be that they are trying to convince other people of their niceness in order to deceive themselves.

Again, overlap between the different types of predominant narcissistic types can occur. For example, an Exhibitionist Narcissist can act as a Communal Narcissist in certain situations if it works to bring in narcissistic supply, say by giving a homeless person a large sum of cash when they have an audience to witness their generosity.

---

[1] *Gebauer, Jochen, Constantine Sedikides, Bas Verplanken, and Gregory Maio, "Communal Narcissism," Journal of Personality and Social Psychology (2012), vol. 103, no.5, 854-878.*
Fatfouta, R., & Schröder-Abé, M. (2018). A wolf in sheep's clothing? Communal narcissism and positive implicit self-views in the communal domain. Journal of Research in Personality, 76, 17-21.

J ill, 50, is a devout Catholic, and will quietly bow her head and clasp her hands together piously as she takes Holy Communion, every Sunday, without fail.

She takes pride in having the barest of wardrobes – just a handful of long dresses hang inside, mostly picked up from charity shops, but you might notice that they do accentuate her ample bosom rather well.

Jill is heavily involved with the church, organising church fêtes and jumble sales, and she bakes a mean lemon drizzle cake; hers are always the first to sell out at the charity cake sale (on account of her secret recipe, which she will be taking with her to the grave).

Jill loves nothing more than to be right hand woman to Father Jameson, her priest, and she loves it when he tells her that she is 'a blessing'. "Ah, what would we do without our Jill?" he will say, and "Of course, a special mention goes to Jill McDonnell, without whom this fête would most certainly not have been possible – there'll be a special place in heaven for you, Jill, so there will …."

Jill works part time at the local convenience shop. Her name badge says 'Jolly Jill' on it, and she has a little sign propped up by her till with inspirational quotes on it, which she changes regularly. "No one has ever become poor by giving (Anne Frank)" is one of her favourites, and "There is no love without forgiveness".

"My empathy levels are off the chart," she will tell you as she scans and packs your groceries. "I just couldn't sit by and watch those poor children in Africa without helping".

The Communal Narcissist

► gives to others publicly

► does good works and deeds

► prides themselves on being 'nice'

► sees themselves as the *most* generous, the *most* caring, the *most* kind

► can be territorial

► is abusive behind closed doors

"There's just something about my face that makes people want to tell me their woes …"; "I just love all animals … a poor bird broke its wing flying into my window last week and I cried for days … that's just the way I am …"; "A sensitive soul, that's me, just trying to make my little contribution to the world … well you have to, don't you?"

Recently, Father Jameson had an appointment at the hospital for his eyes. When Jill discovered, whilst cleaning the church with Margaret Massey, that Margaret had driven him to and from the hospital, and that she hadn't even been asked, she saw it as a personal slight.

Jill went home, kicked their old Border Collie out of the way, and ranted to her long suffering husband, Dave, livid. "That Margaret thinks she's better than me. She's just jealous because he chose *me* as churchwarden. I wonder how she found out about his eye appointment before me. It was so *humiliating* being the last to know. How *dare* they treat me like this. *Nobody* appreciates how much I do. Just because she plays the church organ. She's got ideas above her station…"

Dave was up a ladder, repainting the lounge to Jill's exacting standards, at the time. He knew better than to comment, but made sure he made the right number of sympathetic noises so as to avoid her wrath being directed at him, whilst their teenage daughter, Alice, rolled her eyes and slunk off to her room to drown out the raging with her headphones.

Dave has been worn down by Jill's impatience and judgemental attitudes towards others for years, but he plays his outward role of supportive husband in public on autopilot. He's used to playing second fiddle to 'handsome' Father Jameson too, with his 'fine singing voice' (who he's noticed Jill will always make sure she's got her lipstick on for). He's even had to host various lunches for the man, and tolerate Jill's alternate simpering and coquettish behaviour throughout. "Don't be ridiculous, Dave," she will scoff after such occasions. "The man's a *priest*, for goodness sake, a man of the *cloth*. Of course I don't have feelings for him, although you'd do better to take a leaf out of his book when it comes to grooming and personal hygiene …"

Jill

She's always been that way. Before Father Jameson, it was the 'saintly' manager of the animal rescue centre that she volunteered for that he'd have to be compared to, and hear about endlessly. "He's from Scotland too, but his accent is not at all coarse like yours ..." she would tell him repeatedly. She was devastated when her volunteering services were terminated after she tried to take charge of a fundraising effort for the centre, annoying the staff who had it all under control, but she made out that she had left to spend more time at the church of her own accord.

Alice can't wait to go to university. "The softest thing about *my* mother" she tells her disbelieving friends who have only seen her outward persona, "are her teeth." Of course, only *she* knows that Jill slaps her dad repeatedly, until he cries and begs her to stop, and that she's been controlled herself for her whole life. She's not allowed to wear anything her mother considers to be vaguely 'tarty', and even though she's 18, she's not allowed to get her ears pierced, go to the pub with friends, or 'loiter' in town with them. Even her choice of university was dictated by her mother, who insisted that she knew best, even though she had left school without qualifications herself.

Alice has begged her dad to get a divorce as she can't bear the thought of him being at the mercy of her mother when she leaves for university, but Dave is resolute – Catholics do not get divorced, and he made his vows; "until death do us part." He tells Alice that underneath it all, her mother is a 'good woman', who 'loves her very much', and 'only has her best interests at heart'. Alice doesn't feel that her mother even knows the real her at all, but these assertions make her feel like a bad person for disliking her own flesh and blood, and she goes through cycles of trying to be a better daughter. She tells her friends that she intends to get a nose-ring and dye her hair pillar box red the day she moves out; but whether she'll actually pluck up the courage and risk the disgust of her mother remains to be seen.

Jill, not to be outdone, retaliated by putting Margaret on the church flowers rota for three weeks in a row, even though she knew she had terrible hay-fever, and made a point of visiting Father Jameson with a get well soon card. She put on the voice she reserves for such occasions; soft and breathy. "Father, I wouldn't want to speak out of turn but may we talk *confidentially*? I wouldn't want to burden you with this, and poor Margaret would be devastated if she knew I'd told you but, just between us, she does like the odd sherry in the daytime, and it's a problem that I'm helping her with. But perhaps in the future I should drive you to your appointments? Just to be on the safe side, you know ...?"

Jill McDonnell was never to be upstaged – certainly not when it came to piety and helpfulness. Her very sense of self depended on it.

The Narcissist's Playbook

The cycle of 'idealise' and 'devalue'

Hoovering   RAGE

Shallowness of emotions   Jealousy

Being above the laws and rules

Violating boundaries

Passive aggression

Blameshifting

Lying

Fluctuating morals, impaired conscience and inability to feel guilt

Narcissistic pseudologic and word salad   Difficulty being alone

Gas-lighting   **Projection**

Lack of empathy   Sense of entitlement

Exploiting others

The need to control

Selfishness

The narcissist's playbook

2

N arcissistic abuse is mostly *covert* emotional abuse – subjectively difficult to spot and hard to quantify. Physical abuse, which may also be a feature of narcissistic behaviours is, at least, pretty easy to label by friends and relatives as being wrong, even if it's hard for the victim to be objective.

For the narcissist, the purpose, as ever, is to secure *narcissistic supply*. The abusive behaviours work in two ways: the first is that the narcissist gets supply directly from the sadistic satisfaction arising from drama and conflict; the second is that the abusive behaviours lead to their victims *becoming addicted* to the narcissist, losing their autonomy and becoming trapped in the relationship. They are therefore kept exactly where the narcissist wants them, as a reliable and steady source of supply, too invested and confused to break free. All victims relate to the vampire-like nature of the relationship, and some even describe a feeling of 'soul rape'. Whilst these terms may sound overly dramatic to the casual onlooker, sadly they really do give an accurate flavour of the experience of narcissistic abuse.

But how do the abusive behaviours lead to the victims becoming addicted to the narcissist? Narcissists use 'intermittent reinforcement' to keep their victims hooked to them, and this works due to the flooding of the brain with certain brain chemicals (neurotransmitters) during the initial honeymoon phase of the relationship. What starts as the 'perfect' relationship, with the narcissist being loving and caring, invariably turns sour with (often subtle to start with) abusive behaviours. The victim absorbs the blame for the abuse and becomes desperate to get back the feelings of the initial phase of the relationship (with its associated rise in neurotransmitters). They jump through hoops to placate the narcissist, who gives out varying wins (big or small) at unpredictable times, so the victim begins chasing their tail, eventually becoming grateful for the smallest crumbs of good behaviour or attention from the narcissist. Sometimes just the absence of abuse becomes enough to make them feel at peace.

> **Narcissists use 'intermittent reinforcement' to keep their victims hooked to them, and this works due to the flooding of the brain with certain brain chemicals.**

From a neurochemical perspective, this is an addictive cycle, similar to the one employed by slot machines, and it's precisely the varying unpredictable nature of the wins that keeps the victim 'in the game', chemically hooked to it.

The initial payout at the slot machine keeps the gambler playing, sinking more and more cash into the machine, hoping that the next win is around the corner. Just as they are about to tire of the game, a small win occurs, re-igniting their desire to continue playing for the jackpot. More money is lost, but another neurochemical releasing win follows, as they hoped. It is no accident that these machines are designed to be profitable. The gambler is never really the winner. And in exactly the same way, nor is the victim of narcissistic abuse.

This chemical addiction to the narcissist, as a result of their intermittent reinforcement schedule of rewards, is known as Trauma Bonding. It leads to false hope that things can get better, and a pattern of rumination in the victim about how they can get back to that place of loving calm. It teaches them to try harder. To be better. To give more. To ask for less. To want less. To disappear into the narcissist's void, and to dance to their tune, on demand, like a puppet on a string. And all the while, to look grateful for any scraps tossed their way, and to scrabble on the floor for them, starving and needy. We ask that you do not underestimate the seriousness of this, and to note that cult leaders are all pathologically narcissistic; they use the same tactics as everyday narcissists. It is very easy indeed to be sucked in.

What follows is a detailed description of the trademark signs and behaviours of those with NPD, and how they look in real life.

The cycle of 'idealise' and 'devalue'

This cycle is the hallmark of those with narcissistic adaptations.

The idealisation (love-bombing) phase

The initial stage of a relationship with a narcissist is the 'idealisation' phase, also known as the 'love-bombing' phase, in romantic relationships.

As the narcissist's lawyer, you will also be idealised by the narcissist, and if you are unaware, you will be drawn in by their charm, charisma, likeability, and pity plays. You will be the best lawyer, the most understanding, the one that they will recommend to everyone. The narcissist will be relieved to have found you, and you will be the only one they know they can fully trust, after all that they have been through.

Love-bombing is *always* described at the beginning of a romantic narcissistic relationship. The narcissist will spend excessive amounts of time either physically with the target of their affections or be in constant communication with them. They will appear completely besotted with their target, who will be flattered by their attention, and who will allow other things in their lives, such as friendships and hobbies, to drop away at this stage.

Narcissists appear to have an inbuilt radar for sniffing out the other's vulnerabilities, perhaps their attunement being as a result of their own dysfunctional upbringing. Although, by definition, they have little or no emotional empathy (they cannot *feel* another's pain or joy), they are able to employ 'cognitive empathy' (the intellectual *understanding* that certain situations may be painful for another) to their advantage.

Love-bombing is *always* described at the beginning of a romantic narcissistic relationship.

In the case of Dennis, our Exhibitionist Narcissist, he was able to exploit Jane's grief at the death of her fiancé. He could not *feel* her anguish, but he was able to *understand* that people feel sad when a loved one dies. When he (an atheist) told her (a believer) that he had been sent from God to take away her pain, he knew he was answering her secret prayers. He would have understood that she was worried about becoming an 'old maid' too; he would have seen her as an ideal person to love-bomb.

Manipulation and exploitation are wired into narcissists' brain circuitry at an early age – not only have they learnt them from their parents, but they have used them all their lives as a defence against feeling their own pain and to get their needs met. Contrary to what some victims believe, those with narcissistic adaptions *do not* plot and scheme for hours about how they will manipulate others. It is completely natural and effortless. The ease with which such tactics are deployed, in combination with the believability of the narcissist, make it dangerously easy for *anyone* to be sucked in. As the lawyer, you may be struck by how effectively the narcissist is able to exploit your own weaknesses, and those of their spouse.

In romantic relationships, during the love-bombing phase, the narcissist will monopolise the target's time. Depending on what works best for that particular target, there may be gifts, meals, constant sex, helpfulness, displays of affection, and words of affirmation.

This is the *only* time in the relationship when the narcissist will listen deeply to the target's fears, stories from their past and secret hopes and dreams. The target will feel validated, heard and loved for exactly who they are.

Unfortunately, in exposing their vulnerabilities in this way to a narcissist, they have unwittingly handed the narcissist the key to their future exploitation and control.

Once the narcissist has uncovered the wounds of their target, and they know exactly what the target needs to feel healed and whole, they 'become' that person; the 'perfect' person for the target. It's common for victims to say: "I felt like I had known him my whole life" or, "It felt like he was heaven sent" and, "He was my soulmate". If the victim had lost a parent at an early age, the narcissist will play that role. If the victim had been neglected and unloved as a child, they will shower them with attention and love. If the victim had been cheated on in the past, they will speak of their high morals and faithfulness. If the victim was beaten as a child, they may speak of their perfect childhood, or may invent their own childhood dramas to show that they understand their target's pain. If the victim has a 'rescuer' mentality, they will re-write their own past so that they are the ones who need rescuing.

Targets will also invariably be taken in by the adoration which appears to be coming from the narcissist. Narcissists may stare deeply into the target's eyes, and make proclamations of perfect, true, never-ending love, far too early on in the relationship.

Essentially, the narcissist is holding up a mirror to the target. They are merely reflecting back the target's own adoration and love of the narcissist. The narcissist may *appear* to be in love, and most likely they *think* they are, but in fact, all that the narcissist is feeling is the positive effects of narcissistic supply. Their metaphorical suit of armour is temporarily gleaming and whole.

This is the point at which a reminder that "If it seems too good to be true, then it probably is" would be relevant. But by now, the target is hooked, and would not listen anyway.

As the lawyer representing a narcissistic client, you will also be idealised in whatever way works most effectively for the narcissist. This will be individualised to you. Pay attention to how you feel. You may feel a strong sense of connection to the narcissist early on, and may feel that this person could be your best friend if they weren't your client. You will, most likely, think what a nice person the narcissist is, and may be flattered to be considered to be their lawyer. You may be impressed by their status and achievements. If they are playing the role of hard done by victim, you may feel an almost parental urge to help. You may even find yourself wishing to be of importance to the narcissist, to be somehow special to them.

The devalue stage

This stage follows love-bombing/idealisation. It occurs as the narcissist realises that their target is not the perfect human that they had idealised and put on a pedestal during the initial phase. It is usually not an abrupt change, but a gradual turning up of the heat, so slowly that you may not notice. The victim becomes the proverbial frog in boiling water, and does not jump out.

During this stage, the narcissist begins by employing subtle put downs to see how the target reacts. Remember that at this point the target is very favourably disposed towards the narcissist, so their defences are down. They therefore either completely miss the put downs or when they do notice them, they make excuses for them. The narcissist will devalue the target in those areas in which they have already identified vulnerabilities.

The brain has systems whose jobs are to filter out incoming information that it does not consider to be relevant to the individual. If you noticed every single thing that was happening around you, if every single thing was to reach your conscious awareness, you would be pretty overwhelmed. Therefore, the brain filters out things that are not in line with your beliefs or your view of the world and those around you. These are known as 'deletions'. The brain also distorts reality, in line with our own personal prejudices due to former experiences, magnifying or diminishing our perceptions of things; so called 'distortions'. For example, if a person you like says something negative, "they can't have meant it". And finally, the brain's mental filters lead to 'generalisations' where we make automatic assumptions based on our past experiences, ignoring any exceptions that may be present, for example, "vicars are kind".

It's important to realise that although these processes are going on all the time, colouring our perceptions of reality, we are largely unaware that they are even happening.

These filters are used against the target by the narcissist during the devalue stage to great effect, causing the victim to ignore or misread the devaluing behaviours.

The aim of devaluation is to gradually lower the target's self-esteem, so that they accept more and more bad behaviour from the narcissist, and eventually start jumping through hoops to try to get back the original feeling they had during the love-bombing phase. The narcissist may or may not be aware that they are doing this, and are unlikely to know *why* they behave in this way, unless they have particularly good insight.

Methods of devaluation

Verbal

These may be direct. If the target is a little self-conscious about their weight, the narcissist might say: "Perhaps you should wear something else – that doesn't do you any favours. I'm only telling you because I know you wouldn't want to be seen in something unflattering. *I* don't mind what you wear …"

They may thinly veil the devaluation with humour, delivering it with a jok-ey demeanour, and possibly following it up with: "I'm only joking – you are too sensitive!" For example: "Are you *sure* you should be drinking that full fat coke?!" Our Devaluing Narcissist, Anton, managed to put down his bride on their wedding day by telling the guests in his speech, with a big smile, that she had "scrubbed up well" for the big day, rather than saying that she was beautiful. Her heart had sunk, but she told herself that she was being overly sensitive, and that this was just his quirky sense of humour.

The cycle of 'idealise' and 'devalue'

love-bombing

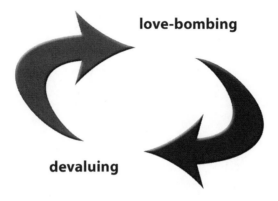

devaluing

There may be indirect insults, for example: "My friend thought that you looked pregnant – you aren't are you?" or "My dad was really offended at the way you didn't thank him enough for dinner" or "My mum is worried that you are making me materialistic." This way the narcissist is devaluing the target but not taking responsibility for it.

The narcissist often uses verbal devaluing to discourage the target from achieving anything that is important to them. If it doesn't impact the narcissist favourably, or threatens to take the attention off them they will not be supportive of their target's ambitions. For example: "Don't be too disappointed when it doesn't work out/you don't get the job/they change their minds."

The narcissist tends to start off feigning concern and having the target's best interests at heart, but if the target accepts these put downs, the narcissist will slowly ramp up the insults, testing how far they can go. Eventually, if the target tolerates this, frank name-calling and insults can become the norm. "You are boring"; "You are spiteful"; "You can't dance/sing/cook."

Being embarrassed by the other's behaviour at social events is another devaluing tactic, for example: "You shouldn't have drunk so much/talked so much/ hogged that person's attention so much/told that story etc". These types of statements make the target feel like they are misreading social situations, and they start to mistrust themselves and to rely upon the narcissist to tell them what is appropriate or otherwise. The narcissist becomes their barometer of what is acceptable, their 'voice of reason.'

The target's taste in clothes, furnishing, houses, art, music or anything else can also be used to devalue them, as can their choice of career, parenting methods and so on. The way you stand, the way you speak, the way you blow your nose; the list is literally endless. Children will be demeaned and criticised, and spouses will be ridiculed for not earning enough, cooking well enough, keeping the house clean enough, being sexually adventurous enough. The narcissist's target will eventually believe that they are not enough *in any way*, as a result of these endless verbal put downs. This of course is true – they are not enough in the sense that they cannot top up the narcissist's narcissistic supply enough to keep them happy – because no one can.

Non-verbal

Examples of non-verbal devaluation can be wincing, pulling faces, looking disgusted, walking away, checking the phone at inappropriate times, watching TV during important conversations, yawning and looking bored when the other is speaking, looking at their watch, lateness, the silent treatment. Physical abuse also falls into this category although not all narcissists employ this.

Our Devaluing Narcissist, Anton, did this all the time to Peter, who, if you remember, was an accomplished classical guitarist. During the love-bombing phase he would listen to Peter's playing with rapt attention, but in the devalue stage he would wince and walk out of the room if he played and even stick his fingers in his ears. This was to undermine Peter's confidence in his own abilities, and ultimately make him dependent on seeking Anton's approval for his own validation and self-worth.

Jill, our Communal Narcissist would employ physical abuse tactics towards her husband Dave, slapping him until he cried and begged her to stop.

Lateness is a common non-verbal devaluation tactic; it makes the target feel unimportant and undervalued, as if their time is not as important as the narcissist's. The target is simply expected to go along with the narcissist's lateness, which is often justified as a result of having important things to do; of being *more important* than the victim. What might start as a few minutes of tardiness could easily regularly become hours. This is surprisingly common, and may well become a feature of the lawyer-client dynamic with a narcissist. The narcissist's sense of entitlement and lack of empathy also plays into this, and it boosts their sense of self-importance and control over others.

Triangulation

This tactic is employed to get the victim to feel 'off balance' and to invoke feelings of jealousy and insecurity, which gives the narcissist a sense of power and sadistic enjoyment.

Triangulation is where the narcissist brings a third person into the equation. That person will often be another unwitting victim of the narcissist, who is being groomed by the narcissist as another source of narcissistic supply. Narcissists generally have multiple sources of supply on the go at any one time, and many of these will be romantic interests waiting in the wings to take the place of the significant other. Others may just be hopeful fans, usually subordinates, who are flattered that the narcissist is shining their light on them. Young secretaries and junior work colleagues often fall into this category, and the narcissist will enjoy innocently dropping their names into conversation and texting them late into the night in front of their significant other who, desperate to not appear mad or crazy, will often downplay their unease about these relationships. Anton, our Devaluing Narcissist, would do this with young gay men he had met on the internet, and Jill, our Communal Narcissist, was triangulating Dave with the 'handsome' Father Jameson. Former romantic partners may be used for triangulation, and even members of the narcissist's own family ("It's not my place to insist that you are invited to my brother's wedding, even if we have been together for five years…", for example). The narcissistically disordered person will always deny all wrongdoing, or having any ulterior motives, if confronted. They may not even be aware of what they are doing or why, so deeply embedded into their subconscious are the programs on which they run.

As the lawyer, be prepared to be triangulated with Counsel, and with other lawyers. You may find yourself rapidly descending from 'flavour of the month' to being devalued and compared unfavourably to other lawyers.

Some narcissists cycle through so quickly that they blow hot one minute and cold the next. As a junior doctor, Supriya remembers working with a highly narcissistic registrar who would delight in praising her openly one day and giving her the benefit of his full charm offensive, and then completely ignore her the next, turning his attention to one of her colleagues instead. (His unsafe practices and tendency to play God with patients' lives got him sacked from that particular job, but he continued working in the medical profession elsewhere and no doubt rose to the highest ranks, due to his charismatic outward persona).

The cycle begins again

Once the narcissist has devalued the target to the point where they are thinking about leaving, the cycle will begin again, and, quite abruptly, the narcissist will start to idealise the target once more. Note that these cycles can be very short (days or even hours) or long (months or weeks), and the narcissist will typically vary the cycle length, which keeps the target off balance.

In romantic relationships, this will never be quite as pronounced as in the initial love-bombing phase, but the target will accept this as normal. The target will experience huge relief at being back in favour, and will make excuses for the narcissist's previous behaviour (they were stressed/tired/anxious/working too hard/stuck between a rock and a hard place etc.) When the devalue stage returns (as it invariably will), the target will be thrown off balance once again, until the next idealisation phase. As these cycles repeat, the target begins to blame themselves for being unable to keep the narcissist happy, and tries harder and harder to do so. Walking on eggshells and tiptoeing around the narcissist's fragile ego eventually becomes the target's daily existence; the new norm. And in many cases, actually, it's not a 'new' norm at all, but a replaying of an *old* norm, most likely one enacted in childhood with a parent or primary caregiver.

Discard

Some describe the cycle not as a two part cycle but as a three part cycle, made up of idealisation, devaluation and then discard. Here the narcissist discards their victim, ending their relationship, before love-bombing them again, to draw them back into the cycle of abuse. However, more usually the narcissist does not actually discard their victim, but just makes them come close to thinking that they are going to do so. The victim then begs them to stay and tries to please them even more, until they are rewarded by renewed love-bombing.

But much more common than repeated discard *by the narcissist* is the situation where the *victim* ends or tries to end the relationship, only to be sucked back in. In fact, it is widely quoted that it takes, on average, seven attempts for a victim to leave their abuser, even one who is physically abusive. Of course, abusers do also leave their victims, but they more usually do this in one 'grand finale', rather than as part of a repeated cycle. For this reason, we do not include the 'discard' phase in our model of the cycle of idealisation and devaluation.

Hoovering

When a narcissist is on the verge of being left, or has been left by their significant other, this will trigger their deep abandonment issues. Hoovering is the term given to the narcissist's tactic to suck the target back into the relationship, so that the narcissist can continue to use them as a source of narcissistic supply. It is another form of idealisation but specific to imminent abandonment.

At this point the narcissist will turn back into the perfect partner. They will become seductive and charming. They will seem caring and helpful. They will put the bins out, load the dishwasher and stop texting their young attractive subordinates in front of their spouse. They will stop all devaluing behaviours and will apologise for the error of their ways, claiming stress or any other suitable excuse. Sadly, the trauma bonded spouse will be fooled by such behaviour, delighted that they still have a future with the narcissist. Of course, this is merely a temporary reprieve.

Given that it takes seven attempts to leave an abuser, if you are representing the spouse of a narcissist be aware that they may well be hoovered back into the relationship *even after you have been instructed to act for them*. They may seem weak or indecisive to those who do not understand the highly addictive, neurochemical nature of trauma bonding (similar to a heroin addiction). Look out for this, as when they re-instruct you it may be a clue to the nature of the person they are divorcing, and be mindful of trying not to judge them for their apparent indecision.

7 *The number of attempts, on average, it takes to leave an abuser*

Rage

Narcissistic rage is another trademark sign indicating that one is dealing with a narcissist. This isn't anger. This is an intense fury that is unmistakable when one sees it. The way that a narcissist expresses their rage varies between narcissists. Some will physically attack. Others will throw and smash things. Dennis, our Exhibitionist Narcissist, would slash furniture with a knife. Some will clench their teeth and repeatedly hit a wall, or punch through a door. Some will scream and shout. Some will exhibit a chillingly quiet, psychopathic sort of fury, like Anton, our Devaluing Narcissist who would whisper threats whilst taking Peter's pulse as a lie detector test, and snarl at him through gritted teeth that he could read his mind.

Narcissistic rage is a consequence of 'narcissistic injury.' It happens when the narcissist's outer bubble is punctured; when the protective suit of armour is penetrated by some external event. It could be a perceived personal slight which brings on the injury, or any situation in which things do not go the narcissist's way. With little insight into what is happening, the rage quickly bursts forth, like a reflex response.

People who have seen narcissistic rage often say the same things – it was terrifying to witness and it made them realise that it was one of only two *deeply, genuinely felt* emotions of the narcissist; the other being jealousy.

Narcissistic rage is generally accompanied by a type of communication known as the so called 'narcissistic word salad' (dealt with below).

Shallowness of emotions

It really does seem that many narcissists have a reduced emotional depth; that they feel most other emotions (apart from rage and jealousy) relatively shallowly, and that they have to sometimes 'play act' other *extremes* of emotions. Think of Dennis, and the way his eyes would well up in a display of emotion, short lasting and superficial. This is not to say that narcissists can't *feel* their emotions at all; they do. It seems to be the *extremes* of emotion (joy, despair etc.) that they struggle more with feeling. Those relatively middle of the road emotions, (happiness, contentment, annoyance, mild irritation) are sincerely felt. But the difference here between narcissists and non-narcissists is the *depth* of the emotion. Narcissists can be happy one minute and angry the next, going right back to contentment in the next breath, depending on external circumstances. Their moods and emotions are *labile*. Think of a non-narcissistic person who is feeling happy in the moment. To them their happiness is deeply felt, like a very thick layer of ice on a frozen lake. It takes quite a bad event to penetrate that thick layer of ice, that feeling of happiness, and to change that feeling into a negative emotion. Now consider the narcissist, who is also feeling happy. Their happiness is shallowly felt; the layer of ice is thin. From the surface, it still looks like ice; it still looks like happiness. But even a minor external event or perceived slight can crack that thin ice and allow another emotion to surface.

Partners of narcissists frequently report occasions where the narcissist switches moods instantly, for example going from a foul mood to transforming into the life and soul of the party with a change in external circumstance such as a third party arriving. Their previous emotion is so shallowly held that it is easy to change. Think back to Anton, our Devaluing Narcissist, who would coldly blank his partner Peter during silent treatments, silently furious with him for his non-existent affairs, but would be able to laugh heartily at whatever sitcom was on the TV.

Going back to *extremes* of emotions, many partners of narcissists report that they never really properly cry. A narcissist who feels they should be desperately sobbing (for example, when a partner threatens to leave them) may make a sobbing sound with slightly watery eyes. A narcissist who recognises that they should be beaming with joy may turn the corners of their mouths upwards, raise their cheekbones, open their mouths and show all their teeth, possibly with a feverish look in their eyes, and tell people how joyful they are. With these *extremes* of emotions, one gets the feeling that one is watching someone deliberately trying to 'act like other people'. It just doesn't feel quite real, and it may seem overplayed or insincere. As a lawyer, if you suspect you may be dealing with a narcissist, look out for these unconvincing displays of extreme emotion, but be aware that *pathological* mood states such as depression can co-exist with NPD, and also blunt the ability to feel extremes of emotion.

We recall the story of an acquaintance being at a party hosted by a highly narcissistic middle-aged couple, who were commonly referred to as 'the beautiful people'. They were acting as if they were having the time of their lives, throwing their heads back and laughing at the smallest things, blowing on party whistles and letting off party poppers continuously. As our acquaintance explained, it felt completely false, as if they were trying too hard to look like they were having fun. Their slightly confused guests (our acquaintance included) mostly felt obliged to join in, dancing feverishly, as they did not want to appear ungrateful for their host's hospitality. But one person just sat and stared at the scene before him incredulously. Our acquaintance later heard that, to the couple, this had constituted an act of war. He and his wife were badmouthed and barred from future events from that day on, labelled as 'jealous' of their success and beauty and as 'boring'.

Jealousy

A healthy, non-narcissistic individual's sense of self-esteem comes mostly (around 70%) from their own intrinsic sense of innate self-worth, with around 20% coming from what other people think of them, and the remaining 10% coming from how they measure up when comparing themselves to other people. These proportions are very skewed in those with narcissistic adaptations, with a much, much higher proportion coming from what people think of them and how they compare themselves to others than from any innate sense of self-worth.

This means that narcissists are always comparing themselves to others; to what possessions others have, to the size and desirability of their houses, to their abilities and interests, to their relationships and social lives, and to their wealth and status.

Narcissists need to feel superior, whether overtly or covertly. They need to be winners.

They do not like it if their partner has a friend, sibling or anyone else in their lives who they perceive to have more than them, or be better than them in some sense. This jealousy manifests in a few ways.

Most commonly, the narcissist will accuse their partner of infidelity. They may also try to isolate them from the person they are jealous of, either by causing problems in the relationship with bad behaviour towards that person, or by manipulating or controlling the behaviour towards their partner. They may directly ask their partner to stop seeing the person in question, giving their partner the silent treatment until they do so, or tell lies about the person they are jealous of, to put an end to the relationship.

Even nights out with long-term friends will be frowned upon or questioned. We recall the story of a woman who was raged at on and off for years about a ladies' only wedding hen night she attended, where the waiter (who she did not even speak to) was scantily dressed in 'Chippendale' style. She was made to feel guilty for being at such an event; her narcissist partner (who paradoxically, was a much better physical specimen than the waiter) simply couldn't deal with his own feelings of inadequacy. Perhaps there was some element of projection there, too, which will be discussed later.

Narcissists are constantly fearful about being replaced by someone else, someone better. They have deep abandonment issues. This will lead to snooping on phones and emails, and, often constant, intrusive phone calls, in order to check up on their partner's whereabouts.

They are also jealous of their partner being successful. Whilst they may initially seem proud of their achievements, this is only because they reflect well on themselves. The narcissist will initially bask in the glory of being capable of having such a successful partner to talk about to others. However, this will soon turn into a deep insecurity. If their partner is successful, he or she may leave them for better climes, after all. And no narcissist (other than the Closet Narcissist) is capable of having a partner who others perceive as being more successful than them. The narcissist will do everything in their power to undermine their partner's efforts to further their careers, by devaluing them, criticising them, attempting to destroy their confidence and sabotaging progress wherever possible. They certainly will not cheerlead them behind closed doors if they think they have a real possibility of success.

In divorce cases where this undermining of career advancement has gone on for years, it is important as the lawyer to acknowledge it. It may take many more years for the non-narcissistic spouse to recover their self-confidence and self-belief and be able to earn independently of the narcissist. Years of devaluing and mind games, such as gas-lighting, take their toll on a person. Healing and moving forwards is a long, drawn out affair and any settlement should, if possible, take account of the extra time required to mentally recover in these cases.

Being above the laws and rules

This is a very interesting pattern, which may appear less marked in Closet Narcissists, except behind closed doors.

It may be seen in many areas of the narcissist's life, from the laws of the land to the laws of physics and biology; from moral 'rules' to the rules of the road. It often results in risk taking behaviours which others are carelessly subjected to, such as risky driving and drug taking.

Narcissists may insist upon having unprotected sex with multiple partners and not care about pregnancy or health risks (thus disregarding the laws of biology). Like our Exhibitionist Narcissist, Dennis, many drive recklessly, attempting to defy the laws of physics (driving through rivers, taking off on humpback bridges). They may accelerate around blind corners, ignore speed limits, and subject their passengers to hair-raising journeys.

They may flout the law (Dennis coerced his wife into accepting points on her licence by falsely accepting the blame for his speeding offences). They may even drive without a driver's licence.

As lawyers you will be subjected to woefully incomplete financial paperwork being presented to the court as a result of the rules not applying to them. They will often flout Court Orders, or refuse to accept them until their own conditions have been added to them, giving them a sense of control.

They may sell themselves as being highly moralistic, but in reality, morals are something for other people to adhere to. If it serves them and doesn't tarnish their reputation, they will lie, cheat, steal and ruthlessly exploit others, violating whatever code needs to be violated. Hypocrisy is a very marked feature here, but a high-functioning, intelligent narcissist can cover their tracks for years. Supriya is reminded of a very junior doctor she worked closely with who would turn up to work several hours late (expecting her co-workers to look after her patients on the wards) and then sneak off at lunchtime for a glass of wine, on the grounds that it was the 'civilised' thing to do. She wasn't an alcoholic, just someone with a huge sense of entitlement and specialness, as a result of her narcissism, who would moan incessantly if anyone left her to do any of their work in return.

Violating boundaries

This can occur on many levels, and is an effect of the narcissist's exploitative nature. 'No' often will not be accepted by a narcissist. In personal relationships narcissists will take up their victim's time and their money. They may violate physical boundaries and sexual boundaries. They may push verbal boundaries, enjoying making others feel uncomfortable with obtuse or flippant comments, 'banter' or rudeness disguised as jokes. They may have inappropriate social relationships with work colleagues and subordinates.

As a result of these blurred lines, secretaries will find themselves working late into the night for them for no extra pay. Subordinates will be flattered to be considered as 'friends' and so may find themselves driving them to the airport at 4am. Narcissists may refuse to tidy up after themselves, leaving others to do it. They may borrow things and not return them, or return them dirty or damaged. The Exhibitionist or Devaluing Narcissist is that person you know who will borrow your car and return it covered in mud, and littered with snack wrappers, and then disarm you with a big smile. The Closet Narcissist might leave it with all the seats in the wrong position, the radio set to another channel, and the sat nav reset to avoid all major routes. And the Communal Narcissist, or any narcissist who wants to impress you in order to gain narcissistic supply from you, will return it fully valeted (by their long-suffering spouse, because they themselves were busy with other, much more important things) and with a fancy box of chocolates on the seat.

As their legal representative, they may push you past the normal professional client relationship, working on you to become their friend. They will then expect you to go the extra mile for them, with out of hour calls and requests, and expectations of free work or reduced charges. You may well be flattered to receive the attention of someone so likeable and charming. You may feel as if you've 'always known them', after just a very short time, and find yourself hoping to remain friends long-term. Pay attention to thoughts like these – they could well be early alarm bells.

Passive aggression

Those with narcissistic adaptions are masters of passive aggression. It serves them on various levels. It enables them to covertly devalue others, in order to control and minimise them. It fuels drama to provide narcissistic supply. And, all the while, its subtlety allows them to justify to themselves and others that what they are doing or saying is in line with their own image of 'niceness', and is not aggressive in anyway.

Silent treatments are a classic example of passive aggression, as is persistent lateness, both commonly employed by the narcissist.

Procrastinating on jobs (such as cleaning or putting the bins out) that the narcissist feels they are above until others do them is also very common. In the work environment, narcissists will often not do the more mundane jobs that do not bring them an easy win of narcissistic supply, leaving others to fill in for them. Many narcissists will often do a household task so ineffectively that their spouse will stop asking them to help, or will deliberately make a mess in an act of passive aggression (think of Anton's daily habit of throwing wet towels on to Peter's side of the bed).

Sabotaging other's work is very common (Anton enjoyed sabotaging Peter's cooking for dinner parties by surreptitiously turning up the oven). Sabotaging relationships is also the norm; most narcissists tell believable lies about their targets as an act of passive aggression, so that others form an unfavourable picture of them and don't want to know them ("She hasn't cooked once in our whole relationship"; "He spends every night at the pub").

Name calling and insults re-framed as jokes are also a common passive aggressive tactic.

> **Silent treatments are a classic example of passive aggression.**

Blameshifting

Those with narcissistic adaptations do not take the blame (except in the rare instances when doing so will give them narcissistic supply). They are never in the wrong, and simply cannot entertain the idea that this could even be a possibility. They will pass the blame on to others with lightning speed, almost as a wired-in reflex response which doesn't register consciously. We have some wonderful current examples of narcissistic politicians (a high risk group for narcissism) who do this beautifully.

They cannot take on blame, so they project it outwards on to others as a defence against feeling their own shame and the consequent deep depression that would result. As another example, during a rage a narcissist might repeatedly punch a wall, whilst blaming their terrified partner, "You are breaking my hand".

Lying

To a narcissist, the truth is not a finite entity. The truth is simply whatever they say it is at the time that they are saying it. This is so different to how most people are wired that it can be very hard to understand. Narcissists live a completely false version of reality every single day, as a defence against meeting and feeling their own shame and feelings of inadequacy. Lying to themselves and others about who they are is core to this personality disorder, so they are especially good at it, which is why lying about other things is extremely common – it's just a short hop, skip and a jump away from what they have to do anyway. When a narcissist tells their version of the truth, they seem to believe it 100% – and that is because they often genuinely do, for the duration of the sentence, at least. It's extremely easy to be taken in.

In the context of family law, this has many ramifications. The narcissist will lie about every single thing if it serves them to. They will lie about their finances, hide money, accuse their spouse of being a drug abusing alcoholic prostitute who is unfit for parenting, claim that they or their new partner is being harassed by their spouse, call the police and claim that they have been assaulted by their spouse. They will lie on legal documentation (as they have no respect for the law) and directly to you. They will even lie about *you* to their spouse saying that you find them laughable, or that you have been calling them names, or that you have predicted a very poor outcome for them. When you, as their legal representative (during the devalue phase) fall off the pedestal they initially put you on, they will lie about your competency to others too.

Fluctuating morals, impaired conscience and inability to feel guilt

The above heading might sound somewhat demonising, so we'd like to reiterate at this point that we state this fact without judgement.

Those with NPD will often purport to have high moral standards, if this is in line with how they see themselves and their 'false self' but, in reality, moral rules apply to others, not to them. They seem to be able to intellectually understand their hypocrisy when acting in an 'immoral' way but again, psychologically bat off the feelings of shame that most people would feel so they don't have to face them. The same is true for guilt – they seem to know that they should be feeling guilt, but with guilt comes shame. They simply cannot take these feelings on board, so they don't, and they intellectualise their reasons instead, using what we call 'narcissistic pseudologic' – a nonsensical, contradictory type of logic delivered with utter conviction.

These impairments also go some way to explaining why the rules do not apply to them, and of course, why they lie.

Narcissistic pseudologic and word salad

Narcissistically disordered individuals can be very opinionated. Many seem to be able to 'change sides' with great ease, and seem to thrive on heated debates. It is almost the norm for narcissists to automatically take the opposite view to an opinion that is being expressed, and for many, compulsively playing 'devil's advocate' is an enjoyable game, precisely because of the frustration that it causes the other party.

Those with NPD need narcissistic supply. Arguing and debating gives them this by making them feel superior, special and clever. They need power struggles to keep things interesting. They need to 'win' in order to prove themselves and others that they are the best, in order to inflate their false self, so that they do not have to face their own feelings of shame and inadequacy.

Those narcissists that pride themselves on their intelligence (the cerebral subtype) may employ a grandiose, wordy, over complicated way of speaking, perhaps often also speaking very fast, in order to convey to the listener the great speed of their mind. They may speak as though they are highly logical, with high intensity. The listener often finds themselves believing the narcissist, as they seem utterly convincing and seem to know what they are talking about.

But, as we all know, the majority of effective communication is *non-verbal*, and this is where many narcissists have a big advantage. Their tone of voice, speed of delivery, and body language convey great conviction, deep understanding and intelligence. But if you look at the *actual words* they are using you may be surprised to see a different picture. Nowhere is this more obvious than in written communication. Here it is easy to see the multiple contradictions, irrational conclusions, and loose associations between ideas that is the hallmark of the narcissist. This is what we call narcissistic pseudologic.

This pseudologic goes a step further when the narcissist experiences 'narcissistic injury' from being slighted, rejected or humiliated. Once the narcissist's defensive armour of superiority is punctured, narcissistic rage ensues, and their style of communication nosedives into full 'narcissistic word salad'.

Here the narcissist loses all sense of logic. They deny that things happened, blame the injured party using senseless reasons and re-written history, project on to the other party things that they themselves have done or have felt, make accusations, go round and round in circular discussions which descend into a downward spiral, say something one minute and deny having said it the next. They introduce new topics frequently or reintroduce old ones and try to logicalise events using nonsensical explanations. They make intimidating threats, and then profess undying love in the next sentence. The recipient of this ranting, raging, nonsensical, accusatory word salad is left reeling and breathless, utterly confused and questioning their own reality. They often feel the need to try to record conversations to prove to the narcissist that they have said certain things, and they find themselves trying to explain basic emotions, decency and empathy to the narcissist.

As the lawyer of the narcissistic client, you certainly will experience the narcissist's pseudologic when it comes to their rationale for punishing the other side, and you will be struck by the rigidity of it. As the legal representative of the non-narcissistic spouse, you will see emails and texts and possibly listen to audio recordings of the narcissist in full meltdown, where the contradictory word salad will be obvious.

There is absolutely no point in trying to respond to either word salad or pseudologic in legal correspondence – you will be doing your client no favours in engaging in costly and unproductive correspondence, and will be playing into the hands of the narcissist who will be trying to run up legal costs for their spouse. The non-narcissistic spouse may wish to clear their name and respond to accusations and allegations if they do not understand that they will be inadvertently giving the narcissist what they need most – narcissistic supply as a result of the drama and conflict, as well as the ability to financially abuse them through you, their lawyer. Your role in managing this effectively is crucial.

Difficulty being alone

Narcissists need narcissistic supply to give them a sense of validation and self-worth. They need *people* to provide that, so they find it very difficult to be on their own where they are left with nobody to give them external adoration or attention. They may insist on their primary source of supply doing everything with them and not wanting them to have any time away from them; this is especially true of the older narcissists. They most likely will have multiple sources of supply on the go at any one time, and will often have a phone that buzzes and pings continuously as they are in constant communication with others. The younger narcissists are often avid users of social media, where one is never really alone. They curate their posts to present an image to the world that will get the maximum numbers of likes, heart emojis and comments, all of which boosts their fragile senses of self. 'Me time', 'alone time' and 'screen free time' are not concepts that narcissists subscribe to. They descend into gloom and depression, or severe restlessness if forced into these situations, and may turn to drugs, alcohol or other addictive behaviours to distract them.

It is characteristic of narcissists (especially the higher functioning, successful, intelligent ones, who are better able to hide their traits) to go straight from one romantic relationship into another with no gap or only a small gap. Because of their lack of emotional depth, they do not need to grieve or heal from former relationships, and they will use the breakdown of their relationship to garner sympathy from their next target who they may well have been grooming to step into their new role as primary supply for months or even years.

'Gas-lighting'

The term gas-lighting comes from the 1938 thriller 'Gas Light', in which a husband sends his wife 'mad' by repeatedly dimming the gas powered lights down to a flicker in their home, and then denying that they were flickering when she questions him.

> **To gas-light is "the act of undermining another person's reality by denying facts, the environment around them or their feelings".**

To gas-light is "the act of undermining another person's reality by denying facts, the environment around them or their feelings".

It is a slow form of abuse which results in the victim questioning what is real, and wondering whether they are going 'mad'. Essentially, the abuser tells the victim that they are wrong on many levels and that they shouldn't trust themselves. It is a method of invalidation, whereby the victim slowly starts to feel unreal, and like a shadow of themselves. They then start to rely upon the abuser as their 'voice of reason', no longer trusting their own perceptions of reality, and only trusting the narcissist's perceptions and point of view. There are a few presentations.

The narcissist will often tell a person that their *feelings* are invalid and wrong; that they shouldn't be feeling a certain way. They sometimes do it by deflection, or by twisting the other person's perspective. Think of the unhappy housewife who is feeling stressed by her mother's terminal illness. The narcissistic husband may invalidate her feelings by saying that she shouldn't be feeling stressed because her mother is old, and that he is the one that is entitled to feel stressed because his job is busy and he is doing long hours. Think of the wife who is upset that her husband has visited a lap dancing club and paid for a private lap dance. The narcissistic husband will tell her that she should be upset instead about the fact that society allows women's bodies to be exploited in venues which allow them to expose their breasts; that it is *society* she should be upset with, not *him* (this one also rather beautifully demonstrates narcissistic pseudologic).

Another common form of gas-lighting is simply to deny a person's *memory* of an event. "That didn't happen" and "I never said that" are common narcissistic refrains. Narcissists are renowned for rewriting history in this way, causing their target to question their memory and sanity.

Gas-lighting can also occur in the present, with everyday things in the environment. We recall a story of a narcissistic husband who would be drinking coffee, but would tell the wife that actually he was drinking tea, when he knew she had watched him make it.

Sometimes gas-lighting can be as extreme as the stuff normally reserved for fiction. I know of a narcissistic husband whose wife was thinking of leaving him, who would lean over her when he thought she was asleep and attempt to 'brainwash' her by repeatedly telling her that she did not want to leave him after all. The example of the (outwardly charming) Anton, telling Peter that he could read his mind, and carrying out lie detector tests on him by taking his pulse and monitoring his breathing rate, is another true story.

Often the victim is repeatedly accused of having personality defects, until they come to believe what they are being told, for example "You are crazy"; "There you go again, hysterical as ever"; "No one could ever love you because you are so unreasonable"; "You are paranoid/such a drama queen/boring/useless/a gold digger/ungrateful/selfish …"

Devaluing can also be used to gas-light victims about their own abilities. Consider the famous opera singer whose partner told her that she couldn't sing. Our Devaluing Narcissist Anton, who made Peter believe he couldn't cook by apologising about his food to others. The woman whose partner criticised her poor taste in interior design, although the house was featured in a design magazine. These victims had the reality of who they were, and what they were good at, deeply eroded, to the point where they had lost confidence in their own sense of themselves.

The narcissist starts small at first and slowly turns up the volume on the gas-lighting, which can reach epic proportions. At this point, those outside the relationship may find the assertions outrageous and nonsensical (see the famous opera singer example above; a true story). However, to the long term, worn down victims, the narcissist's assertions seem true and believable.

In family law, although it may not be directly named, gas-lighting may well be included in the non-narcissistic spouse's list of unreasonable behaviours in a divorce petition, and may give an early clue as to the personality of the other spouse.

Projection

Projection is a psychological defence mechanism unconsciously used by many people, but by *all narcissists*. Anyone who finds it difficult to accept their failures, weaknesses and their own less flattering traits may unwittingly use projection as a way of feeling better about themselves.

In the case of narcissists, their sense of safety and self-worth depends upon maintaining a superior view of themselves. They are completely unable to accept the parts of themselves which are imperfect or flawed, as doing so would lead to an existential crisis, emotionally. They therefore assign those parts of themselves to other people, essentially giving away the feelings of deep shame that would come with acknowledging their flaws ('shamedumping').

So, when a narcissist accuses their partner of infidelity, it is actually the narcissist themselves who is cheating, or thinking of cheating. When a narcissist accuses a work colleague of stealing their work, they are the one who has considered doing that to someone or has done it. When a narcissist comments on a larger person's weight when they themselves are overweight, once again they are projecting their own disgust at themselves on to the other person. When they tell you that you are just like their mean-spirited father, they mean that *they* are just like their father. When they accuse you of being materialistic, they are inadvertently revealing this trait in themselves.

They project their thoughts, feelings, behaviour, insecurities about themselves, shame and fears on to their target. And the more intelligent ones may manage to do this by using a third party so that they absolve themselves of the act of projecting. "I've heard people say that you are arrogant…"

If a victim has also been gas-lit for years, it is quite common for them to actually take on and identify with whatever it is that the narcissist is projecting on to them. This is called 'projective identification'.[1] They can start to believe the accusations. They apologise for transgressions they never made in the first place. They feel guilty for them. We knew of a woman who was so frequently accused of having affairs and making a fool out of her husband that she would feel great shame and apologise to him profusely even though somewhere, deep down, she knew that she was innocent.

Note that it is also common for a narcissistic individual (most likely who has been identified as such by their spouse) to project their narcissism on to their spouse. This complicates things for you as the lawyer, as it may be that a charming and plausible narcissist initially convinces you that it is their *spouse* who is the narcissist. This is always worth bearing in mind when seeing new clients. However, if you are familiar with the 'narcissist's playbook' it will become very clear over time who the real narcissist is, as the behaviour patterns in divorce are unmistakeable. Be wary of the 'victim of narcissistic abuse' who seems oddly intent upon annihilating their spouse, with no regard for their feelings

> **Projection complicates things for you as the lawyer, as it may be that a charming and plausible narcissist initially convinces you that it is their *spouse* who is the narcissist**

---

[1] *Projective Identification in Couple Therapy, Arthur C Nielsen, 2017.*

Lack of empathy

All narcissists, without exception, lack empathy, which is of course *how* they are able to carry out their abusive and exploitative behaviours above without guilt or remorse. Lack of empathy is one of the 'Triple Es' of pathological narcissism, the others being entitlement and exploitation.

Those with narcissistic adaptations are unable to *actually feel* other people's pain or joy, or any other emotion. *They are therefore unable to really care about any other person*, other than in the context of what that other person can do for them, or how that other person can contribute to their own inflated sense of superiority (by making them look good, by giving them adulation, or food, or shelter or sympathy etc.) People are merely *tools* for those with NPD to use to obtain narcissistic supply, the oxygen that keeps their false selves alive, and so keeps them from facing their own deep insecurities, inadequacies and shame.

However, narcissists can *feign* empathy, and often do, particularly in the early stages of a relationship when they are seeking out to target another's vulnerabilities. This is because life experience and the careful study they have made of watching other people's behaviour has taught them under which circumstances they should *appear* to be sympathetic, and what they should do and say to convince others of their compassion. In other words, they have 'cognitive empathy' but not emotional empathy.

> **Lack of empathy is one of the 'Triple Es' of pathological narcissism, the others being entitlement and exploitation.**

For example, if your mother died, a narcissist would be aware that this is a situation in which others would express sympathy, and would therefore have a stock phrase for dealing with this (for example, "I'm sorry for your loss"), and a behaviour to go along with it (perhaps a hug). However, they would not be able to really connect at all with how you were feeling, even if they had experienced bereavement themselves, and this might show itself fairly quickly. Perhaps straight after expressing their sympathy they would tell a funny anecdote, suggest that the bereaved person get on to a dating website or change the subject and talk about themselves. Some narcissists, in situations like these, miscalculate their responses in the opposite direction, and behave in an overly sympathetic manner, ringing people they barely know to offer their condolences and trying to be involved in helping with the funeral arrangements. The Closet Narcissists and the Communal Narcissists often fall into this latter category, and are completely unaware of how inappropriate this seems to others.

A big 'tell' of lack of empathy is that narcissists tend not to take care of their significant others when they are ill, and are very unsympathetic in these situations. They will not bring you soup and mop your brow. They will not massage your back for more than a second. They will still expect a meal on the table when you have the flu. Very often, if they can be persuaded to help, they will expect something in return (things are transactional to a narcissist), and they will usually point out how nice they are being.

Conversely, any opportunity to demonstrate how kind and compassionate they are to a new source of supply may be relished. We recall the story of the professional woman who rushed to her boss's hospital bed on Boxing Day after he broke his hip to sit by his bedside with his family for the day. She had left her own ill family including two young children (all of whom were incapacitated by the flu) in order to do so. She had been covertly grooming her boss as a source of supply for months at this stage, and he was beginning to fall in love with her, although she had been careful to ensure that she had *said* nothing that could be misinterpreted. All her advances had been non-verbal, and she had no intention of leaving her own husband and family. She just needed his adoration, and sadistically enjoyed devaluing her own husband by triangulating the pair. "But he's my *boss*," she told her husband when he questioned her actions. "It's the least I could do – he's been so good to me…" Here she was feigning empathy for the boss, and having none for her sick family, all to obtain narcissistic supply.

Narcissists will often give away their lack of empathy by being cruelly inappropriate, with no idea that what they have said or done may be off the mark. Consider the narcissist who, on hearing that a family friend's teenage daughter was in hospital being tube fed for anorexia nervosa, felt it absolutely appropriate to suggest that letting the daughter die would be the best outcome all round. Or the narcissist who cheerfully suggested to the vet who came to the house to put down the family dog that he didn't believe she *really* felt sympathy for the family but that she must be putting it on, whilst the rest of the family sobbed. Or the narcissist on a boat who picked up his very young daughter unexpectedly and threw her into the sea. When she surfaced in floods of tears from the shock, he stormed off, for hours, furious that she could not take a joke, as her long suffering mother consoled her. Consider Dennis, our Exhibitionist Narcissist, and how he would drive so erratically that his wife Jane would suffer neck pain from being thrown around in the car. Narcissists are careless and thoughtless unless they stand to benefit in narcissistic supply terms, and those who are the closest to them are the ones who pay the biggest price.

If a narcissist is having a good day, they will not thank you for bringing their mood down if you have not had such a good day. You may be struck by the poignancy of the story of the very little boy who was crying about his hurt finger. As soon as he heard his narcissistic mother coming home he said, "Quick everyone, act happy – mummy's home."

Sense of entitlement

Another of the Triple Es of narcissism, this can take many forms. What lies at the core of this is the powerful, all pervasive need to *feel* special. They need to be *treated* as if they are special in order to prop up their fragile belief that they *are* special, and as all their validation comes from external sources, *how they are treated by others is the key* to this. This feeling does not, in narcissists, come from within.

It is often quoted that narcissists expect the best table at the restaurant due to their sense of entitlement, and that they will throw a tantrum if they do not get this. Another common example is that they may jump queues or complain loudly if they have to wait in line. Being rude to waiters and waitresses is another oft quoted red flag of NPD. Whilst this is true of many narcissists and should definitely be looked out for, in many cases their sense of entitlement to being treated as if they are special is much more subtle and they may much more cleverly manipulate situations to make sure that they are treated in the manner they desire, or so that they artificially create that feeling of specialness.

Lateness is one example of this. Arriving to an event late so others are left anxiously waiting for them to arrive, postponing the festivities until their grand entrance, is a great way to feel special. If part of a narcissist's sense of specialness comes from believing themselves to be the *nicest* person in the world, for example, they are not going to stamp their feet at having to wait in a queue as this would bust their own myth. They are going to arrive at the very last minute so that they don't have to wait at all, being publicly ushered in as the bride is walking down the aisle, as the curtain is lifting, as the judge is about to call you in, or as their child is about to blow their first note into their clarinet at the school recital. They are *entitled* to arrive late, as they are special.

Other narcissists, rather than treat service staff badly, treat them especially *well*, so that they are fawned over and receive special treatment as a result. Tipping the girl who sweeps up the hair at the hairdressers a fifty pound note can have *all* the staff at the hairdressers positively disposed towards you, and bending over backwards for you; sending someone out to get your special type of herbal tea, for example. Being extra charming to the waiters at the restaurant will mean that they will always find you the best table on subsequent visits, without you having to throw a tantrum. These intelligent narcissists will find the work around to ensure that they get this feeling anyway rather than risking putting themselves in a position where they aren't treated as if they are special. Remember the transitional nature of narcissistic interactions with others here.

As much as narcissists may feel entitled to be treated in certain ways and to have certain things, they also feel entitled to *not have to do* certain things. To not have to work, to not have to pay their way, to not have to tidy up after themselves, to not have to do domestic chores, to not have to get up in the night for the baby – each narcissist has their own unique list of things they feel entitled not to do. Many will work very hard in some areas (the ones which bring in the most narcissistic supply), and not at all in others. Of course, in order for these other important things to happen, they have to exploit others to get them done for them.

If you are representing a narcissist, you will find yourself being expected to treat them as if they are entitled to special treatment. As if their case is the most complicated. As if their spouse is the most unreasonable. As if they are the individual who has the most difficult job (so expecting you to talk with them outside of office hours). They will arrive at court at the last minute or will be late (if they arrive at all) and may make a big show of having to leave early. They feel entitled to being treated as if they are special and they will make sure that this happens on their own terms. When dealing with these frustrations, as ever, try to take a breath and spare a thought for that screaming child within the narcissist. Please pick *me*. Love *me*. Notice *me*. Let *me* be your favourite.

Exploiting others

Exploitation: a natural follow on from entitlement, and another of the Triple Es. Again, depending the individual, this can have many presentations. Narcissists are able to exploit others for their own benefit because they do not care about other people's feelings, due to their intrinsic lack of empathy. Add to that their need to feel special through external means, and their sense of entitlement to have certain things and to not have to do certain things, and you have a recipe for interpersonal exploitation.

Work colleagues will pick up the slack for them and have the credit for their work stolen by them. Subordinates will be used in whatever way benefits them, and partners will find themselves doing whatever the narcissist feels entitled not to do, be that domestic chores, parenting or earning a crust. The list of exploitative behaviours is endless, and empathic givers who just keep giving are prime targets to be manipulated here.

As the lawyer, be prepared to be manipulated into working for free, or giving free advice. We estimate, from experience, that family lawyers representing narcissists end up billing for only around 70% of their time spent on the case.

The need to control

Narcissists need to control their victims. They do this in order to make their targets dependent on them in some way, so that they can keep them in place as reliable sources of narcissistic supply.

In the case of our Exhibitionist Narcissist, Dennis, he stripped his wife Jane of her autonomy by taking over all her roles, such as cooking, choosing home furnishings and décor, and all financial decisions and driving. This had the effect of making her dependent on him; unable to live without him, especially as he had isolated her from her family. He de-personalised her, even deciding what hairstyle she would have. Many narcissists will appear to have strong feelings about what clothes suit their partner (which may initially be interpreted as caring for them), but which again is merely a control tactic and a manifestation of the fact that the narcissist only sees others as objects to be used for their own ends.

Narcissists typically control many areas of their targets' lives. An important point to make here is in regard to financial control. Whilst most narcissists tightly control their partner's spending, some (particularly affluent narcissists) use what looks (from the outside) like *generosity* to control their partner. They may give their partner full access to bank accounts etc, and encourage them to leave their jobs and stay at home, in reality making them completely financially dependent on them. Once the narcissist has them trapped, they turn up the volume on many or all of the horrendous abuse tactics described in this section. At first the target feels that they should be grateful to the narcissist for 'looking after' them financially but eventually they realise that they have been gifted a Trojan horse. The narcissist will expect them to do exactly what they tell them to do and to give up their own lives, hopes and dreams in return for their financial security. On the outside, these victims might look like spoilt, ungrateful brats; far from the birds in the gilded cages that they really are. Emotional support for them, when they try to leave, will be thin on the ground as a result. With narcissists there really is never such a thing as a free lunch.

Narcissists will also control how their targets spend their day, often by giving them time consuming tasks to do (perhaps under the guise of "you would do this for me if you loved me, as I don't have time myself"). They will often constantly check up on their partner's whereabouts, and control who they are friends with, by directly alienating friends through bad behaviour or by disapproving of them, making it difficult for their partner to maintain contact.

They may control what their partner does for a living, or even sabotage their chances of success. The children of narcissists suffer here too – their hobbies, university courses, careers and choice of friends may be dictated by the narcissist, as external appearances are desperately important. If a narcissist can control it, and it ultimately contributes to their own narcissistic supply, then they will. Children are merely an extension of themselves, and are not separate from them. Therefore, if the narcissist wants it, the child should want it too. And if the child wants it, but the narcissist does not, then the child should not want it either.

On the subject of control, some narcissists are also driven by a need to be perfect. These narcissists, as well as demanding perfectionism from others, demand it of *themselves* too, in various areas of their lives. These narcissists are prepared to work incredibly hard to be perfect.

> **The need to control often plays out in the narcissist having to have the last word on everything.**

We recall the example of a facial aesthetics doctor, who was highly narcissistic, but was convinced that she was a kind and wonderful boss, wife, friend and mother. She needed to be those things, in her own mind. She wore flawless make-up every single day, even when not at work, and there was never even so much as a single hair out of place. She was immaculately dressed in designer wear at all times. She had built up a string of highly successful practices, with multiple people working for her, of whom she demanded absolute perfection. She was a notoriously difficult boss, and even minor mistakes would make her employees feel like they had gone from 'hero to zero' overnight, and they would constantly be walking on eggshells. Her grand home was like something from the pages of a magazine, and staff would scuttle around continuously, scrubbing and polishing white floors and gleaming mirrors. When a married member of her live-in staff had an early miscarriage, she coldly fired her for having the audacity to get pregnant, which would have been highly inconvenient for the running of the household, and the distraught girl was given just a day to move out. Her children were also expected to be perfect in every way – high grades, the clothes they wore, the instruments they played, the level of sporting prowess achieved. She had been this way from childhood, brought up by a narcissistic father. Even as a medical student she had ironed her bedlinen and underwear. Look out for this type of perfectionism in your clients – it may be a warning sign of narcissism.

This need to control often plays out in the narcissist having to have the last word on everything. If they cannot have everything their way, they have to have at least some of it their way. In the divorce process, you will find them putting their stamp on all manner of things; your letters, which they will have you re-draft endlessly unless you allow them to write them for you in the first place; the dates they are available for court; insistence on trying mediation even though it is unlikely to work in cases such as these; variation upon variation of consent orders before they can be finalised; total disregard for deadlines; absolute refusal to complete paperwork or provide financial disclosures. The list will be endless and the process of being controlled, exhausting.

Selfishness

Narcissists only do what *they* want to do, and they will drag others with them kicking and screaming. Because they have no empathy, they simply cannot fully understand other people's feelings, and so if they want to do something/go somewhere/have something/build something they will insist that others comply with their wishes, trampling all over their boundaries and needs.

Work colleagues will feel abused and unheard by them as a result of this, and partners and children may give up trying to object, developing 'co-dependency issues' where their own needs are so infrequently heard, and never met, that they stop having them altogether, instead focusing on meeting the many needs of the narcissist.

Narcissists are biologically wired to have no qualms about using others for their own ends, and genuinely feel completely entitled to exploit others to get what they want. They seem to have little or no insight into these behaviours.

The world revolves exclusively around them, a point made in the tongue-in-cheek joke we include here, for emphasis: *How many narcissists does it take to screw in a lightbulb? One. They just hold the bulb up in the air, and the whole world revolves around them.*

How they view others

Narcissists fluctuate between seeing people as either 'all good' or 'all bad'.

Here they are struggling with a healthy psychological phenomenon called 'whole object relations'.

They are unable to see people (or indeed themselves) as having both good and bad points at the same time – in other words, they cannot integrate both the liked and disliked parts of a person into a single stable picture. Instead they alternate between seeing the person (and themselves) as either being 'all good', when they are on the narcissist's pedestal, or 'all bad', when they have fallen off the pedestal and are exhibiting an annoying human flaw.

Related to this is the fact that narcissists also have problems with what is known as 'object constancy'. This means that they are unable to have positive feelings towards someone when they feel disappointed, angry, hurt or frustrated by them. It's as if any positive feeling there was instantly evaporates, leaving the victim walking on eggshells, scared to be anything less than perfect. In a healthy relationship, if your husband forgets your anniversary because he is swamped at work, you might be hurt, but you still love and care for him. Not so with the narcissist, who will vilify that husband for his cruel act.

Those who have struggled at the hands of a narcissist will recognise this instantly. They can feel as though the narcissist loves them one day, and then feel utterly despised the next because they have exhibited some minor human imperfection or have offended the narcissist in some way. Children (who inevitably misbehave) can feel these fluctuations acutely, and, as the development of whole object relations and object constancy occurs in childhood, poor modelling of it by their narcissistic parent can cause them to suffer from such problems themselves, as adults.

Legal professionals representing a narcissist may also be struck by this; worshipful reverence one minute and disdain, or worse, the next.

The narcissist's experience of 'love'

Narcissists do not experience love deeply, if at all.

This is a very tricky one for the spouse of a narcissist, and one of the hardest things of all to come to terms with as a victim, especially one who has given the narcissist years of their life and had a family with them.

If you ever question a narcissist about their concept of love, you might get some interesting answers. Many (if not most) will idealise it, fantasising about a Disney-style, perfect, love at first sight, never-ending, til death do us part type of love. A minority may reject the concept entirely, if pushed. And others may bring a slightly more bizarre notion to the table. We remember a Devaluing Narcissist once telling us about a husband and wife team he had known who had both contracted the same type of bowel cancer, the wife just a few months after the husband. His eyes welled up momentarily as he explained that this was an unmistakable sign of true love (see also 'narcissistic pseudologic' above). To him this was the ultimate beautiful romantic gesture from the wife; dying from the same cancer.

Narcissists do not experience love in the same way as healthy adults. To them, love is completely conditional. It's dependent on whether the recipient of their charms is giving them enough narcissistic supply, by doing what they want, being a flawless human being, and by adoring them, regardless of the abusive behaviours they are being subjected to. Of course, no one person will ever be enough to keep the narcissist topped up adequately with narcissistic supply, and the narcissist's partner has an impossible task in trying to meet the terms above. Love is transactional, and this also applies for the children of a narcissist.

Narcissists do not experience love in the same way as healthy adults.

It often causes the victim of narcissistic abuse much confusion when they first realise this, and they alternate between memories of the narcissist in the early days of love-bombing, staring deeply into their eyes and vowing their undying love, to those when the mask of the narcissist finally drops. They start to see the devaluing, and the gas-lighting, and all the other behaviours described above, but they cannot reconcile this with how the narcissist behaved towards them at the beginning (and in all the subsequent times when the narcissist 'hoovered' them back in, just as they were about to leave the relationship). "It looked so much like love" they will say, "but how can it have been?"

At this point, the victim is experiencing a difficult psychological phenomenon; so called 'cognitive dissonance'. Here they are struggling to hold two opposing beliefs about their relationship or marriage in their brains at the same time. This is still likely to be going on when they come to see you, their lawyer, and they may fluctuate wildly in their beliefs on any one day to begin with. "He loves me, he loves me not."

At this point, we want to mention the grief process. Divorce or loss of an important relationship will trigger a grief process in healthy people. The five-stage Kubler-Ross model consists of denial, anger, bargaining, depression and finally, acceptance. But the spouse divorcing a narcissist has a particularly traumatic process to go through (even greater we would say than in 'normal' divorce, and perhaps even in many cases of bereavement). This is precisely because the spouse is grieving the loss of a relationship that was not at all what they had believed it to be. *They are grieving the loss of something that was never real*, which makes it especially difficult. Many simply cannot process their grief, as they believe they are not entitled to it. When these people try to revisit happy memories, through their new lens of awareness, they see the darker side of that same image; the bad behaviours that they had filtered out and ignored at the time. Everything they had previously thought of as a 'good time' may be negated, essentially wiping out years or even decades of their past.

Others will prefer to believe that the good times were genuine and that their partner just took leave of their senses. They may choose to romanticise the relationship, and may not move on, remaining wedded to the image of their partner as they were in the idealisation and love-bombing phases. This is their choice and should be respected.

If a partner of a narcissist tells you, as their lawyer, that they have been living a lie, respect their point of view. Well meaning comments such as "but surely you can't regret all? There must have been love there for you to get married in the first place?" are not helpful or true in these cases. These are people who have had their feelings, thoughts and beliefs invalidated for years – they do not need more of the same, especially not from you.

It's important for you to be mindful of the traumas that this person has been through in the relationship, as well as the grief reactions that they are experiencing when they come to see you, especially when it comes to your expectations regarding their cognitive function *in relation to giving you your instructions*. They will be experiencing severe stress and panic reactions, with cortisol and adrenaline coursing through their bloodstreams. Not only are they dealing with their loss, but with nonsensical goalpost-changing and accusation-laden correspondence from the legal professionals on the other side. Add to that the intense fear of the future, probable issues with their children, and poor sleep. Now throw in the effect that the stress hormones in the blood are having on their brain, diverting blood away from the rational thinking parts and towards the instinctive parts as part of their fight, flight or freeze response. They are likely to seem a bit 'irrational' and 'reactive' to you as a result, possibly even fluctuating between 'highs' and 'lows'. This is a very specific type of response, and having a suitable third party recommendation to hand, such as a narcissistic abuse coach or a therapist who specialises in narcissistic abuse (not just a regular therapist or counsellor) would be extremely helpful, all round.

Living in the 'drama triangle'

Karpman's drama triangle was first described in the 1960s as a description of conflict in social interactions. There are three roles within the triangle – victim, rescuer and perpetrator. In high conflict relationships people tend to move around the triangle taking up the different roles at different times, perpetuating the drama, so that it continues on and on. If one person switches role, the other person has to also switch role to take up one of the vacant positions in the triangle, often completely unwittingly. People tend to get stuck in the drama triangle, unable to break out, and nowhere is this more apparent than in a relationship with a narcissist, who manipulates the triangle to their own end with great skill, sucking people in to fill the vacancies.

The Drama Triangle

Victim

Rescuer   Perpetrator

For example, narcissists will often enter a person's life when they are vulnerable, and they will play the role of rescuer; the knight in shining armour. They will help their target sort their affairs, and take care of them. Notice the way our Exhibitionist Narcissist Dennis swept Jane off her feet after the death of her fiancé, claiming that he had been sent by God to take away her grief. Here Dennis was the rescuer and Jane, the helpless victim of her awful circumstances.

Once the rescue has been effected, the narcissist will at some point take on the role of perpetrator, gas-lighting and devaluing their target. The target, rather than being the victim of circumstance, now becomes the narcissist's victim, and is utterly confused. But as soon as they try to address the issue, the narcissist will pull a quick role shift out of the bag, and play the role of victim themselves, for example telling their target that "they do not understand how difficult life is for them at the moment, how stressed they are, and how they are making it all even worse". The target has been made the perpetrator now – everything is their fault. The empathic target, without even consciously registering it, feels their heartstrings being pulled, and they move into the role of the rescuer themselves, placating the poor narcissist and trying to solve their problems.

Often there will be other people in the triangle that the main target may know nothing about. For example, the narcissist may be telling his young new secretary that his wife does not love him. Here the wife (in his mind) is the perpetrator. The secretary puts herself in the rescuer role, flattered to be important enough to be confided in, and hoping for more, and the narcissist happily plays the victim. When the wife finds him texting his secretary late into the night, she becomes angry, reinforcing her position as perpetrator. The narcissist continues to play the injured party (victim), and the wife feels guilty about her anger and tries to rescue the narcissist from his own pain, at the same time blaming the secretary (now the perpetrator) for obviously trying to steal her husband.

There are an infinite number of permutations of the exact ways in which the narcissist can play in the drama triangle, and divorce provides the perfect backdrop for multiple triangles to be in motion at any one time. As the lawyer, you will be sucked in. Counsel may also be sucked in, and your opposing legal team, as well as the spouse of the narcissist. You cannot step out of the drama triangle if you do not realise that you are in it in the first place, but simply noticing what positions you are taking up in it is all that is required to make major shifts in the game. And make no mistake – for the narcissist, sadly, it is just that; a game.

The dropping of the mask

As we have already mentioned, narcissists wear a mask (or sometimes many different masks depending on who they need to be in a given situation to secure the most narcissistic supply). I've previously referred to this as their 'armour' to illustrate the protective nature of it, but it is more commonly referred to as a mask.

The mask is the outward projection of the narcissist's false self. But when the narcissist does not get what he or she wants from their target, the mask will drop to reveal their true nature. Some narcissists can keep their mask on for years, fooling their long-term partner, for example, although they may drop it at work or in other situations. Others are less stable and drop their masks more frequently, whenever they experience narcissistic injury. Some are able to only partially drop their masks in response to mild narcissistic injury, showing relatively controlled rage, but others will drop the mask entirely.

During the divorce process, especially if it is the narcissist who has been left, triggering deep abandonment issues and severe narcissistic injury, the mask will drop, most likely completely.

The narcissist's target, the recipient of their abuse, will finally get a true glimpse of the person that they have slept soundly next to in the marital bed and it is usually a moment that they will never forget. You may even get to see it for yourself.

Here is an account from a woman who had been married to a narcissist for 20 years, who had finally plucked up the courage to leave:

> *He turned around and looked straight at me. His eyes, normally a washed out blue, were black; suddenly beady, boring into me with a hatred I didn't think any human could have for anyone else. I know that doesn't sound possible, them being black, but they were, or at least I thought they were. His upper lip was curled upwards in a vengeful snarl, like a creature from the bowels of hell. A vile creature, full of rage and mockery and loathing. The closest thing I'd ever seen to the devil; I hadn't even believed in <u>him</u> before. I remember trying not to recoil in horror as he hissed (yes hissed) at me that he was going to take the children, and that I would be left with nothing. And that the police would be coming to take me away. There was a chilling emptiness there. A bottomless void of darkness from which venom emanated. This snarling, spitting, hissing, ridiculing creature was the <u>real</u> man I had married. 'Smiling Death', someone had once called him, and now I knew why. Finally I understood how all those other times of*

fury and rage had barely scratched the surface of what really lay beneath. It lasted barely a minute. And in the next moment, he was promising to change, declaring undying love, saying we could make it work. Eyes blue once again, pleading.

Who do narcissists target?

Anyone can be targeted by a narcissist, but the people who tend to fall the hardest and for the longest tend to have some or all of a number of specific traits.

Rescuers

Those people who need to rescue others are often taken in by the narcissist's pity plays, time and time again. Rescuers usually need to rescue others to feel needed and to matter and, although they may think their rescuing tendencies are generous in nature, in fact, even with non-narcissists, they are dis-empowering to the recipient. A narcissist will exploit this trait time and time again, pulling the target into the drama triangle and keeping them there.

Those who are blindly compassionate and empathic

Despite being hurt by the narcissist, or seeing others hurt, these people (who tend to believe that all people are intrinsically good) continue to forgive poor behaviours endlessly. They believe that 'love conquers all', and they give more and more of themselves to the narcissist. The problem is that, in terms of empathy, this is one-way traffic. A severely narcissistically disordered person will not be cured by love or kindness, no matter how much they receive. And in repeated forgiving, they are actually giving the narcissist *permission* to reoffend, ad infinitum. (Forgiveness is not something that should be given to another person so that they can continue to abuse. For those who have been narcissistically abused, it is something that may be given, without telling the narcissist, some months or years down the line, when they are safe from the narcissist. And here, it is not for the narcissist, but as an act of love for *themselves*, to save themselves from the toxicity of their own bitterness).

Those who were brought up in narcissistic households

You can only know what you know, and these people have been wired to accept poor narcissistic behaviours from an early age, to dance to the tune of their narcissistic parent, and to develop work around strategies as second nature. These people are very attracted to narcissists, and feel a strong 'chemistry' towards them. They probably don't realise that what they are actually feeling is *familiarity*, especially as the narcissists they are drawn to may be superficially very different to the type of narcissist they grew up with. Our brains subconsciously draw us to what feels familiar and safe to us; to what we *know*, in order to re-create the patterns of our upbringing. These people may be surrounded by narcissists, unwittingly collecting them and bringing them into their lives as friends, clients, colleagues and partners.

Echoists

The term 'Echoist' was coined in 2005 by Dean Davis, an American psychoanalyst. In Ovid's myth of Echo and Narcissus, Echo had a curse put on her so that she wasn't able to speak her thoughts, and could only repeat the thoughts of Narcissus (who she was in love with, but who could never love her back). He famously fell in love with his own reflection and drowned as he dived into the pool to try to be with himself.

Echoists are essentially the polar opposites of narcissists, on the opposite end of the spectrum. They have poor interpersonal boundaries, and do not like asking for or accepting help or gifts. They feel uncomfortable having needs at all, and prefer to focus on fulfilling other's needs and wishes. Unlike Closet Narcissists, they do not feel special at all – quite the reverse; they have an aversion to feeling special. They feel under entitled and undeserving, and are emotionally fragile. They find it difficult to accept compliments and can suffer from anxiety and

Echo and Narcissus (1903), a Pre-Raphaelite interpretation by John William Waterhouse
(courtesy of Wikipedia)

depression. Like narcissists, echoists suffer from low self-esteem, but they do not create a false self of superiority to mask this. They overlap with the category above in that they are also the sons and daughters of narcissists. (What determines whether a child of a narcissist becomes a narcissist or an echoist or indeed a healthy individual with good self-esteem is not yet fully understood. Even within the same family, three children subjected to the same parenting may grow up to be one of each of the types above).

Co-dependents

Those people who have previously been in co-dependent relationships are particularly prone to repeating this pattern, and falling for a narcissist. Co-dependency is a specific relationship addiction characterised by preoccupation and extreme dependence – emotional, social and sometimes physical – on another person. Co-dependents feel extreme amounts of dependence on loved ones in their lives and they feel responsible for the feelings and actions of those loved ones.

Who is likely to be a co-dependent?

Co-dependents are essentially caretakers of another, and they are themselves addicted to needing to take care of the other person.

Often, the person they are taking care of also has an addiction of some sort. Partners of alcoholics and substance addicts are co-dependent. Partners of narcissists are also likely to be co-dependents. Interestingly here, some see *narcissism itself as an addiction to needing to feel superior*, in which the cravings to feel superior are like the incessant cravings for a drug. Just as drug addicts need more and more of the drug to satisfy their cravings, narcissists require more and more narcissistic supply in order to feel superior.[2]

So, if you are someone who has previously been in a relationship with an alcoholic or drug addict, you are at risk of becoming the partner of a narcissist, and vice versa. People who have had to take care of a close family member with a chronic illness may also become co-dependent, as can children who were forced into a caretaking role with their own parent. It also seems that any type of deeply traumatic upbringing can result in co-dependency issues. Those who have developed co-dependent personalities often find themselves repeating relationship

---

[2] *Baumeister and Vohs. Narcissism as addiction to esteem, January 2001 Psychological Inquiry 12(4):206-210.*

patterns in their new relationships with different alcoholics, substance addicts and narcissists. If you've been with a narcissist in the past, until you break your co-dependency issues, you may well find yourself with another in the future.

It's as if the co-dependent person is almost defined by the other person's addiction or needs. They are those who have a hard time saying no, who have poor boundaries, and who deny their own needs, thoughts and feelings. They confuse love and pity, and have a need to control others and to take care of others. These types often fear abandonment and have a need to always be in a relationship. They are typically so busy taking care of another that they forget to take care of themselves, and so lose their own sense of identity. Indeed, many long-term partners of narcissists report feeling as if they didn't really know who they were anymore. The good news is that co-dependency can be overcome with awareness and some work. (See the Further Reading section at the back of this book).

The spectrum of narcissism

By now, you may be wondering whether *you* are a narcissist. After all, every now and then, perhaps *you* secretly feel that you are a bit special.

Well, as it happens *most* people do not see themselves as being merely average. Studies have consistently shown that *most people think of themselves as being exceptional.* This is known as the 'better than average effect'.[3]

People who see themselves as being better than average are happier, more sociable and often healthier than those who do not. They are confident, more able to endure hardship, creative, good leaders and have high self-esteem. They also see their partners as being more special than they really are.

Conversely, the opposite is true for those who do not feel special; they have higher rates of depression and anxiety, and do not admire their partners as much. Not feeling special is officially bad for your health.

It is interesting that the biggest predictor for success of a romantic relationship is one or both people in the relationship thinking that their partner is better than they actually are by objective standards. People in successful romantic relationships think that their partner is more beautiful, more intelligent and more talented than they actually are, and as a result, they feel special by association.

---

[3] *Brown JD. Understanding the better than average effect: Motives (still) matter. Personality and social psychology bulletin 2012, vol 38(2) p 209-19).*

So it would seem that feeling special per se isn't actually a bad thing after all. It is a question of degree. *It's a question of to what extent a person clings to the **need** to feel special **at the expense of others**.*

So, narcissism exists on a spectrum. Those at the lowest end of the spectrum who do not feel special are the echoists, after Echo, the voiceless, presence-less character in the Myth of Echo and Narcissus. They have little sense of self and of their own needs. They are 'negative narcissists', as it were, with *not enough* healthy self-belief and self-advocacy skills.

Those at the opposite end of the spectrum are the narcissists, after Narcissus, who are blind to the needs and feelings of others, concerned only with meeting their own needs to feel special.

And those in the middle of the spectrum balance their own inherent healthy sense of specialness with the capacity to care for and meet the needs of others. *This is the ideal place to be on the spectrum; in a place where your own sense of self-worth keeps you boundaried, healthy and happy, with a healthy amount of self-advocacy.* (Some people call these traits 'healthy narcissism'. We believe that this is a confusing oxymoron, and that the term 'narcissism' should only ever be used in its correct, pathological sense).

In Dr Craig Malkin's book, *'Rethinking Narcissism'* he describes a spectrum from 1 to 10. The echoists lie at the left hand side of the spectrum, with those who are the least able to be seen, heard and self-advocate occupying position 1. Those who are better at self-advocacy and expressing needs are at 2, 3 and 4. These people could still do better for themselves, however. Positions 5 and 6 are where the optimally healthy people lie, and the narcissists lie at 7 through to 10, with the most pathologically narcissistic at 10.

Interestingly, narcissism is not fixed. People can move up or down the scale a few notches depending on their life circumstances. Some moves may be permanent, others not.

For example, consider the heart surgeon, who started his adult life off as a 7. He may have been selfish and arrogant, but not always at the expense of those around him. He may have only occasionally devalued others, and may not have been overly entitled, perhaps not expecting too much in the way of special treatment. As he progresses up the career ladder, getting ever closer to the top, he gets more and more narcissistic supply. More and more young nurses may see him as a better prospect, and will fawn over him, vying for his attention. He will thrive on this, and feel more special as a result. He may have his pick of them,

The spectrum of narcissism

0 Echoist   Pathological Narcissist **10**

and may conduct affairs with them, discarding them as more attractive ones come in. He has just hit an 8 on the spectrum.

His empathy for those he has discarded may decrease. He may start to feel entitled to have these affairs as his wife is no longer worshipping him as much as these ladies at work. Concurrently, as his surgical ability increases, he will cure more patients of their conditions, and they will be grateful to him and impressed by his ability. His narcissism may increase further. He may start devaluing his other surgical colleagues, commenting on their lack of skills relative to his. He may start to look as though he believes his own hype, although underneath this, his intrinsic self-esteem is low. He deflects from this feeling by acquiring more and more narcissistic supply. He earns more money, and buys fancy cars and holidays, impressing his junior colleagues who suck up to him, hoping that one day he will recommend them for a job. He is now at a 9.

By the time he reaches the upper echelons of his surgical career, he is regularly saving lives and people around him are hero-worshipping him. His wife has not been on her pedestal for a long time, and he now feels far too important to participate in mundane domestic tasks. He runs her ragged. He starts to gaslight her, demean her and criticise her. He projects his own affairs on to her. At work, he is considered a God, and he starts to expect to be treated like this as the bare minimum. Those around him cater to his every whim, laugh at his jokes, and want to be associated with him. He grandiosely sweeps in to work to see his patients late. He does not bother to learn the names of his junior colleagues. He keeps his staff working after hours and performs operations which are so risky that no one else will do them. Some of his staff are starting to feel abused by his demands on them. He needs to believe he is the best of the best. His secretaries are exhausted, chasing him for paperwork which he feels he is too important to do in a timely fashion. He is at a 10.

He chases even more power, wealth, status and possessions to feel special. He needs a younger, prettier wife who is more of a trophy; your cue as the lawyer, to enter stage left. And at this point, to the narcissist, to paraphrase Shakespeare, all the world is indeed a stage, and all its men and women merely players. Sadly, at this stage, *all* empathy has left the building.

At this point, it is probably far too late to bring the narcissist back down the scale to his original 7. It may, however, have been possible for a specialist psychotherapist to have made some progress earlier, perhaps when he was at an 8.

Note that *all* of us have times in our lives when we slide, usually temporarily, up the scale a few notches. If we have been bereaved, for example, we will feel entitled to be treated with special care. We may be selfish and introspective, focusing on how we are feeling above all else, putting our own needs first.

Adolescents also typically slide up the scale, becoming selfish and unempathic, relying on a sense of artificially feeling special to get them through. Once adults, they slide back down again, able to consider others once again.

The elderly also experience a surge in narcissism, often as ill health takes hold, making them feel vulnerable, sad and self-centred as they struggle to hold on to their sense of self-worth.

It is also possible for those at the lower end of the spectrum to move up, towards the healthy zones of 5 and 6, with awareness and perhaps therapy.

If you wish to know where *you* currently are on the spectrum of narcissism, please refer to Dr Craig Malkin's book, '*Rethinking Narcissism*' in the Further Reading section of this book.

Representing a client with NPD

3

I n Chapter 4 we consider how to achieve the best possible outcome, alongside the provision of considered and appropriate support, when the spouse or partner of your client suffers from NPD.

However, from the point of view of the family practitioner, it can be even more important to understand this personality disorder when it is your *own* client who is affected. It is not just about how they treat the other half of the couple involved, but what sort of behaviour *you* will be subjected to; the extent to which you will become a pawn in their game and subjected to their manipulation, and what effect this has both upon you as an individual and upon the way in which you provide them with legal representation.

Due to the nature of the work involved, family law practitioners are highly likely to find themselves working alongside individuals who suffer from narcissistic personality disorder, to a greater or lesser degree. Such people are more likely to experience relationship breakdown and, as a consequence, require advice and support. The purpose of the information contained below is to increase your awareness of what to expect when you are so instructed, and to improve your skills when confronted by a case which involves one party who has this disorder.

Family law practitioners are multi-skilled, and each individual case represents a new challenge. It is not the intention of this publication to dissuade you from acting on behalf those with NPD – just to enable you to recognise and deal with them without allowing your own well-being to suffer as a result.

How can you identify that a potential client is suffering from NPD before you accept the instruction?

The narcissistic client is likely to become:

- One of your most demanding clients

- One of your most difficult cases

- The sort of case which intrudes on your thoughts when you should be 'off duty' and troubles you unduly

- Unduly acrimonious

- Constantly changing goalposts so very difficult/almost impossible to provide any accurate costs estimate

- A bad debt

- A negligence claim against you

If at all possible, it would be beneficial to evaluate before accepting instructions whether this really is the sort of client for whom you want to act. As family lawyers we are naturally empathic; we regard all clients as equal and would hesitate to turn work away. We have a natural inclination towards dispute resolution and an assumption that with the right guidance every dispute is capable of being resolved, even if ultimately that, regrettably, requires some form of intervention and adjudication. As will be explained below, representing the narcissistic client will provide an entirely different experience. It may be one with which you are entirely unable to cope as a professional. An evaluation at the outset will therefore be extremely useful.

It is so important, not only for you as a professional, but also for the spouse and the family of the client with NPD, that you do not take on the case unless you have an understanding of the behaviour with which you will be confronted, and how to deal with it to achieve a satisfactory outcome for the case. *The lasting damage to which your lack of understanding may contribute is not something to be ignored or disregarded.*

As a family practitioner, you need to arm yourself with the skill set either to identify that this is not a case for you, or know that you have the knowledge and ability to be a participant in something which will be a roller coaster ride for all concerned – and potentially draining and debilitating for you, as the narcissist's representative.

What to look out for

Be wary of the client who has previously instructed a number of other lawyers. Why did that solicitor/client relationship break down? Sometimes it can be for entirely valid reasons, for example:

- **There was a clash of personality or style between the lawyer and client.** Family law is an extremely personal discipline. The solicitor and client are likely to be working together for many months, perhaps even years, and it is consequently important that, at the very least, they have a good working relationship, if not a close bond. The client will be making life-changing decisions based on the advice and guidance of an individual whom they must trust, if not like. If the necessary minimum chemistry just isn't there, then a change may be essential.

- **Financial reasons.** The original lawyer may have become unaffordable for a perfectly legitimate reason.

- **Recommendation.** After instructing their initial solicitor you may have come very highly recommended by a friend or other source, and the client would prefer to go with that recommendation.

If, however, there appears to be no good reason, be wary of falling into the trap of thinking that you might succeed where others have failed. We are all human

---

It is so important, not only for you as a professional, but also for the spouse and the family of the client with NPD, that you do not take on the case unless you have an understanding of the behaviour with which you will be confronted.

---

and we all appreciate praise for being good at what we do. But beware of the slightly excessive, almost sycophantic praise which is likely to be showered upon you by the narcissist when you first speak and/or meet.

The narcissist will be overwhelmingly flattering and full of charisma, even to the point of being slightly flirtatious. They will overplay the 'victim' card. They may be unduly charming (holding doors open, letting you sit first etc). They may hold eye contact with you for a length of time which feels ever so slightly uncomfortable. They will want to tell their story and may appear entirely oblivious to anything which you have to say.

Do they appear over confident? They are likely to have no regard at all for the feelings of their spouse/partner and may, through the telling of their story, reveal a disproportionate desire to inflict what they see as deserved retribution. Do they present as having an air of arrogance and entitlement? If they are aware of NPD as an entity it may even be that they tell you that it is their *spouse* who is a narcissist, as they project their own personality traits on to them. They will, very likely, appear to completely believe their version of reality, initially making getting to the bottom of things even harder for you

As family practitioners we are told so often of the importance of listening. Never will this skill be as important as when you are trying to identify the narcissistic client at the outset of a case and decide whether this is a case in which you want to become involved. The detail set out in this chapter is intended to demonstrate just how very important this is, particularly for your own personal well-being.

In addition, be prepared to listen to others with whom you work. You may have a PA who has a 'sixth sense' when it comes to spotting a client who should be avoided in an initial phone call. Be prepared to have regard for the concerns or observations of others before accepting an instruction.

If you decide that this is an instruction which should be declined, provide a simple reason for doing so. This might be that 'at the present time you do not have the capacity to take on such a complex case', for example. Have to hand the details of other family lawyers whom you might recommend.

If the narcissistic client has decided that they want to instruct you, they may not be put off easily, and will see this first encounter with you as one which they intend to 'win'. Watching how this plays out may strengthen the wisdom of your decision.

Your narcissistic potential new client may increase the flattery, or be prepared to wait as long as it takes, because you are 'the only person/the right person/the best person to fight their corner and provide them with the support and expertise which they need'. If you have been recommended to them as an 'expert' in this field they will see themselves as entitled to 'the best' representation.

If you are determined that this is not a case in which you intend to be involved, you must hold your position rigidly, at the same time being similarly charming and helpful.

If you are able to remain resolute, be warned that the narcissist will not appreciate this rejection and there may be some backlash. At the very least, this will involve telling anyone who is interested that you were unhelpful (or worse) and, as a consequence, are a solicitor who should be avoided. If they were recommended to you by another lawyer or professional contact, rest assured that they will tell that person never to recommend anyone to you again. Do not be unduly concerned about this. People tend to form their own judgement and such repercussions are almost certainly preferable to that which may lie ahead for you in the event that the instruction is accepted.

How the narcissist will behave towards their lawyer

If you have not worked out the nature of the client behind this new instruction and have therefore taken the matter on through ignorance and/or a lack of understanding, you are at the start of a very rocky ride. You may, however, have made a conscious decision not to step away from the challenge. Either way, it is important that you have some grasp of what lies ahead and how best to deal with it.

Family lawyers tend to embark upon a career dealing with the issues encountered by separating couples and their children because they are naturally empathic and have a willingness to try to make things better. Unfortunately, this makes them ideal targets for the narcissist. The narcissist will have spent the duration of their relationship with their spouse or partner manipulating them, and behaving in an identifiable set way. This behaviour is not, however, reserved for members of their family, and the empathy of the family lawyer will be used to manipulate them also, throughout the conduct of the case.

The narcissist will initially present as charming and plausible. They will be keen to tell their story, often presenting themselves as the victim and leaning on the lawyer for support. They will seek to draw them in and explore, in the early stages of the retainer, how malleable they might be. Be under no illusion that this is no more than a game to the narcissist – but a game, which, on every level, they must win at all costs.

The behaviour cycle of the narcissist is to place the person in focus on a pedestal, then devalue them, eventually discard them (or come close to discarding them) and then repeat the cycle. Initially the narcissist will be full of praise for the lawyer. They will want to be viewed as a valued client with issues of particular complexity. They will be keen to tell the lawyer that they came very highly recommended; that they are so pleased to have found you; that together you will make a great team.

You would be a very unusual person not to be at least slightly pleased to hear that you are so highly regarded professionally. We all have egos, to a greater or lesser extent. Each year, as professionals, we compete for ratings in either the Legal 500 or Chambers and Partners (or both). Such a process is driven by our professional desire to be well regarded amongst our peers. The narcissist will tap into this and exploit it to the fullest extent.

Narcissists thrive on pushing boundaries at an early stage, to take control. They will want to test what, as a professional, you are prepared to put up with. They will try to take you out of your comfort zone at every opportunity, to reinforce to themselves that they are in control of you, and that you will bend to their demands.

They will want to speak to you outside of office hours, and may just drop by the office without an appointment, on the off chance of discussing something with you in person. They will try to blur the edges of your professional relationship, treating you as a friend and confidante, and telling you that no one has ever understood them like you do.

You may find that they invite you for lunch or to a social event, the purpose of which is to push the boundaries of your professional relationship and, at the same time, secure an hour of advice for the cost of a reasonably priced lunch rather than the usual hourly rate. If you are not careful, you may even find yourself manoeuvred into paying for the lunch yourself.

This 'honeymoon' phase, however, will not last long.

Most clients seek legal advice to be helped to resolve their disputes and reach a fair and reasonable outcome, so enabling the parties and their family to move forward with their lives separately. *The agenda of the narcissistic client is very different.*

Narcissists tend to collect people along the way in their lives. Even if they have discarded a person, their discard may not be permanent, as they may well draw the person back in at a later stage in order to obtain narcissistic supply from them. But narcissists do not cope well with being discarded *themselves*. So, the suggestion that their spouse or partner might leave *them*, even if the narcissist is the party involved in another relationship (or often several other relationships), gives rise to what is described as 'narcissistic rage' in the narcissist. Remember that a narcissist suffers from a personality disorder due to a trauma which occurred early on in their life and which adversely affected their own attachments – to the extent that they feel intense shame and dislike of themselves. This is at the very core of their being. It causes them to doubt that anyone can really care about them and creates within them an inability to care for others. The only value which other people in their lives have to them is the extent to which they momentarily mute those feelings of shame and rejection, and make them feel better about themselves. For a narcissist to be left is, therefore, in their eyes, unacceptable. The narcissist will want to punish their spouse or partner in a way

Be wary:

► **if the client has previously instructed a number of other lawyers**

► **of falling into the trap of thinking that you might succeed where others have failed**

► **of slightly excessive, almost sycophantic praise**

► **if the client appears over confident**

► **if the client has an air of arrogance and entitlement**

► **if the client tries to push the boundaries of your professional relationship** they will never forget, for having the audacity to inflict pain upon them. *But*, at the same time, *they will not want to let them go.*

Their lawyer will be manipulated into performing a role in the performance which will ensue. All will be carefully and skilfully orchestrated by the narcissist, who will have an extreme attention to detail. The experience of the lawyer will not be dissimilar to that of the spouse in the process. The narcissist will see both as tools to be used to achieve their own objectives.

The first lesson for both the spouse and the lawyer (both lawyers in fact) is that an outcome (satisfactory or otherwise) is unlikely to be the end goal sought by the narcissist who is, in fact, much more interested in prolonging and controlling the process. Paradoxically, the lawyer and the spouse or partner will both experience the same block, the complete intransigence of the narcissist.

So, at the outset of the case, the lawyer is subjected to a charm offensive as the narcissist tells their story, seeks sympathy and empathy and weighs up how to ensure that their lawyer is completely under their control. Almost certainly most lawyers will be drawn in by this.

The narcissist is firm in the belief that he or she knows better than the lawyer; in fact they have no real need for advice, but they do need a lawyer to play a necessary role in their constructed process.

The lawyer representing the narcissist ideally needs to remain one step ahead of their client; able to identify their behaviour patterns and respond accordingly. When you have a detailed grasp of narcissistic behaviour traits you will realise that they are repetitive and predictable.

You will need to be cognisant of the following signs:

- A refusal to accept advice unless it concurs with the action which they wish to take.

- A refusal to listen or change their stance.

- An insistence that their specific wording is included in correspondence, or even that they write the letters which are then put on headed paper and signed off by the lawyer, insisting that their advisor's input is not needed. They may do this under the guise of saving time and therefore cost. Generally, such correspondence will be self-contradictory, raging in tone and riddled with unreasonable demands.

By now you may begin to feel uncomfortable; caught between an obligation to act in accordance with instructions and a client who refuses to recognise the benefit and purpose of your advice. In fact, your client is starting to take charge of the way in which the case is being handled.

Of course, any separation will cause either or both parties to encounter the bereavement cycle, resulting in a plethora of emotions ranging between anger, hurt, frustration and despair. If you don't comprehend the nuances of the situation in hand, it is easy to justify irrational behaviour by simply convincing yourself that the client is upset and things will settle down.

It is, at this juncture, important to remember that the agenda of the narcissistic client is not what you would ordinarily expect. Their objective is to lock the other person in a protracted and expensive process. This then forces them to engage with the narcissist. It allows the narcissist to be omnipresent, when actually their spouse/partner needs to go 'no contact' and sever all ties with them at as early a stage as possible, for their own psychological protection and well-being.

Regrettably, the toxic behaviour patterns of the narcissist can also start to have an immense effect upon the personal well-being of you, as their lawyer.

Having started by complimenting the lawyer and being charming, almost flirtatious, at the commencement of the retainer, the narcissist will build on this. Emails requiring immediate and urgent attention will be sent at the end of the working day, or even outside office hours, as the narcissist tests how boundaries can be pushed and just how much control they have over you. Phone calls will similarly be made late in the day, demanding a return call before you leave the office. They will then extend the duration of the call for as long as possible, with irrelevant and often repetitive conversation, again pushing boundaries, in order to hook you in and maintain control of you. The narcissist will allude to feeling very supported by you. They will explain that they have come to regard you as so much more than just a lawyer but as a friend; a further attempt to blur professional boundaries and exercise and extend control.

Flattery will continue, but this may begin to be tinged with criticism if you continue to seek to provide advice which is not in line with what the narcissist wants to hear. You need to understand that it is the narcissist who is calling the shots, and what will begin as gentle, but firm, reprimands will start to creep into the narcissist's general manner.

In these early stages of the case it is as important for the narcissist to groom their lawyer as it is for them to deal with the matter in hand. The narcissist may call to discuss strategy, or perhaps for no real reason at all, the purpose being to test how malleable you have become and how much more work they need to do in order to ensure that you are fully under their spell and compliant.

A narcissist is likely to offer a significant sum to be held on account if they are affluent, or pay all interim bills by return, or by credit card if they do not have the available funds. They want to be perceived as a reliable source of income, another method of duping their lawyer into liking them and seeing them as a good client; someone for whom they are prepared to ignore their professional boundaries, work outside office hours and go the extra mile. Do you see the picture that is gradually building?

Once the narcissist is comfortable that their lawyer will do as they are told, they can turn their attention to the meticulous and calculated demise of their spouse/partner, secure in the knowledge that they have, in their armoury, legal representation which will support those objectives, pretty much on demand.

The narcissist's approach to financial remedies

In the financial remedy process it is, in essence, necessary to work out broadly what the assets are and then decide how to divide them. That sounds fairly simple. The narcissistic client will do everything in their power to ensure that it is not.

The first step for the narcissist is *not* to provide disclosure. Rest assured they will not provide anything on time or in complete form. Be prepared for paperwork to arrive in incomprehensible dribs and drabs. They may insist on incomplete paperwork being provided i.e. an incomplete Form E with vital information being described as 'to follow'. If the narcissist has done their job well on you in those early stages you will find yourself sympathising with the unreasonable requests for financial information and becoming the shield behind which the narcissist will hide. The narcissist will *tell* you which documents are reasonable to provide. They may, seemingly plausibly, explain that their company accounts just won't be ready. They have, of course, been trying to run a business to stay financially afloat while trying to deal with the irrational and hysterical behaviour to which they have been subjected, at the hands of the other side. How are they supposed to maintain an income stream in such difficult circumstances and deal with all these unreasonable requests for obvious information?

It is worth pausing here to note that many narcissists are either self-employed or in a form of employment which allows them considerable autonomy, as they do not conform well to regulations or restrictions. Their personality disorder often drives them to be successful, inevitably at the expense of others.

Slowly, you will find yourself with no choice other than to provide poorly prepared and incomplete documents both to the court and to the other side, and then seek to justify the omissions. The narcissist feels in control of the process and everyone involved.

Sadly, if you are in the court process, the delay occasioned by the court system also plays into the narcissist's hands. A penal notice attached to an order for disclosure can take a long time and the tendency therefore is to hope that inadequacies and omissions will be rectified along the way. Not so with the narcissist. They will hold off providing vital documents for as long as possible and may, in fact, never produce them at all.

The narcissistic client will want to explore your professional relationship with the solicitor on the other side. "How well do you know them?" "What are they like?" "Do you get on well?" "I can see you are easily a match for them". "They clearly don't know what they are doing." Once again, the narcissist is testing boundaries, gaining knowledge and using flattery to cause you to drop your guard and perhaps be more candid then you might otherwise be with this client. The narcissist will remind you that you have developed a close and quite special working bond; in fact they have come to regard you as much more than just their lawyer – they see you as a friend.

Or so the narcissist wants you to believe. The narcissist is subtly reaching into the professional relationship between the two lawyers in an attempt to 'pull the strings' of all parties involved in the case. The narcissist will see this as a challenge and an opportunity to demonstrate their superiority in a situation where they are also regarded as a victim. Never forget that the narcissist's sole objective is to feed their need for supply from whatever source or, better still, multiple sources which might be available.

We have looked at the narcissist's obdurate approach to disclosure on the basis of an assumption that the case is in the arena of the court. This is the 'battleground' which the narcissist will prefer. In due course we shall consider why out of court methods of resolution, most particularly mediation, are not suitable where one of the couple is a narcissist.

As the stage is set, the behaviour of the narcissistic client will become even more challenging for their representative. The following are particular points to be aware of:

- They will expect you to respond to them in an unreasonably short time frame. This is the follow on from the unexpected visits to the office and out of hours phone calls. What was used to create a slightly over familiar relationship with you is now used to make unreasonable demands; to push you further and further out of your comfort zone, placing the narcissist more firmly in control, both of you and of the process as a whole. You will find yourself wanting to please this client and at the same time unwittingly falling into their clever and pre-meditated trap.

- They may request the repeated re-drafting of letters and suggest that they should not be charged for the time involved, as it is due to your incompetence. Notice here that the devalue stage is beginning to creep in. The client who placed you on a pedestal is now gently, but effectively, pulling you down. The client who was keen to place money on account and pay their interim bills by return is now critical of the fees incurred.

- You will find yourself having to compose letters to defend the unacceptable actions of the narcissist towards their spouse/partner. The narcissist will refuse to listen to any advice which suggests that they might curb such behaviour, maintaining that their actions are totally justified. They will demand your support notwithstanding the fact that they may be removing joint funds without consent; refusing to pay school fees; removing items from the home; bugging the home; or stalking their spouse/partner. You will inwardly recognise that this behaviour is inappropriate, even outright abusive, and may find yourself writing letters to the other side which are fuelling the fire between the couple. You realise that you can see no way out of conforming to the instructions of your manipulator. The narcissist will revel in the drama which this scenario creates. They will present as the victim, with their spouse/partner being the perpetrator – and you will be shoe horned into the role of rescuer. In reality, they are the perpetrator and their spouse/partner, the victim. When you try to diffuse the situation by providing measured advice, the positions shift again. The narcissist retains the role of victim, but now you are cast in the role of perpetrator. The narcissist feels that they are no longer receiving positive and unconditional support from their lawyer, which is a loss of supply. They experience narcissistic injury, just as they did at the hands of their spouse/partner when they decided to end the marriage/partnership. This acute and very real pain can lead to narcissistic rage.

- The narcissist may insist that any court hearing is adjourned, usually because they have another very important and unavoidable commitment. If this cannot be achieved they may arrive at court late or explain that they have to leave early. This gives them a sense of control over the proceedings and underlines their total disregard for authority. They do not expect to be bound by the rules adhered to by others, as they are far too important. They rarely comply with Court Orders, as their sense of entitlement allows them to believe that the terms do not apply to them. Alternatively, they will seek to impose their own restrictions.

None of the above does much for your reputation as a lawyer. You are being driven into presenting as either someone who fails to produce clear disclosure or properly and promptly completed court documents, or alternatively as a poor advisor, unable to persuade your client to listen to your wise counsel. None of this bodes well.

The narcissist, on the other hand, is in their element. At the centre of the debacle, they are gaining high level supply from everyone involved. They would prefer that this feeling did not subside and will therefore do everything in their power to maintain the chaos.

The relationship between lawyer and client will start to deteriorate, heading towards the devaluation or discard stage. The narcissist may re-apply their charm, apologising for their behaviour, which clearly stems from all the stress they are under, as a result of the abhorrent behaviour of their spouse/partner. If you are hooked in by the narcissist at this stage you will welcome the reprieve and, just like any other person involved with a narcissist, will crave the restoration of how things were at the outset of the retainer. You will return to being empathic and the narcissist will have you back under control, to start the cycle again.

If, however, you stand your ground, maintain your advice and remain in conflict with the narcissist, this will again lead to narcissistic rage and discard. The narcissist may seek alternative representation, leaving behind them unpaid bills and almost certainly a complaint about the service/advice received. This is dealt with in greater detail below.

The drama of court proceedings

The narcissist's aim will be to take the proceedings to court. This will be for a number of reasons, which are inter-related:

- A court hearing is almost certainly not what their spouse/partner would want. By leaving them with no choice, the narcissist retains financial and emotional control.

- A trial is a great source of narcissistic supply. They are centre of attention.

They can show how special/clever/charismatic they are. They will try to impress the judge and get them on side. They have the opportunity to win and also bring down the other side, teaching them a lesson for daring to stand up to them, supported by their professional team.

- Psychopaths have reduced activation of the amygdala in the brain and this may also be true of many narcissists, particularly those at the high end of the spectrum. It means they have a reduced fear or fight/flight/freeze response to a situation where most would feel nervous or uneasy. This makes them quick thinking on their feet and exceptionally calm in the witness box. They are also extremely accomplished liars. Their idea of 'truth' is the version of events which best suits them at any particular time, and they will completely believe their own skewed version of reality and demand that others do the same.

Appearance is everything to a narcissist. They may ask you what you think they should wear to create the right impression. You may find that they also comment on how they feel that you should present yourself, again to create the right impression. Another example of boundaries being pushed and crossed, in order to exert control.

Introduction of Counsel to the proceedings

So far we have examined the relationship between the narcissistic client and their instructed solicitor. Due to the combative and litigious approach craved by the client, the instruction of Counsel is inevitable.

Having identified (or suspected) that your client suffers from NPD, you may want to get Counsel on board at an early stage. This is as much for your own protection as for the benefit of the client.

The involvement of Counsel will appeal to the grandiose side of the client's personality. They will already hold a belief that their situation is complex and exceptional, and therefore engaging what they view as a superior level of legal representation will support this perception.

You need to be aware that the narcissist is not really interested in the nature of your advice; they are playing a game with an entirely different agenda to that which might be expected. Any advice is likely to be ignored and/or challenged.

Obtaining a second tier of advice early on has the advantage of being a point of reference throughout the case, and an early 'test' for the initial views which you have expressed. It also enables the client to decide whether they are happy with the individual barrister selected, before they are required to attend court.

Do bear in mind that narcissists are very fickle and quick to apportion blame. Nothing is ever their fault. The barrister who was subjected to the narcissist's charm and flattery in conference may become incompetent, and even negligent, in their eyes later if things don't go their way.

Counsel have much less choice than solicitors over the cases in which they become involved at the early stages as instructions/briefs are received and distributed by the clerks. Barristers build up good working relationships with their instructing solicitors and, as their careers develop, the solicitors from whom work is received tend to be those with whom they have an established rapport. Due to their participation in the more contentious side of family law work, their potential exposure to clients suffering from NPD will be consequentially high.

As Counsel's working relationship with the client tends to be in 'spikes' rather than ongoing, it is easier to remain detached. It remains vitally important for Counsel to recognise the personality disorder of the client whom they are representing, to enable them to be prepared both for what will be expected of them and how to deal with the situation.

You might include tell-tale signs in the instructions/brief, with this in mind. As instructing solicitor, remember that your client is entitled to see the papers sent to Counsel on their behalf and therefore care needs to be exercised regarding what is actually said. However, it will be useful to make it clear that:

• You are the most recent in a long line of instructed solicitors

• Managing expectations is important

• The client has a strong personality and is keen to challenge advice

Counsel needs to understand the clues that may be provided. You may also wish to speak with Counsel by telephone in advance of sending written instructions.

The narcissistic client will want their barrister to be 'better' than Counsel for the other side. This may mean they need to be more senior, but certainly 'punchier'.

Again, they will push boundaries and blur the edges of the demarcation within the professional relationship. They will suggest that Counsel can contact them direct if required. They will want to work closely with Counsel. This might be a point where you, as the solicitor, with (allegedly) care and control of the case, experience devaluation, as the narcissist cosies up to their new found, and far superior, legal representative. The barrister becomes an even better stick with which to beat the other side, and battle lines will be drawn. The narcissist will love the oppositional nature of the court process and the opportunity to undermine the other side via their legal gladiator.

Of course, as practitioners, we know that the court process in family proceedings is geared to settlement, and that a contested trial should be something which takes place in only a handful of cases.

But the narcissistic client is not looking for settlement. *They are interested in annihilation.* They will struggle with discussions during which they are not present which take place between opposing Counsel.

Counsel must be warned that their instructions most likely will change. If they feel that things are not going their way, they will be quick to suggest that Counsel has misunderstood what they have

> **Never fall into the trap of sending Counsel to court with the narcissistic client, even for the most simple hearings, without someone from your firm to take a note.**

been told, or that they have not been correctly instructed by you. They may seek to suggest that Counsel has misrepresented their position to the other side. As instructing solicitor, make sure that you keep a careful contemporaneous note at all times, and ensure that Counsel does the same. Never fall into the trap of sending Counsel to court with the narcissistic client, even for the most simple hearings, without someone from your firm to take a note. If the client balks at the cost of this, it is even worth sending someone at no cost to the client for the protection of the firm (an example of how profitability can be eroded when acting for someone with NPD – but a vital precaution to take). Such a suggestion will almost certainly find favour, as it appeals to the feeling of entitlement and self-importance. The scenario does, however, have to be handled with extreme care, as it could give rise to the narcissist expecting other services free of charge.

Always ensure that Counsel's fees are agreed in advance with the narcissistic client, and obtained on account prior to the hearing. Even if the hearing goes well the narcissist is likely to quibble over the fee, as to do so feeds their need to feel superior and to 'win' in all circumstances. They thrive on a 'deal' and feeling they have come out on top. If the hearing goes badly in their eyes, they may be unlikely to pay.

Just bear in mind that the only acceptable outcome for the narcissistic client is a means of prolonging the misery and upset which they are able to inflict on the other side. If this can't be achieved they will lash out at whomever they think they can most easily blame. The lawyers (both Counsel and solicitor) must guard against being pushed into the role of either victim or perpetrator and not allow the narcissist to attempt to drive a wedge between their own professional team.

Out of court processes

It may be your mode of working to endeavour to keep clients out of court and assist them in resolving their disputes out of court via mediation, collaborative practice and arbitration. You may be thinking that a client who suffers from NPD would not be interested in selecting a representative who has a reputation for a conciliatory approach but rather one from a more litigious background. Unfortunately, that may be unlikely for a number of reasons:

- A lawyer who is known to settle matters out of court is far more likely to be empathic and therefore a better source of supply for the narcissist

- The narcissist will enjoy pushing the lawyer's boundaries and driving them out of their comfort zone

- The narcissist will welcome the opportunity to present to their spouse that they have selected a representative with a reputation for out of court dispute resolution in order to 'wrong foot' them

It's vital to be aware that an 'out of court' process such as mediation or collaborative practice is likely to be highly unsuitable where one of the couple suffers from NPD.

Mediation

From your own perspective, you may be keen to 'off load' this difficult client to someone else, to see if they can achieve a settlement with you simply providing advice in the wings. It is important, though, to understand that mediation is a process which is unlikely to result in a settlement of any kind. As the narcissist's lawyer, therefore, you would need to think very carefully about whether mediation is appropriate to consider.

Let's pause to consider the dynamic which you may be helping to create in attempting to secure a mediated outcome.

Mediation is likely to be welcomed by the narcissist. It brings a new player to their game. It provides an opportunity for direct contact with their spouse/partner, from whom they may be separated. Rather than seeing mediation as a forum for constructive negotiation, a narcissist will see it as one through which to increase costs and wear down the other side towards the desired capitulation.

The narcissist may insist on their own choice of mediator, thereby having the opportunity to imply to their spouse/partner that the mediator is on their side. Alternatively, they may accept the suggestion made by the other side, as this presents an opportunity for blame when the process breaks down.

The narcissist, of course, does not want to settle the case, and mediation gives them the ideal opportunity to delay reaching an outcome. Not only will they be presented with a new and probably empathic professional to charm and manipulate, there will be the added benefit of their spouse meeting 50% of the cost.

The narcissist will be aware that the discussions in mediation cannot be referred to outside of that context, and may therefore delight in pretending to explore options and build up the hopes of the other side – only to constantly change the goalposts at the last minute and then suggest that the others involved in the process, including the mediator, did not properly understand what they had intended. There is also the joy of spinning the wheel for three people, alternating the roles of victim, perpetrator and rescuer; maintaining control of the alternation and therefore the process itself.

The objective of the narcissist will be to take control of the process and to manipulate both their spouse and the mediator. It provides for a highly toxic environment, and not one within which a reasonable outcome can be constructed.

How the narcissist will manipulate the mediator

If the mediator is sufficiently astute to recognise at the intake session that one of the couple suffers from NPD they may unilaterally decide that the case is not suitable for mediation. But what happens if they are unable to see through the charming story telling at that stage?

The narcissist will do their best to get the mediator 'on side'; to form an inappropriate relationship with them within the process in order to undermine their spouse. This may start with contacting the mediator direct either by telephone or email with an innocuous query, perhaps about the timing of the meeting, which then develops into exploring what sort of person the mediator is and how to use them to their advantage. If the mediator appears pliable they will pile on the charm and play the victim role, as a person just trying to do their best for their family in difficult circumstances, but being presented with hostility and unreasonableness from the other side at every turn. They will be keen to cause the mediator to become tacitly sympathetic to their situation.

They may arrive very early for a meeting, in the hope of engaging the mediator in private conversation, or take a long time to pack their bag and put on their coat at the end of a meeting while their spouse quickly departs, again in an attempt to have a private conversation. This unlikely alliance will play into the narcissist's hands and they may even report the irregularity to their spouse/partner, to undermine the mediator and, therefore, the process.

The narcissist will seek to undermine and challenge the mediator at every opportunity. For example, they may challenge the mediator's GDPR compliance, or refer to specific process guidelines, to make the mediator feel uncomfortable. They will attempt to manipulate them into questioning their own judgement by trying to prove them wrong.

The mediator must be on their guard and make sure that they religiously follow the practice code; the narcissist will be constantly tempting them to deviate from their standard practice, and when the inevitable neutrality of the mediator rises to the fore the narcissist is likely to turn on them and metaphorically lash out. At this point the narcissist is highly likely to bring a complaint against them.

They must not be afraid to 'call time' as soon as they have a hint of what they are potentially involved in, if they feel outside their comfort zone and out of their depth.

Albeit rewarding, mediation is challenging and often draining work. Where one of the couple is a narcissist, the process can become an experience which adversely affects the mediator's well-being. The mediator, like everyone else involved, will need to be extremely resilient and confident in their capabilities to take on such a case, and prepared to terminate the process if their instincts indicate that they should do so.

Does mediation ever work with a narcissist?

It would be wrong to say that a mediated outcome is an impossible achievement, but it would need to be extremely carefully managed by the mediator. It is a situation which may better lend itself to hybrid mediation with lawyers present. But even if 'shuttle/hybrid mediation' is proposed (where the parties remain in separate rooms and are accompanied by their respective lawyers) the process is unlikely to work.

> **Rather than seeing mediation as a forum for constructive negotiation, a narcissist will see it as one through which to increase costs and wear down the other side towards the desired capitulation.**

For the best chance of success, the following factors would need to be in place, as a minimum:

- The mediator fully understands NPD and the consequential behaviours which are likely to manifest

- The narcissist has their eye on an outcome which they would like to achieve

- That outcome is within the bracket of that which the court would see as reasonable

Collaborative practice

Adopting the collaborative approach is something which also should be considered with extreme caution where one of the couple is narcissistic. It may, in fact, be even less appropriate than mediation.

If collaborative practice breaks down, both parties must change their legal representation. We already know that narcissists are highly likely to change solicitor often and therefore this will not cause them a problem at all. For their spouse/partner however, it brings in a very subtle and unattractive form of control. Their spouse/partner may have formed a strong working bond with their own lawyer, in whom they have confidence and from whom they gain support. This, in turn, may provide them with the strength to stand up to their narcissistic spouse/partner; perhaps something very uncharacteristic and which the narcissist really doesn't like. The perceived bond between their spouse/partner and their own lawyer may be a bond which the narcissist badly wants to break. The collaborative approach provides the perfect opportunity to do that.

Collaborative practice may appeal to the narcissist for additional reasons:

- It provides an otherwise unusual chance to meet the solicitor on the other side at an early stage. The narcissist can charm and flatter them in the hope of creating a relationship of friendliness and 'banter' which unsettles their spouse/partner.

- Having met the lawyer on the other side they can be critical and undermining of that lawyer through direct reference to their spouse/partner outside the meetings, pretending to be helpful.

- They can perpetually move the goalposts, prolonging the process and increasing the cost.

- By behaving badly, they can try to force the other side's lawyer to call time on the process. This makes their spouse or partner's lawyer look like the 'bad guy' for causing their own client the added distress of having to find a replacement lawyer.

For all of these reasons the collaborative approach should be viewed with extreme caution. This is particularly the case if you are acting for the narcissist's spouse/partner.

How your narcissistic client will behave towards their spouse

It is perfectly possible that your narcissistic client shows none of the potential 'tell-tale' signs of direct behaviour in your dealings with them, so that you have no idea of the sort of individual you are dealing with. *Things may, however, become very much clearer when you pay careful attention to the correspondence which you receive from those representing the other side.*

Of course, we all know that divorce or separation can be one of the most traumatic life experiences which anyone can suffer, and that the situation can give rise to uncharacteristic, and even hysterical behaviour by someone who at all other times is entirely rational and level-headed. However, the behaviours which a client who is narcissistic will be subjecting their spouse to are typical, and should not be confused with hysteria from the other side.

The sorts of things to look out for are as follows:

- Having inappropriate conversations with the children about possible future financial arrangements which unsettle them, in order to manipulate them into supporting their narcissistic parent. This may include things such as saying that they will have to leave their (private) school and move somewhere else, away from their friends; that they are going to be very poor due to the behaviour of the other parent; that they will have to move to a much smaller house.

- A suggestion of stalking the other spouse, both online and in reality.

- Bugging the house/car/computer.

- Threats of or actual violence to the spouse or property, such as threats to burn down the house, have pets put down etc.

- Enlisting the help of others ('flying monkeys' – called such from the helpers of the Wicked Witch of the West in the Wizard of Oz) to report on the activity of the spouse, or spread untrue and detrimental rumours about them to others.

- Intercepting the spouse/partner's post or having it re-directed to themselves.

- Hacking into spouse/partner's emails.

- Refusing to move out of the family home after separation, yet openly conducting extra marital relationships, often in front of the children.

- Denying the spouse/partner access to any paperwork including their own.

- Conducting a smear campaign against the spouse/partner and attempting to isolate them from their support network by telling/writing lies to friends/family/work colleagues and anyone else who features in the life of the spouse. They may make extreme claims of secret unacceptable behaviour which they have had to silently bear such as affairs, drug abuse, alcoholism, violence, child abuse or mental health issues.

- Reporting their spouse/partner to the police for alleged assault (this is very common indeed).

- Removal of property from the family home (particularly items of sentimental value such as photographs or jewellery) without agreement.

- Removal of vehicles without explanation or agreement.

- Threats to move abroad with the children.

- Manipulative correspondence, which feels like blackmail, and other 'scare tactics'.

It is important to remember that the narcissist almost certainly did not want the relationship to end – even if they have a new partner (or partners). If their spouse/partner found the strength and resolve from somewhere to bring things to an end, the narcissist will be reeling from how this makes them feel, bringing back all the early feelings of rejection and shame which almost certainly caused the personality disorder in the first instance. They will be thrown into narcissistic rage and, through their lawyer, will do everything in their power to punish their spouse/partner. They hope that this will cause them to break and either change their mind and reconcile or, alternatively, make them understand just what a rocky road this will be. The narcissist will do everything in their power to make sure they are tied up in an expensive legal battle for as long as possible, as they try to destroy them.

It is so important that you, as the representative of the narcissistic client, are able to recognise exactly what you are dealing with, and do not allow yourself to enable and support the narcissist's abuse of their former partner.

The narcissistic litigant will want to inflict pain, suffering and hardship upon their former partner who, in their eyes, needs to be punished for failing to continue to play by their rules. They will want to starve them of funds by a number of means including the following:

- Instructing you to write numerous letters on peripheral issues requiring a deadline response, intended to both unsettle the other side and cause them to incur unnecessary legal fees as they defend themselves over small, but hurtful or irritating points, which do not affect the overall resolution of matters. Don't forget that the narcissist is not really looking for an outcome of resolution.

- Getting close to an agreement and then suddenly and inexplicably wanting to change the goalposts.

- Refusing to agree to the role of Respondent in the divorce proceedings no matter what, even if they have committed adultery and this would be the simplest ground. They will want to be the Petitioner in an 'unreasonable behaviour' petition because the breakdown of the marriage cannot be their fault.

- Not wanting to pay any form of interim financial support, even if they are clearly the stronger financial party in terms of income.

- Making wholly unreasonable financial demands if they are the weaker financial party.

- Messing around with the payment of school fees to render the children's future education uncertain and demonstrate that it is something of which they are in control.

A narcissist will want to do anything possible to keep financial resources away from their spouse/partner. They are highly manipulative and their expressed high moral standards, in fact, only apply to other people. They are very convincing liars and resolutely believe their own 'truth', becoming angered (narcissistic rage) if they are not believed. They actually have no understanding of the difference between the truth and a lie, which can be very alarming. They adhere to their own version of events and seek to impose this on everyone else involved, inflicting cognitive dissonance when their 'truth' is validly questioned (see page

It is so important that you, as the representative of the narcissistic client, are able to recognise exactly what you are dealing with, and do not allow yourself to enable and support the narcissist's abuse of their former partner.

181 and page 264 for an explanation of cognitive dissonance). A high earning narcissist will happily reduce their own income and assets in order to punish their spouse/partner. Do not underestimate this.

Some of the tactics employed are:

- Excessive spending, giving money away, buying expensive gifts

- Selling assets to friends/family at vastly reduced prices

- Hiding money in a business or investing in hopeless business ventures

- Delaying taking payments from their own business

- Forgoing a bonus

- Reducing their own income through working part time/having less work/ contemplating retirement

- Overpaying tax

- Overpaying subordinate workers – especially if they are in some kind of relationship with them

- Driving down the value of the family home by refusing to maintain it properly; publicising that this is a divorce situation so a quick sale is required; refusing to properly engage with an estate agent

- Running up joint credit card bills

- Withdrawing large sums from a joint account without proper explanation or reason

Do you want to act for the narcissistic client?

We have already identified that those who suffer from Narcissistic Personality Disorder are likely to be involved in a relationship which breaks down and therefore in need of legal representation. Hopefully you are now gaining an insight into what that may involve for you as their instructed lawyer. Lawyers are trained to use their expertise to present the case of their client in the best possible way and seek to achieve the best possible outcome, taking account of all of the circumstances.

It is appropriate to pause at this point to consider what will be deemed by the narcissist to be a successful outcome. Probably not a fair and reasonable resolution. They will want to punish their spouse, either as part of a 'final' discard process or because they had the audacity to end the relationship of their own volition without permission or agreement.

You may feel that, on balance, everyone has the right to professional representation, the case may be lucrative and you know what potentially lies ahead and welcome the challenge to deal with it. And that is ok. It could even develop into a niche specialism for you.

Be aware, however, that when you are acting for a narcissist you are likely to take a hit on fees. As well as sending copious emails and calling around the edge of office hours, they will ensure that they talk about matters which have nothing to do with their case on the phone. This is, in part, to build a relationship with you, and in part to blur the lines between what is and what is not chargeable. Be sure that they will be the first to challenge your fees, when it suits them.

You will, however, want to take special care to protect yourself and your firm:

- You may want to amend your terms and conditions (something perhaps to consider in any event) to provide that you do not deal with emails or take phone calls except between the hours of 8am and 6pm Monday to Friday.

- Make sure that your terms and conditions are signed.

- Ensure that you always have sufficient funds on account of costs to cover all work which you are about to undertake, and disbursements which you will incur.

- It is very difficult to give written costs estimates to a client with NPD because their demands and instructions are likely to change suddenly, and without warning or reason. They are also likely to challenge invoices raised. For this reason, keep a written note of every conversation which takes place in relation to the file, even if at a social event.

- Update your costs estimate more regularly than usual.

- Never allow Counsel to attend a hearing without someone from your firm present to take a note, even if it is at the expense of your firm.

- Avoid giving out your personal mobile number (although it will probably be requested). Narcissists do not respect boundaries.

- Try to ensure that the file is dealt with by an experienced fee earner at all times – this is not a case for a junior assistant (see below).

- Make sure that your workload is such that you can devote proper time to this case, without allowing it to take priority over other matters.

You may decide at an early stage that this is not a case in which you wish to become involved – and that is absolutely fine. Do not remonstrate with yourself for reaching this decision.

Bear in mind that if the narcissist decides that you are the right lawyer for them (i.e. one who has the sort of reputation to which they are entitled and/or whom they believe they can manipulate) they can be very persuasive and insistent.

The narcissist might seek to persuade you that matters can be concluded swiftly and amicably. You, in turn, might suggest that you will be unable to work to their timeframe; that you do not have the capacity at the present time to take the case on.

You could ask for a very large deposit on account of costs (which is not a bad idea in any event) and hope that they are reluctant to pay and look elsewhere. If they surprise you and pay what is requested, at least you are well in funds to proceed. This will provide a certain level of protection (at least from a financial perspective) from the difficulties which lie ahead.

An experienced PA is often very adept at identifying potential clients who suffer from NPD during an initial telephone conversation. Narcissists view those who they perceive to hold a subordinate role as individuals with little, or no value, and are likely to be rude and dismissive to them. Listen to the views of those with whom you have worked for a long time and whose judgement you value. (Compare this to the wholly different approach adopted towards the lawyer's PA when the case is underway. They will represent an opportunity for triangulation and be someone to flatter, manipulate and have on side; someone to call, ask for favours and through whom to further create the 'special' client relationship which they so badly crave).

Passing the case to a junior assistant

Be warned that this is not the sort of case that you can pass to an inexperienced practitioner, however much you might want to, despite the fact that you may have many reasons to do so. The narcissist will be a needy and demanding client; you may feel that it would be more cost effective for someone with a lower hourly rate to deal with the endless emails which they send, so that the fees do not become disproportionate. From a business perspective it would make obvious sense to pass the matter to a more junior fee earner. You may tell yourself that this will be fine because you will be supervising them. Indeed, it may be even something suggested by the narcissist, or they may well query why you have not done this when they start to contest your fees.

However, a narcissist will run rings round your junior assistant. They will almost certainly raise a complaint about them at some stage, and this could have a very damaging and lasting adverse effect on the career of a young lawyer. You could even lose a member of staff as a result of the experience they have suffered at the hands of this client. Don't forget that any kind of impact is supply for the narcissist, and the opportunity to play games with an inexperienced lawyer will add another enjoyable facet to the game which they are playing.

Terminating your retainer with a narcissistic client

If you do not recognise the nature of this client initially, either because you are just too busy to pay proper attention, or their 'mask' is just too good, it may be very difficult to extricate yourself at a later stage. The Code of Conduct prevents you from terminating a retainer without good reason and you must, even in those circumstances, consider the effect which such action may have on the individual client. Timing may be crucial. It would not be reasonable to leave your client in an invidious or detrimental position due to your desire no longer to act.

It is likely that you may, at some point, receive correspondence from the client which will become tantrum-like towards you, particularly if the advice provided is suggesting a contrary approach to the one the narcissist wants you to take on their behalf.

Demonstrating a breakdown in trust between lawyer and client is probably the best reason to end the retainer if you need to, and will probably be evidenced by the sort of correspondence which you may receive – likely to be highly critical if you are not simply agreeing to be the mouthpiece for the client's wishes and whims.

It is in this situation that an understanding of the sort of person you are dealing with becomes crucial. Whether or not you feel comfortable to continue to act, or have a need to extricate yourself, you must proceed with caution and care.

Do be aware that if your decision is to terminate your retainer, you may be on the receiving end of retaliation borne out of narcissistic rage. This is most likely to be in the form of a complaint or even a negligence claim. Remember to always retain a complete copy of your file if instructed to send it on somewhere else, once all fees have been discharged.

Also bear in mind that you don't have to send on the whole file. Attendance notes which have not been charged for are for your benefit and can be retained. The client already has a copy of everything which has been sent to them and is deemed to have retained a copy of their own correspondence. You may decide to be awkward and only forward on that which you absolutely have to. Alternatively, you may feel that is not the way you choose to behave and simply send the complete file. Whichever course you take is your choice, but make sure you think about what you want to do carefully in the first instance. Do not allow another member of your team to just send the file out in your absence, even if the narcissist is putting them under pressure to do so.

During the course of the case, the behaviour of the narcissist is likely to have created a feeling of fear in your support and junior staff, as a result of the way they are spoken to and dealt with by the narcissist. This is done to create a desire to please and thereby gain approval of the difficult narcissistic client. All staff need to be clear that they *only take instructions from you* where this file is concerned and *not* from the narcissistic client themselves.

Representing the narcissist in the court process

We have already examined the fact that the narcissistic client will be extremely dilatory when it comes to disclosure. Information will be provided piecemeal and will be incomplete. This is not a Form E to pass to an assistant solicitor for completion or, if it is, it must be meticulously checked.

Narcissists refuse to be bound by time deadlines imposed by others or authority; they are self-confessed rule breakers. Expect, therefore, to be provided with information and/or documents at the last minute, and to be placed under time pressure to get the Form E out to the court and the other side. Your narcissistic client might even instruct you to file documents late, seeing this as a good tactic to place the other side under pressure. Try to resist any games you are instructed to play, emphasising your obligations as an officer of the court.

It is very likely that the narcissistic client will want to plead conduct at section 4.5 of Form E. In almost all cases this will not be relevant. Remember that you are being instructed to provide advice, not to simply follow instructions which are to the detriment of the client and the case generally. Have your strategies in place to deflect this. Appeal to your client's need to feel superior and explain that to plead conduct inappropriately will detract from the very strong points in their case, and could give rise to a costs order against them which would needlessly make their spouse/partner feel like they had won round one. Explain that if financial conduct is relevant, this can be raised differently at a later stage.

This will be another example of an early battle for control between yourself and your client. The more of these you lose, the greater the manipulation will become moving forwards.

The First Directions Appointment

It may be that directions can be agreed with the other side and the issues resolved on paper. If, however, a hearing is required, ensure that it is attended by the solicitor with conduct of the file. If you decide to instruct Counsel it may be a good idea to have a conference first, so Counsel has an opportunity to get the measure of the client in advance. Do not send Counsel to court without someone from your firm to take a note – even if that ends up being at the expense of the firm.

Discuss all of the issues with the client in advance. If you think you may need any form of expert evidence, such as a pension sharing report or property/business valuation, either agree this with the other side or make your Part 25 application.

Your client will probably want to raise an inordinately lengthy questionnaire, designed to frighten, intimidate and raise costs. This will be another occasion when you will need to impress upon your client that they are paying for your advice and guidance, and that they should rely on your experience to present their case in the best possible way.

You are likely to find yourself arguing with your own client. This will be another moment when the narcissist will want to take control and you will need to attempt to resist. It may become a moment when you consider whether trust has broken down and the retainer should be brought to an end. If this is something which you are considering in the run up to a hearing, remember that your obligation to provide a reasonable level of client care means that, if you feel that you can no longer act, the client must have sufficient time to instruct someone else without it being detrimental to their position.

If you are agreeing directions either at court or in advance of the hearing, make sure that you go through this carefully with the client and keep a note to confirm your explanation. This is the sort of client who is likely to say that they did not agree to something – notwithstanding the fact that they clearly did – after the event.

When preparing replies to questionnaire in accordance with the directions order, make sure that they are signed by the client and not you or a member of your firm. A narcissist will be keen for you to do things for them such as sign documents on their behalf. It makes them feel superior and it gives them someone to blame if they feel like it later. Given their propensity to lie, some of the narrative answers given may be untrue and you would not therefore want to confirm accuracy on behalf of your client.

Negotiation and the FDRA

The first point to bear in mind is that the narcissist is unlikely to have any interest in negotiation. What they will want to do is work out what is important to their spouse/partner in the overall potential outcome and do everything in their power to make sure that they don't get it, even if such course of action could be to their own detriment.

The narcissist will do everything they can to thwart the negotiation process. They will fail to comply with directions for as long as they can get away with it (and here they are assisted by the delays inherent in the court system). They will refuse to agree anything, ensuring that everything has to follow the difficult and expensive route.

They will tell you that they want things done 'their way'. Everything will be done at the last minute. They will not want to make a proposal because they will want to test the other side first and find out what it is they want. They will move the goalposts. If assets involve resources such as shares and share options where the values change daily, they will swamp you with confusing spreadsheets to repeatedly challenge the asset schedule produced by the other side.

A narcissist will have an over attention to detail and will delight in wasting time and costs over small points, such as the recovery of a possession or the regular payment of a very small sum of money.

The narcissist will love the fact that the FDRA judge cannot impose anything and will not be the judge dealing with the Final Hearing. This means an arena where they can do whatever they want. They can totally ignore the indication given by the FDRA judge if they wish to do so. They can undermine their spouse/partner by telling them after the hearing that they have been told by their solicitor/Counsel that the FDRA judge is well known for being useless, and thank goodness the trial judge will be someone different. They will know that the solicitor/Counsel on the other side cannot give any guarantees about the outcome, and so the discretionary nature of the jurisdiction absolutely plays into their hands, as does the delay factor.

In the unlikely event that your narcissistic client is, for some reason, prepared to do a deal at the FDRA (perhaps the other side is prepared to agree a deal at the low end of the bracket from their perspective and it is too good a deal to miss), make sure that you do the following:

- Ideally, draft the full order at court, but if you can't do so, make sure that you enter into very clear heads of terms which are signed by your client after you have taken them through them line by line. Don't fall for "Oh I trust you – no need to go through it". Don't forget that they are likely to lie about what happened and to change their mind.

- If the order is drafted later, make sure that it is done as quickly as possible and also make sure that there is no room for any ambivalence in its terms.

- Keep a clear contemporaneous note of everything which is discussed, and record this in writing with the client as soon as possible after the hearing.

- Be prepared for the client to suggest that you misunderstood their instructions at court.

The Final Hearing

When you come to a trial where you are acting for a narcissistic client you are almost at the 'what will be will be' stage. The case ought to have settled earlier. If your opponent's solicitor understands what motivates a narcissist, their client may have been prepared to accept a low offer just to bring matters to a conclusion and stop costs spiralling out of control.

Ahead of the Final Hearing you need to attend to the following:

- Comply with all directions. If your client refuses to do so, make sure you have documented your written request that they must, and have warned them in writing of the repercussions should they chose to ignore that advice.

- Make sure that everything you do is done in a timely fashion – delivery of the trial bundle; Counsel's papers etc. so there is no room for criticism if the client does not like the final decision.

- Explain to your client the 'golden rules' of giving evidence – answer the question, tell the truth and do not get emotional. When they get into the witness box you will have no control over what they do. Take a very careful note of what they say.

- Make sure you have money on account to cover not only Counsel's fees but the overall cost of the hearing, and that the request is made well in advance of Counsel's deemed brief delivery date. Don't be afraid to apply to come off record if this is not provided.

We all know that there are rarely any 'winners' in the court process. Prepare yourself to take the client through the outcome and brace yourself for the reaction should the court not decide in your client's favour.

Communication strategies when representing a narcissistic client

The narcissist will want to communicate with you on their own terms. You are dealing with a client who is looking for narcissistic supply, through adoration, drama and conflict, and who is suffering from episodic narcissistic injury and rage at being in the process of losing their spouse, formerly their best source of supply. Narcissists do not go quietly in divorce or separation, regardless of who made the petition. They are looking for extra narcissistic supply at times like these, when they are running at an all-time low.

You will not be listened to, after the initial idealisation phase, just talked at. You may experience the narcissist's nonsensical pseudologic, and a complete breakdown of all logic during a 'word salad.' What follows below are a few strategies to keep your communications as civil and effective as possible, with a view to maintaining your own sanity at the same time.

Do not be tempted to confront the narcissist with your suspicions of their personality disorder

This is never a productive course of action. It may lead to narcissistic injury and rage, if the narcissist, as is likely, is unable to face the reality of their condition. Commonly, narcissists react to suggestions such as these with 'projection'. You may find yourself being accused of being a narcissist yourself, or of being controlling or manipulative.

Occasionally, a grandiose narcissist will have insight into their narcissism to some degree, but they are likely to view it as an asset, not a flaw. They may even believe themselves to be 'better/nicer/cleverer/more successful than all the other narcissists'. Either way, expressing your suspicions to the narcissist will not be helpful.

Take a time out

If you are having a face-to-face or telephone conversation with a narcissist, and they have pushed your buttons, you may well be triggered into feeling fear, anger or despair. If feelings threaten to overwhelm you, de-escalate the situation by taking a time out. Quickly and politely completely remove yourself from the conversation until you have had a chance to calm down and let the narcissist know that you will resume the conversation later on. A simple, "I will have to go away now to consider the points you have made. I will get back to you later," will suffice.

Communicate by email where possible

A ranting, raging, accusatory narcissist in the throes of narcissistic injury is very difficult to manage in real time conversations, whether it is you, the legal system or their spouse who is the current target of their wrath. Communicating by email gives you an email trail that may be useful in demonstrating that trust and communication has broken down, should you need to terminate your retainer with the narcissist. It gives you time to calmly respond to communications from the narcissistic client, and may serve to moderate the way the narcissist behaves towards you, as everything is in writing, and the narcissist may not want you to have written evidence of bad behaviour. Most importantly, it allows you to dispassionately view the narcissist's communications, without giving the narcissist the opportunity to gain narcissistic supply from your immediate reactions.

'We' is a magic word

Research has shown that using words such as 'we', 'our' and 'us', rather than 'I', 'my' and 'me' seem to temporarily remind narcissists that other people and relationships exist, and makes them more empathic. Wherever possible try to use these collaborative pronouns, particularly when facing challenging situations. Never say "I need you to do X" – in doing this you are setting yourself up as being more important than the narcissist. Your needs are irrelevant to the narcissist and this will result in a knee jerk reaction where the narcissist feels that their authority is being challenged. Say "We need to…" instead.

Remember that the narcissist's inner child is running the show

Try to remind yourself, when the going gets tough, that this person was a child who was treated badly, and this is why they are so difficult.

If you are struggling with a ranting email from the narcissist, copy and paste it into a document in a child's handwriting font. (See page 261, 'A Narcissist's Prayer', for an example). Take some time away from it and then come back to it in this format later – it's amazingly effective in taking the heat out of a situation and bringing back perspective.

The tantrums, the self-centredness, the grandiosity, the fantasy world of superiority – all of these stem from an abandoned, neglected, invalidated child who needs to make their mark on the world to feel that they deserve to be here. They are wired to be like this. Try to call upon your own compassion at these times. Try to be the adult in these interactions, and do not descend into a childlike state yourself in response to the child-bully the narcissist becomes when things are not going their way.

Do not take *anything* personally

When the narcissist accuses you of being incompetent, stupid, inefficient or a thief, remember that they may well be *projecting*. It is never about you. It is always about them. They are batting off their own feelings on to you.

Even if they have not specifically accused you of being a certain way, pay close attention to how you are feeling. Narcissists are experts at passing their own feelings on to you. Question whether this is actually your feeling to be burdened with, or theirs. For example, if you are feeling rejected or questioning your own abilities, just notice this and ascertain whether these feelings are your own. If you only find yourself feeling this way with this particular client, or type of client, the likelihood is that you are experiencing transference of the narcissist's feelings on to you.

Be task focused

The narcissist will try to take you off task chatting about irrelevancies, on your billable time, in order to win you over and groom you for abuse later down the line. Also, be aware that the narcissist's agenda is not the same as yours. They do not wish to find a resolution to problems or to move forwards. They wish to prolong the proceedings for as long as possible, in order to punish their spouse and gain supply from the drama. The narcissist's spouse was, most likely, their most reliable source of narcissistic supply. It may seem counter-intuitive, but they do not want this aspect of their relationship to end.

To get them back on task, and away from rants, tantrums, accusations, complaints, talking about themselves etc, try asking "Can we work out what we need to do to collaborate effectively with the task at hand?" or "Can we focus on the current problem that we need to be solved, and how we best stay on track to solve it?" or "Could we prioritise what needs to be done so that we can sort out the current issue?"

Note the judicious use of *closed questions* here – the narcissist has to respond with a yes or no. Open questions can work against you with a narcissist if you are trying to get them back on task, for example, "What do we need to do to move forwards with the task in hand?" could open up a whole spectrum of answers, wasting yet more time, especially as 'moving forwards' is far from what the narcissist really wants. Also note the use of the 'magic we.'

If possible, start as you mean to go on. If you have allowed the narcissist to ramble on with pleasantries in the initial stages of the relationship with them, it may be harder to establish communication boundaries later.

Don't disagree with a narcissist – use the 'Fogging' technique instead

There is never any point telling a narcissist that they are wrong – they have to believe they are always right in order to maintain that fragile sense of superiority. If you challenge this, you cause narcissistic injury and rage, which is entirely unproductive.

Fogging is a technique you can use if people are behaving in a manipulative or aggressive way. You do not argue back – you give a calm response which is placatory but not defensive, whilst not giving in to their demands. It involves acknowledging any parts of the criticism that are true whilst not responding to the other parts. In other words, you acknowledge the *literal* truth in what the narcissist is saying, but you don't react to any implicit suggestions they are making, and you don't agree to do things they may want you to do.

For example, if a narcissist comes into your office and tells you that you need to completely redecorate and change the layout of your furniture because it's dated and uninviting, instead of justifying why you don't want to do that, being drawn in or feeling insulted, you could simply say, "Yes, the office could certainly be redecorated."

Here you haven't justified yourself, contested the criticism, criticised them in response or become defensive, and you haven't agreed to do what they say; you have merely agreed with the part of their statement which is true. This helps you to remain emotionally detached from criticism, whilst placating them.

Imagine that the narcissist's insult is a stone they are throwing at you. Instead of reflexly throwing it back, you envelop it in the fog that is surrounding you, so that it simply disappears.

Do not start a sentence with 'no' (unless you are being frankly abused or in danger)

Following on from above, if a suggestion is being made that you do not agree with, or a question being asked to which the answer is 'no', do not start the sentence with 'No'. 'No' inflames a narcissist. It gives them the sense that you are seeking to take the control away from them, and that you believe yourself to be superior to them. Implicit in this is that you do not see them as special/clever/right/superior, which is a big challenge to their sense of self, and can cause narcissistic injury and rage. Indeed, you may not get any further than saying the word no, if you put it first in a sentence. Many narcissists, if told they cannot do something will make a point of doing it anyway, just to prove you wrong, and assert their superiority.

Do not react emotionally to a narcissist

To a narcissist, reacting emotionally is a sign of weakness, which will be used against you, if not immediately, in the future. The narcissist needs to get narcissistic supply out of every single interaction, even with you as their lawyer. That could come in the form of feeling important, clever, special, appreciated or nice, or it could come in the form of conflict and drama.

To keep things calm, you need to stay away from giving supply through drama and conflict. No matter how much they push your buttons, do not be drawn in.

If you have found yourself being swept into the narcissist's drama, and are feeling out of control, the 'Grey Rock Technique' is a valuable method to employ. It quickly cools things down by cutting off the narcissistic supply you have hitherto been providing your narcissistic client. Here you deal only with the matter in hand, giving no emotional response at all – not even the merest hint. The aim is to appear as interesting to the narcissist as a boring grey rock. Lifeless and dull, giving out zero energy. Think of a robot, completely devoid of human emotion.

You can do this by:

- Reducing eye contact, or making no eye contact at all

- Making your voice flat and boring, with no variation in tone

- Speaking slowly and deliberately

- Discussing only the relevant points, using as few words as possible

- Completely ignoring and not responding to any inflammatory statements

- Consciously immobilising all facial expressions to a mask-like exterior – no smiling, no raised eyebrows, no brow furrowing – narcissists are experts at reading and feeding off non-verbal cues

It is common for those with narcissistic adaptations to quickly slink away to find better sources of supply when subjected to the grey rock technique. If you have got to a stage where you are hoping to be dis-instructed by your client, it may well be that the grey rock technique, if consistently employed, is the most effective way of making this happen.

Praise the narcissist

Instead of giving narcissistic supply through drama and conflict, you must appeal to the narcissist's sense of importance, cleverness, specialness, or niceness to keep things civil. It may feel wrong, pandering to them in this way, but this is not the same as being sycophantic. Simply praise things that are true, and no more. (Overdoing the praise where it is not warranted, with constant flattery, will only feed your client's unhealthy narcissism). Make sure your praise is in line with how the narcissist likes to see themselves.

Avoid hyperbole, and words such as incredible, amazing, wonderful etc. Be measured and proportionate in your praise. "I see that you are a quick thinker"; "You are good at formulating strategies"; "You speak eloquently on this subject"; "Your job is clearly very demanding and difficult."

When praising a narcissist, you are trying to point out their real strengths. If you do not know them well, you first need to give them the *evidence* that you have seen of them having the strength. For example, "From what I see about how you have built up your business from scratch into the success that it is today, I can tell that you are very determined and hardworking…"

Praise goes a long way to disarming a narcissist, even when they are being downright rude. You may have to learn to swallow your pride and overcome your natural resistance to offering it, however.

Positively reinforce the narcissist's good behaviour

In much the same way as you might work with a child, catch the narcissist's good behaviour as soon as it happens, bring attention to it, and voice your appreciation for it. This will positively reinforce the good behaviour and will also give the narcissist a little boost of narcissistic supply. For example, if the narcissist arrives on time for a meeting, you could say "Thank you so much for making sure you are here on time today – it's very helpful in keeping us on track with our case."

Note that here we are using the 'you' pronoun at the beginning of the sentence. This should be reserved for when you are giving the narcissist ownership of their good behaviour, in order to reinforce it.

Contrast current bad behaviour with past good behaviour

Start with the good behaviour first, using the 'you' pronoun. Then insert the behaviour you want changed, using the collaborative 'we' pronoun. Finally, sandwich it in with another piece of praise, using the 'you' pronoun.

Think of it as a hamburger – compliment, confront, compliment. For example, "It was so helpful last week when you were able to complete your paperwork and get it to me quickly. I've noticed that this week that it's been a bit harder. It would be great if we were able to go back to completing paperwork quickly, so that we can be as effective as possible. I really appreciate all the effort you put in with this."

Narcissists often respond well to this hamburger method of persuasion.

Ignore blame, focus on solutions

There is no point trying to defend yourself or anyone or anything else that a narcissist may be blaming. Narcissists have a fixed mindset regarding their opinions, and you cannot change this.

Completely ignore the blame, no matter how difficult this might be, and look for the solution instead.

For example, "You have charged me for 2 hours work on that letter you wrote. It's not my fault that you kept getting it wrong and had to keep rewriting it. It's your own incompetency that's the problem here – I would have expected more from a supposedly qualified lawyer, on such ludicrous rates of pay. Do I have to write my own letters from now on so that you don't rip me off? This is just ridiculous…"

You could reply, "Letters that need repeated re-drafting do take more time, it is true. Perhaps we should communicate by email rather than phone regarding the content of letters from now on, so that we can be clear on what we want included before the letter is written?"

Note that here you have validated the bit of their statement that you can without actually agreeing with the blaming portion of it. This is another example of 'fogging.' Here you have also used the 'magic we' to encourage a collaborative response when suggesting a solution.

Become thick-skinned

Ignore slights, frank insults and put downs. It is in the narcissist's nature to devalue others – it helps them to feel superior. Where the narcissist has devalued you ("You are incompetent"; "I don't need you to write my letters"; "I don't want your advice, I just want you to do as I say"; "I will not be paying you for that") you need to *ignore any insults*. Employ the use of fogging if you can, to placate the narcissist, so that you can move forwards more productively.

"I notice that you never seem to answer emails after 5pm. How I wish I had a job that allowed me to be so lax. But some of us have actually got to really work for a living, and not just clock off whenever we feel like it. If I stopped work at 5pm it would feel like a half day. No wonder the legal system is so full of delays…" "Yes, the legal system is full of delays" would be a reasonable 'fogging' answer here.

Employ empathy

If you cannot find anything that can be agreed with in the narcissist's statement, you cannot use the fogging technique.

For example, "I think I should threaten to have the kids removed from her. That'll scare her. Tell social services that she is an abusive alcoholic and unfit to be a mother…"

In the example above, try using empathy and validation to try to disarm the narcissist where necessary. Then follow with a dose of praise. After this, make it all about what is good for *them*. Finally, try to steer the narcissist to a reasonable action by using the 'we' pronoun.

For example:

"I really understand how upsetting this is for you and how angry it makes you" (empathy).

"It's good that you are able to think outside of the box" (praise).

"Let's find solutions that will be helpful to you" (making it about them).

"For this we need to work on your form E" (reasonable action).

Use this three-step procedure instead of arguing or correcting

If you try to set a narcissist straight regarding the law or what the right or best thing to do would be in a situation, you are asking for trouble, and communication will break down. It doesn't matter how gently or diplomatically you do this – the narcissist wants you to adopt *their* beliefs and attitudes, full stop. The narcissistic client believes they know best, and you cannot change this.

Step 1

So instead of correcting or arguing, first *mirror back* whichever of your client's words you can that are true, with praise, without adopting their point of view.

For example:

"I've worked my whole life for that b***h, building up a company from nothing, and now she thinks she can take half of it? That house is mine – all mine and she's getting none of it. I'd rather burn it to the ground than let her see a single penny from it..."

Rather than explaining how the law usually sees division of assets, stop. Take a breath and then *reflect with praise*, picking out the bits from their statement that are true and ignoring the bits you disagree with.

"You certainly have worked hard to build up an impressive business and lifestyle..."

Step 2

Pause, to give the narcissist time to assimilate this praise. The next phrase you utter must *not* start with 'but'. 'But' implies disagreement. The narcissist will use it all the time – you must not. *Instead use 'and'*. You are now getting on side with the narcissist, implying that you want what they want, making it all about them. This is important – you have to state why it is in the narcissist's best interests.

"… and we want to handle this case so that you can continue with your success."

Step 3

Now you've got them on side, and you lead by telling them what needs to happen. Here you enlist the 'we' pronoun.

"For this, we need to…"

Tell them how you are feeling in order to change their behaviour

This technique will not work with those narcissists who are very high up on the spectrum. Because it involves you alluding to how you *feel*, a narcissist who is at a 9 or 10 on the spectrum, with no empathy at all, a sadistic attitude and no ability to feel remorse, may use your feelings against you. You may be shamed or ridiculed for them, or badmouthed to others. However, it can be very effective in those who are less narcissistic.

There are three steps; A, B and C – Affect (feeling), Behaviour and Change.

Step one: A – Affect (feeling)

Describe your feeling. Never accuse, simply take ownership of how you are feeling and express it. Try not to use language that is too emotive in this context. Keep it simple. Tone is key – do not sound accusatory or angry. Be calm and gentle.

Examples might be: "I feel on edge"; "I feel nervous"; "I feel upset"; "I feel sad"; "I feel disrespected".

Step two: B – Behaviour

Describe what it is that has made you feel this way – their behaviour that has led to the feeling.

Examples might be: "when you shout"; "when you talk over me"; "when you criticise me"; "when you say that I am incompetent".

Step three: C – Change

Describe the change you want to see, by *asking nicely* for it. Don't tell them what you want stopped (so not, "Can you stop shouting at me?") but tell them *what you want instead.* "Can you lower your voice?"; "Can you tell me what steps you want me to take?"; "Can you adopt a kinder tone?"

Understand the fight, flight or freeze response

If you were confronted by a tiger, your innate reflex survival mechanisms would kick in. You would either try to fight him, run away, or stand there rooted to the spot, unable to move; the fight, flight or freeze responses.

When attacked by narcissist's abuse tactics, you can experience the same reflexes – you either counter-attack, avoid them, or you surrender. One person might always have the same response to narcissistic behaviour (for example, they might always surrender), or their response may vary depending on the precise nature of the attack.

When the brain senses a threat (as it can when interacting with a narcissist), the older parts of the brain (from an evolutionary perspective) are activated. You may have heard of terms such as the limbic system, the brain stem, the reptilian brain and the amygdala in this context – all old structures.

Humans have a very big cortex, the big outer part of the brain that sits on top of the old structures described. From an evolutionary perspective, this is a very new structure, and is the thinking part of the brain. This highly developed large cortex is the reason why humans have done so well as a species. It's also the reason why only humans and chimpanzees (who also have a large cortex) can cry.

But when our brain sees a threat, which it perceives as a threat to our life, the old brain gets activated first, and without even thinking, we are thrown into an instinctive fight, flight or freeze response, with the release of various stress hormones, such as cortisol and adrenaline. Blood is diverted away from the cortex (the thinking part of the brain) to other areas of the body, such as muscles, so that we can fight harder or run faster. The prefrontal cortex (the bit of the cortex at the front of the brain) is normally responsible for thoughtful reasoning, insight and reflection as to what is really going on, and self-soothing.

So when the fight, flight or freeze response is activated, the prefrontal cortex is shut down, and we lose logic and perspective, and instead get sweaty palms, palpitations and a feeling of fear.

The old brain does not know that the narcissist's behaviour is not actually a threat to life – it *perceives* it as such in some people. (Just as some peoples' old brains get activated by being stuck in bad traffic – we all know of those who panic in such situations and get angry or desperately want to run away). It is merely an early warning safety system that is a little too easily triggered in certain situations. The old brain cannot think for itself; it is the keeper of evolutionary, hardwired, reflex survival tactics.

However, with awareness of what is going on, it is possible to overcome these initial reactions and modify the way you respond to a narcissist's attack. In the book '*Disarming the narcissist*' by schema psychotherapist, Wendy T Behary, various communication strategies are given to modify these instinctive responses, as explained below.

Modifying the counter-attack (fight) reflex

If you find that your instinct is to counter-attack when ignored, devalued or threatened by a narcissist, once you've noticed this, resolve to stand up for your rights in a different way. *Your new mantra is "I have rights"*. Assert those rights by saying something along the lines of, "I feel devalued by your words and actions, although I appreciate that this is probably not your intention. You do not need to put me down/ignore me/be aggressive/be rude to let me know that you are uncomfortable with me. You have rights and so do I. I'd appreciate it if you could speak to me with more consideration and I'll do the same for you."

Modifying the avoidance (flight) reflex

Running away from the narcissist's attacks may be your natural instinct, and you may find yourself palming them off on a junior colleague or not returning calls. This is not a long-term strategy that works, and a junior should certainly not be expected to deal with such a client.

If this is your default reflex, rather than running away, you need a temporary reprieve, a time out, in which to gather your thoughts and work out a strategy before you return to the battleground. *Your mantra is "I need a time out"*. Assert this need as follows: "I know that this point is very important to you. It's also important to me but I'm feeling flooded. I need some time to gather my thoughts so that we can speak productively. Perhaps you would also benefit from this."

Modifying the surrender (freeze) response

People who accept the blame, agree with narcissist and just give in are those whose natural instinct is to surrender. They tell themselves that the narcissist is right and that it is all their own fault. *Their new mantra should be "I may not be perfect but it's not all my fault".* "I see that you are upset with me. When I sense that, I have a tendency to give up and give in. However, I may not be perfect but this is not all my fault, and you have to take responsibility for your share too. I'd appreciate it if you could be more thoughtful towards me."

If the narcissist you are dealing with is very high on the spectrum and you think they may mock your feelings or use them against you, you may wish to use these script examples without mentioning your emotions.

Summary: Communication strategies when representing a narcissistic client

▶ Do not be tempted to confront the narcissist with your suspicions of their personality disorder

▶ Take a time out

▶ Communicate by email where possible

▶ 'We' is a magic word

▶ Remember that the narcissist's inner child is running the show

▶ Do not take *anything* personally

▶ Be task focused

▶ Use the 'Fogging' technique

▶ Do not start a sentence with 'no'

▶ Do not react emotionally

▶ Praise the narcissist

▶ Positively reinforce the narcissist's good behaviour

▶ Contrast current bad behaviour with past good behaviour

▶ Become thick-skinned

▶ Use the three-step procedure instead of arguing or correcting

▶ Tell them how you are feeling in order to change their behaviour

▶ Understand the fight, flight or freeze response

Case History

Solicitor – Kate

Client – Mike

Kate is consulted by Mike on the basis of a recommendation from a friend of his. At the first meeting Mike explains that his wife of 34 years, Naomi, has told him that she wants to separate. Mike has received a letter from a solicitor instructed by Naomi.

Mike finds this all very surprising and believes that Naomi is having some kind of breakdown or personal crisis. He tells Kate that Naomi has been behaving very strangely of late. He believes that this may be as a result of hormonal changes consequent to her age or perhaps as a result of a new group of friends whom she has met through her yoga class.

Mike explains in some detail how he has always provided well for Naomi and their three daughters, now all over the age of 18, to the extent that Naomi – who has not worked throughout the marriage – has been the envy of all their friends. Mike explains that he has privately educated all three children and that they have a beautiful five bedroomed home which is now mortgage free.

Mike tells Kate that she comes very highly recommended and states that he needs someone who will set Naomi's solicitor straight and make Naomi understand that she doesn't know when she is well off. Mike tells Kate how he will be relying on her to put his life back on track.

Kate finds Mike to be an ebullient personality. He is a charming man and she is flattered by the fact that she seems to have been so highly recommended by his friend. It quickly becomes apparent that Mike is not minded to listen to what Kate may have to say but rather is keen to tell her his 'story' and to lay out what he expects her to achieve. He has prepared some notes which Kate might find helpful when responding to Naomi's lawyer, Emma.

Mike asks Kate whether is Emma is known to her, to which Kate explains that the world of family law is a small one, and that professionally most lawyers locally do know one another. Mike asks what she is like, but then, cutting across himself, says "No – sorry you probably can't answer that – I already know that you are a match for anyone in this field – after all that is why I am here to see you!"

Kate starts to feel slightly uncomfortable but isn't sure why. She continues to go through the background of the marriage but increasingly feels that Mike has a need to take control of the meeting. He talks a lot, and not all of the information is relevant at this stage, but Kate's style is to let the client do most of the talking in this initial session, so she can get a feel for what they are like and what is important to them.

The meeting was arranged for 12 noon. As 1pm comes and goes, Mike suggests that they go across the road from the office to an Italian restaurant that he noticed on the way in. He needs to eat and assumes Kate does too. It appears that Mike has already checked Kate's diary commitments with her PA and understands that she has nothing else until 4pm. He would like to continue the discussion in a less formal environment. He feels that if he and Kate are to work together to put his personal life back on track to where he wants it to be, they need to have a good working relationship and Kate needs to understand 'what makes him tick'. He would like to buy Kate lunch.

Kate feels uncomfortable again. She is acutely aware that Mike has been recommended to her by a friend of her managing partner. There is some suggestion that he may instruct the firm on his corporate work, which could be lucrative. Mike is making it very difficult for her to decline. She agrees to go to the restaurant where they remain for about an hour and a half.

During the meal Mike tells Kate how difficult life has been on occasion with Naomi and how, because she doesn't work, she

Kate & Mike

doesn't understand the pressure he is under. He also tells Kate how jealous Naomi is and jokes that if she were to see them in the restaurant together she would assume that they are having an affair. He quickly points out what a ludicrous assumption that would be, but explains that this is the sort of thing he has had to deal with for years.

Mike goes on to explain that Naomi, although an excellent homemaker and mother, has not always provided him with the support in his business that he has needed and has, on occasion, refused to accompany him to evening business social events because she has claimed to be too tired. Mike goes on to say that he loves Naomi deeply and that he couldn't imagine life without her. He feels that she has found a new life and new friends at the gym and is forgetting that it is his hard work which has allowed her the lifestyle which she now enjoys.

When Kate returns to the office she realises that she doesn't have all the financial information from Mike which she would like and resolves to write to him setting out what she has and asking him to fill in the gaps. She has asked him for £2,000 on account of costs. Later that afternoon she is informed by the accounts team that £2,500 has been paid on account. Kate decides not to record the time spent over lunch as Mike picked up the bill.

Kate does know the solicitor acting for Naomi. Emma has a reputation for being conciliatory. Kate, on the other hand, tends to issue court proceedings in most cases as it helps her clients if they have a clear time framework in place. She realises that Mike would like to reconcile and thinks she might be able to persuade Emma to at least consider a 'cooling off' period before any steps are taken. She does not stop to ask herself why Mike might want to instruct a lawyer with a more litigious reputation if his preference is to try to save the marriage.

Kate prepares a draft letter to Emma and sends it to Mike for approval – at the same time thanking him for lunch. She decides not to adopt Mike's proposed wording. Mike responds promptly and queries why Kate has not used his draft. He readily concludes that Kate is the expert and says that he will do what she suggests. He reiterates that he feels fortunate to have found Kate and believes that they will make a great team. He thanks her for taking the time to understand his situation. He says that their conversation has made him realise that he has been bullied and manipulated by Naomi for years and that he has been working hard while she has been able to do what she likes and he pays for it.

Kate's slight feeling of discomfort rises again, but she is not sure why.

Mike has been recommended through a commercial contact. He has clearly inferred that he will instruct the firm to act on behalf of his business if his matrimonial affairs are handled well. That may or may not be true, but it puts Kate under pressure which is what Mike wants. He doesn't want his marriage to end. He is keen to present to Kate as a 'victim'. He flatters her saying she comes very highly recommended and he is keen to try to form a bond with her. He probably deliberately arranged a meeting in the 'slot' before lunchtime. He has asked Kate to have lunch with him to blur the professional boundaries. He has paid more on account that he was asked for. Kate hasn't recorded the time spent over lunch as Mike paid the bill but this has resulted in a free hour of advice for Mike. Mike has successfully made Kate feel uncomfortable which is what he wants. He needs to be in control and for Kate to do exactly as he asks.

Mike rings regularly to see if a response has been received from Naomi's lawyer. Kate asks her PA to explain to him that she will call him as soon as she hears anything.

Mike wants everyone to see what an important client he is.

Within a few days a reply is received. Naomi is not prepared to consider reconciliation. On behalf of her client Emma states that Naomi has found it astonishingly difficult to take this step and has only done so with support. She is seeing a counsellor. A draft divorce petition is supplied on the basis of 'unreasonable behaviour'. Emma states that Naomi will only claim costs if the petition is defended. She is preparing voluntary financial disclosure on Naomi's behalf and invites Kate to do likewise for her client. She hopes that, as the children are all independent, matters can be resolved swiftly and cost effectively. She says that she would propose mediation as a process for resolving matters if an agreement cannot be readily achieved.

Kate calls Mike to tell him about the response. He says that he needs to see her immediately to discuss. He can't go home without having talked this through with Kate, and he will get in the car now to arrive at her office as soon as possible. If she is busy, he will wait. This is just too important. Kate says that she can see Mike briefly at 5pm. Mike arrives at 5.20pm blaming heavy traffic for his tardiness.

By buying Kate lunch Mike now thinks that he can call on her time out of hours if he needs to. Kate feels a bit obligated and is also conscious of the need to impress the client. Mike arrives late to emphasise that he is in control.

Kate sees Naomi's allegations of behaviour as being quite 'low key' as she states that Mike has put his job before her, which has made her feel isolated and unloved. She feels they have drifted apart and she wants to start a life without Mike.

Mike, however, is incensed and feels that Naomi has thrown everything he has done for the family back in his face. He insists that Kate draft a petition for divorce 'now' and that it is lodged with the court tomorrow. Kate explains that it is good practice to provide the other side with a draft before lodging anything with the court. Mike appears disturbed, almost frantic, and tells Kate with a raised voice that she must protect him from these lies and that if the marriage is to be over the court must know the real reason.

Kate tries to explain that nothing turns on the content of a divorce petition and that 'no fault divorce' has now received royal assent. She advises that she would want to provide Emma with a copy of the petition so she can take instructions.

Mike's mood becomes more insistent. He tells Kate that he wants the petition issued in the morning and that if she won't do it he will find someone who will. With that he leaves the office.

Kate & Mike

Kate decides that she will think about the situation overnight and decide how best to proceed in the morning.

Mike is pushing Kate out of her comfort zone. She is unsure what to do for the best. She is giving herself reasons why she might be prepared to act in an uncharacteristic way. At this point she should be asking herself whether she really wants to act for this client. Were she to decide that she would prefer not to, she will have a difficult conversation with her managing partner. She would have to present a very clear case as to why she might decline to act, and why that would be beneficial for the firm. She might even go so far as to warn the managing partner that accepting commercial work from this client might not be a good idea. She will have to be clear in her explanation if she is to be listened to.

The following day Mike calls just after 9am, insisting on speaking to Kate. He apologises profusely for his demeanour the following day, stating that he was so upset that he couldn't think straight. He reiterates that his family mean the world to him and it was just such a shock that Naomi would do this. He goes on to say that he has been thinking about nothing else all night and he now realises that Naomi is not the person he thought she was.

Mike understands what Kate has told him about providing a petition in draft first, and he would not want to cause Kate any professional embarrassment, but he has concluded that he must put a 'marker in the sand,' and the petition must be issued today. He is sure that Kate understands how he feels. He asks Kate if she 'must' provide a draft petition to the other side first or is it just 'good practice'. Kate confirms the latter. In that case, whilst Mike does not want to put Kate in an awkward position for his sake, he must insist that his petition is issued immediately.

Kate finds herself feeling that she has no choice. She is keen to make the client happy. She has been told by her managing partner to 'look after him' as there may be a good commercial work stream from him. In her head she decides that when she next sees Emma she can explain. After all, as she has explained to Mike, 'nothing turns on the content of the petition.'

Mike is apologising to ensure Kate is 'on side' and under control. He needs to keep her on a professional pedestal, at the same time doing his bidding. He stresses that he doesn't want to put Kate in an awkward position. The fact that she will do something for him which conflicts with her professional boundaries gives him 'supply'. Kate, in the meantime, is experiencing cognitive dissonance, and giving herself reasons why what she knows is wrong is actually ok here.

The following day the petition is lodged with the court via the online portal without providing the details of Naomi's solicitor. Kate tells herself that this will speed up the process and be a good thing for the couple. She sends nothing to Emma.

The petition is issued and sent to Naomi at the home address, where the couple continue to reside together – although Naomi has moved into the guest room. Naomi is astonished to receive this. She contacts Emma.

Kate receives a letter from Emma expressing concern about the issue of a petition and also explaining that the situation is intolerable. She invites Mike to move out while matters are resolved. He is away a lot for work purposes so this should not be too inconvenient for him.

Kate contacts Mike, who asks to come to the office for a 'face to face' meeting to discuss as quickly as this can be arranged. He is prepared to 'drop everything', the implication being that Kate should do likewise. Kate arranges a meeting at the end of the working day. Mike again arrives a few minutes late. The traffic was terrible, apparently.

Mike refuses to move out. He asks Kate if he can be made to do so. She explains the process and grounds under the Family Law Act 1996. Mike says that Naomi's behaviour is causing him concern, and he blames her friends at the gym. He feels that she has 'had it too good for too long' and he wants to make some changes. He thinks she should get a job. Mike says that he will pay the bills on the house and provide Naomi with £500 per month for her other expenditure. He thinks that should be more than enough. He has seen an entry on the joint bank account which must be a payment to Emma's firm,

Kate & Mike

and he makes it clear that he will not be paying Naomi's lawyer to make his life miserable. He tells Kate that he will only pay enough into the joint account to pay bills and the £500 allowance. She must notify Emma immediately. Kate advises caution, but Mike is quick to say that Naomi has brought this on herself, and must face up to the consequences of her actions.

Somewhat reluctantly, Kate drafts a letter informing Emma of the new financial arrangements for her client.

Emma writes back stating that she will have to apply for interim financial support for her client. Naomi realises that she has much more limited access to funds that she realised. She speaks to her eldest daughter, Sophie, whose husband Tom recently received an inheritance from his late father. Mike disliked Tom from the outset (for no tangible reason save that he had won the affection of his eldest daughter). Sophie has provided her mother recently with a great deal of support, her own relationship with her father having become increasingly more difficult since her marriage.

Tom and Sophie agree to loan Naomi the sum of £10,000 to help her through this difficult time.

The couple's middle daughter, Nathalie, has become Mike's favourite since Sophie married. She has been looking to upgrade her car following a bad MOT failure. Mike offers Nathalie the money to buy a new car, which she is delighted to accept. Mike tells Nathalie that Naomi has become so ungrateful that she wanted to divorce him, and that she has even threatened to throw him out of the house. He tells her that it was because he was away a lot on business, trying to pay for everything, while Naomi enjoyed her extravagant lifestyle, with no financial contribution. Now her older sister and her odious husband are lending their mother money to persecute Mike with lawyers. Nathalie takes her father's side and speaks to Sophie, and a wedge is driven between the two older sisters. The youngest child, Olivia, is away travelling in Asia for the foreseeable future with a group of friends whom she met at university.

Mike is deliberately disrupting the family dynamic. He is punishing Sophie and turning the sisters against one another. He wants Naomi to feel responsible for this and to show her that he is in control.

Emma writes to Kate asking for voluntary disclosure via Form E. She says that as there are no dependent children and reasonable assets, resolution of financial matters should be pretty straightforward. It seems that she has 'parked' the interim maintenance suggestion for the moment. Kate asks Mike to provide the necessary documents. She is very conscious that the complication will be his interest in the business, of which he is one of 3 directors. Mike receives an income, on average, of circa £270k per annum gross.

Mike is suddenly very busy with work and it is now Kate who is pressing him to respond. She passes the task of chasing Mike and completing Form E to her very able junior assistant solicitor, Amelia, who is 2 years PQE. Amelia hears nothing from Mike. In the meantime Naomi, who has decided that she just wants to be out of this marriage, has returned her form of acknowledgement of service to the court indicating that she will not be defending the petition. A copy of this is sent to Mike with the certificate in support of application for pronouncement of decree nisi. This he returns promptly but there is still no sign of the disclosure documentation.

Emma contacts Kate to see when Forms E can be exchanged. Kate explains that she is waiting for Mike's documents. Naomi's form is ready. At home, Naomi asks Mike why he is holding things up. Mike flies into a rage and tells Naomi that Kate's assistant is dealing with this to save money on legal fees which are being run up needlessly by Naomi's lawyer. He maintains that he has provided all documents required and will speak to Kate in the morning to see what has happened. Naomi relays this information to Emma who in turn contacts Kate. Kate speaks to Amelia who assures her that she has received nothing. Kate contacts Mike who tells her that he has sent everything electronically to Amelia some time ago. Nothing can be found on the system. Kate asks Mike to resend the documents. He is annoyed by this and says it will take him some time to do this. He tells Naomi that Amelia has lost the documents and that in future Kate will be doing everything, which will make it much more expensive. He contacts Kate,

Kate & Mike

insisting on a reduction in his most recent invoice due to this inefficiency. He demands that Amelia go nowhere near his file in the future, and that everything is handled by Kate. He threatens to complain to the Managing Partner.

If Kate is certain that the documents were not provided by Mike she should be supporting Amelia rather than accepting his word. Mike is annoyed that Kate has involved her junior assistant – arguably she should not have done so had she realised the personality trait of her client. Mike is blaming his lawyer so that he can tell Naomi that it is not his fault. In the meantime he has no intention of providing disclosure. Again he is taking control, threatening Kate with a complaint to the Managing Partner to undermine and unsettle her. Another point when Kate should seriously consider whether she wants to continue acting for this client. If she chooses not to do so, the most obvious reason is a breakdown in trust and confidence. Timing is, however, important as she must not leave Mike in an invidious position. It is probably good practice not to terminate a retainer if there is a major event on the horizon, such as a court hearing two weeks away or less. Kate must also consider whether she should reduce the fees as requested for a 'quiet life' or whether she should stand her ground as everything has been properly incurred.

Weeks go by and no progress is made. Emma writes again about the interim financial position. Mike instructs Kate to suggest that Naomi finds herself a job and says that in the meantime she is being 'bankrolled' by their eldest daughter and her husband whom he has never liked and who wants to appear 'superior'. Mike says that if Tom wants to take over the financial support of Naomi, he is more than welcome to do so.

At home, however, Mike tells Naomi that he doesn't know what is going on, and as far as he is aware, he has done everything necessary to progress the case. He tells her that he has taken advice about the appropriate level of financial support, and is just doing what he has been told is fair. He points out to Naomi that she started this, and that now that he has been forced to instruct a solicitor, he would be rather foolish if he did not take their advice.

Kate then receives an issued Form A and a date some five months away for the First Directions Appointment. There is also a Part 25 application for a valuation of Mike's business interests and for a pension sharing report. When Kate informs Mike he seems quite pleased at this litigious turn in the proceedings. He asks if he will need a 'QC' to represent him in court.

Kate explains that a conference with Counsel may be useful but that a good 'junior' would be the right level of qualification for the case. Mike expresses some scepticism but confirms that he will follow Kate's guidance as she is 'the expert'. Kate informs Mike that the disclosure process must now be completed. The documents are produced on a piecemeal basis. Documents requested in relation to the company are not available. Mike blames his accountant. A Form E is put together with some omissions. Mike refuses to agree to Forms E being exchanged until the conference with Counsel has taken place. It proves difficult to find a mutually convenient time, as Mike seems to have a string of unexpected, but immoveable, meetings. It becomes clear that Form E will be filed late. Kate writes to Emma to confirm that it will be filed as soon as possible. She knows that it could be filed even if the conference has not taken place, but events have 'beaten her' into just following instructions with little intervention. Kate tells herself that this is the right thing to do with this particular client – another example of cognitive dissonance.

The day of the conference with Counsel arrives. Kate would usually have asked Amelia to attend to take a note but, on this occasion, bearing in mind the history, she decides to go herself. She finds herself telling Mike that she will charge her time at Amelia's rate. In her head she wonders why she is doing that, but pushes the thought out of her mind and tells herself that it is the right thing to do.

The facts of the case are actually fairly straightforward. The family home is worth £1.6m mortgage free. An equal division will house Mike and Naomi. There are other cash assets in Mike's sole name totalling about £60k. Mike has a SIPP with a CETV of £900k. Naomi only has state provision. Mike has a Range Rover and Naomi has a Golf. Naomi also has some jewellery the value of which Mike wants to take into account. The complication is Mike's interest in a company and his income ongoing. Mike is 59. He says that he plans to retire at 60 and always has. Naomi is 57 and has not worked since Sophie was born.

When Mike meets with Counsel he is, in his view, suitably deferent. He seeks to form an alliance with his new 'gladiator' and at the same time is somewhat dismissive of Kate's role. Kate has come to expect this, and gets on with taking a note, secretly pleased that she has the involvement of another professional who Mike seems to like and with whom she can liaise moving forwards.

The conference starts well, but then Counsel moves on to the detail and is critical of Mike's somewhat 'wanting' disclosure. Mike is of the firm view that the outcome is simple. Naomi gets half of everything. For a clean break. The business should be ignored because Mike will leave there in about a year's time and the income will stop. Naomi is over 55 so can draw on her share of the pension and if that is insufficient she can get a job.

Any view which Counsel might hold in the alternative to this approach is met with disdain.

At the conclusion of the conference Kate tells Mike that she needs to speak to Counsel about another matter, but she will be in touch. Mike leaves. Counsel tells Kate to wait and see what questions the other side raise following Form E exchange, and that he would be happy to settle a Questionnaire of Naomi's disclosure, should the client so wish.

Kate leaves Counsel's chambers, pleased that her giving a fictitious reason to hang back for a few minutes had caused Mike to leave in advance. As she turned the corner onto the Strand, however, what should she find but Mike, waiting for her. On the return journey he cross questioned her about the advice given, queried why a QC had not been instructed who might have had a better handle on things, and generally criticised Kate's handling of the case. Kate found that she didn't have the energy or the inclination to do anything more than listen.

The following day Mike was again on the phone first thing to apologise to Kate for his reaction. He again said that he was just incredulous at the unfairness of the situation when all he had done all his life was to work hard to support his family. He was, however, critical of Counsel, who he didn't feel was 'on his side'. As a consequence he didn't want Counsel to deal with the First Directions Appointment but would prefer Kate to do so, 'in whom he has absolute trust'. He would speak to Kate on a separate occasion about Counsel's fee for the conference, which he felt should be reduced if Counsel was not going to be instructed for the hearing.

Kate has a client who is querying fees at every stage now. Mike has an unrealistic view of a 'fair' outcome. Kate had hoped that Counsel would be the buffer for this. She feels as though she is not in control. This is of course exactly what Mike wants. Now he can turn his attention to Naomi whom he intends to punish for having the audacity to bring their relationship to an end. Is this another moment when Kate could terminate her retainer? This depends on how far away the First Directions Appointment date is. Might she terminate the retainer after the First Directions Appointment? Or does she think she has the strength and resolve to see the case through to the end?

Kate decides to 'park' her decision for a couple of days and to speak to a colleague about how representing Mike is making her feel. The colleague to whom she speaks is the Managing Partner with whom she is good friends. Kate discovers that the head of the CoCo team has been contacted by Mike, expressing his disappointment in the manner in which matters are being handled by the Family side of the practice. Claire, the Managing Partner, explains to Kate that she hadn't raised anything with her as she felt sure it was just a misunderstanding, but warns her that terminating Mike's retainer would not be a good idea at this point. She tells her that she is entirely confident Kate can handle it.

Claire has no understanding of what Kate is being subjected to. She is keen to keep everyone happy and retain the client, both in the short term for the family team and longer term for CoCo. She has every confidence in her colleague. Kate has not been candid about her concerns. She does not want to show Claire any sign of weakness. There has always been some tension be-tween the CoCo and Family teams, and Kate does not want to be blamed for the loss of a client. She reluctantly decides to push her reservations to one side and persevere.

Ordinarily Kate would ask Amelia to provide a first draft of the First Directions Appointment documents as indicated previously. The facts of this case are relatively straightforward. Kate's way of working has, however, been thrown completely off balance and she decides to deal with the case herself. She contacts Counsel's clerk to confirm that Counsel will not be needed for the First Directions Appointment. She alludes to the fact that the hearing may be adjourned in order to avoid causing any offence, and asks for the fee note for the conference. She sends the First Directions Appointment documents to Mike for his approval. Mike comes back saying that he does not think that sufficient questions have been raised and criticises Kate for allowing Amelia to have a hand in the preparation of the documents. He provides his own draft questionnaire. After a deep breath, Kate responds confirming that she prepared the documents, as Amelia is not now having any involvement with the case. She further confirms that she has done so at Amelia's hourly rate – a saving of £180 per hour – so that Mike is not adversely affected by this. Mike's immediate response is to say that Kate has not given proper attention to the documents as a consequence, as they are not 'of her usual high standard' and suggests that she uses his document.

Kate has now been disingenuous to Counsel's clerk with whom she has a good relationship. She is reducing her fees because Mike is causing her to alter her normal working practice. Mike is criticising her work and she is being asked to file a document with the court which has been prepared by the client and with which she is not happy.

Kate decides to file Mike's questionnaire without alteration. She doesn't have the energy for the battle with him over the content as she has a number of other very complex matters which require her attention. She writes to Mike explaining that the judge could amend the questionnaire at the First Directions Appointment. Kate feels better leaving the judge to remove the unreasonable questions which Mike seeks to raise so the paperwork is filed and served.

Kate receives an email from Emma, Naomi's solicitor, querying some of the questions raised and expressing surprise about the content of the questionnaire. Kate puts this to one side, thinking that she will deal with this later. She reads Emma's questionnaire and sends a copy to Mike. The questions principally focus on Mike's business and are entirely reasonable. Needless to say, Mike does not agree and phones Kate (on her mobile after 6pm) to say that he expects her to ensure that the judge removes these 'ludicrous' questions from the document at the First Directions Appointment, as Kate has explained the judge has the power to do. Kate tries to explain that the questions are OK but Mike refuses to listen and ends the conversation, saying that he won't hold Kate up as he is sure she has more important things to do than be told how to do her job properly, and he also doesn't want to incur unnecessary fees. He tells her he is confident that she will perform splendidly on the day of the hearing and achieve the 'right' outcome.

Kate prepares the position statement, setting out the case which Mike would like to advance, i.e. that there is no need for a pension sharing report or company valuation because everything is so straightforward. She explains that there should be a clean break as the daughters are all over 18, and both parties should work to meet their needs. She doesn't send a copy to Mike in advance as she has no appetite to spend time drafting and re-drafting the document, not does she have the time. Ordinarily she would ask Amelia to attend the hearing with her to take a note but she decides not to do so. She thinks that Mike will be critical of any costs which might be incurred, and she thinks that she can manage the day on her own.

Kate is now in a situation where she has a client who is praising and devaluing her almost in the same breath. She is altering the way she works to accommodate his unfounded criticism. She knows that Mike won't like the outcome of the hearing, and has decided not to take Amelia with her to court. Is this because she knows the day will be difficult and does not want Amelia to witness that? Or is it because Mike has criticised Amelia's involvement in the case and she doesn't want to expose Amelia

Kate & Mike

to more criticism? She should be taking someone with her to take a note – maybe not Amelia – even if it is at no expense to the client, to protect herself and the firm.

The First Directions Appointment goes ahead. Naomi is represented by Counsel and Emma is also present. As Kate had expected, the judge allows the questions raised by Emma on behalf of Naomi but deletes some of the questions in Kate's questionnaire (the majority of those inserted by Mike). An order is made for there to be a pension sharing report on joint instruction, and also a valuation of Mike's business.

Mike is already at court when Kate arrives. He clearly arrived very early. He makes the point that he has been waiting for over 15 minutes but clearly arrived well in advance of the agreed time. He then makes light of this and says that he enjoyed watching the "comings and goings" of the court waiting room.

Mike queries whether actually it would have been appropriate to instruct Counsel as Naomi has Counsel instructed. Kate gathers herself together and reiterates to Mike the decision which *he* took, not to instruct Counsel, following the conference. Mike says that whilst he understands this, he would expect to have guidance from Kate. He says that he will see how the hearing goes. Kate, who has already felt anxious about this morning's court appointment, feels that anxiety heighten. Prior to going before the judge she explains to Mike again that many of the questions which he wanted to raise are not appropriate and are likely to be deleted by the court.

Unfortunately, during the course of the hearing, it becomes clear that the judge has had limited time to read all of the paperwork, and confirms that he has read the position statements for both parties and also the First Directions Appointment documents. He says that he has 'skim read' Forms E. Although Kate knows that, unfortunately, this can often be the case she finds herself thinking about how she will explain this to Mike once the hearing is over.

At the conclusion of the appointment Mike, as expected by Kate, expresses dissatisfaction about the way in which the matter was handled by the judge. He asks if there is anything that can be done, first of all to revisit the order made and secondly, to ensure that this judge does not deal with any future hearing. He says that he has an important meeting to attend and leaves court in a 'flurry', informing Kate that he will speak to her about this later.

As a consequence of Mike's departure Kate has an opportunity to speak briefly with Emma about the case. Perhaps surprisingly, Emma informs Kate that she may be instructed to put forward a proposal for settlement. Kate half hopes that this might be the glimmer of an opportunity to bring this matter to an end.

Mike telephones Kate, again late in the day. He reiterates his dissatisfaction about the court hearing. Kate does her best to explain that unfortunately the court system is riddled with delay and inefficiency at present, but that the judiciary do their utmost to perform their role, sometimes in the face of adversity. Kate reassures Mike that, in her view, the outcome of the hearing was entirely correct and she refers Mike to her previous correspondence dealing with the draft questionnaire. She also explains that valuation evidence together with a pension sharing report are both essential if the court is to be assisted in making an adjudication at a later stage.

Kate is aware that Mike has outstanding fees and that she will need to render a further invoice to him following this morning's hearing. She explains this to him by telephone. Mike again expresses his dissatisfaction, says that he has to end the call as he has a pressing engagement and confirms that he will come back to Kate.

Kate and Mike are jostling for control of the conduct of the proceedings. Mike is refusing to take advice. Kate is struggling to deal with this. Kate ought to have taken someone with her to court to take a note unless she is absolutely certain that she has been able to keep a clear note of what has happened. Mike, undoubtedly, is unhappy with the outcome and may raise criticism of Kate's handling of the hearing itself. There appears to be an issue growing over payment of fees. Should Kate have perhaps considered terminating her retainer ahead of the First Directions

Kate & Mike

Appointment when Mike questioned her judgement in relation to the preparation of the First Directions Appointment documents? Could she have said that trust had broken down between herself and Mike?

The following week Kate receives a proposal for settlement from Emma on behalf of Naomi on a without prejudice basis. Apparently, a purchaser has been found for the family home. Mike has not mentioned this to Kate. Naomi seeks 70% of the net proceeds of sale of the family home together with maintenance for an extendable term of three years. She also seeks a pension sharing order which would provide her with 50% of the pension assets. She is prepared to leave Mike's business alone. Kate finds the proposal in some ways surprising, but forwards it to Mike for his instructions. Mike tells Kate to go back offering 60% of the net proceeds of sale of the house. He will agree to the maintenance provision and the pension share. Kate is surprised that Mike does not quibble over the maintenance. She drafts a response to Emma's proposal.

Suffice it to say that matters are resolved on a basis that Kate feels is at the bottom end of the bracket for Naomi. Emma promptly provides a draft application for Order by Consent. Mike takes an eternity to give instructions on the draft, and the document proves time consuming to finalise. It is 'touch and go' as to whether the purchaser for the house might be lost. The same applies to the drafting of the pension sharing annex. Eventually, the documentation is finalised. Immediately the order is sealed Mike defaults with regard to the payment of maintenance. Kate however is delighted when Mike informs her that he will deal with this aspect of the matter himself.

Kate receives a detailed note from Mike about her fees. He asks for an overall reduction of £1,500 + VAT to cover the points about which he has been unhappy. Kate finds herself accepting this simply to bring the matter to a conclusion. It is a file that she simply wants to close and put into storage. She feels aggrieved, however, as she believes that she actually undertook work over and above that for which Mike was charged as a consequence of his approach and manner, and now she is having to reduce her fees. Overall, however, her objective is to close the file and put it behind her. She feels that this is worth the reduction in fees, notwithstanding the fact that this may have an adverse impact on her own personal income as a consequence of the bonus structure of the firm.

Kate & Mike

Representing a client whose spouse has NPD

4

S o far, we have considered your position if you are contacted by the narcissist in a relationship. Now we are going to look at the situation from the other side.

Specific challenges faced by the partner separating from a narcissist

Even if you are not instructed by the party suffering from narcissistic personality disorder, your involvement in the case, as the lawyer instructed by the *other* party, will still necessitate an understanding of exactly what you are dealing with. More importantly, you need to understand what your client has been subjected to (for, probably, a prolonged period of time) and the effect this will have had, and will still have, on them moving forwards.

It is also important that you comprehend what an enormous step your client has taken to bring the relationship to an end, if it has been their decision.

If it is an outcome that has been forced upon them, it is vital to consider the pain (probably physical as well as emotional) they will be suffering. It is also crucial to recognise how difficult it will be for them to make the logical decisions which are required of them, and which are in their own interests. Bear in mind that the same areas of the brain light up in the emotional pain of separation as in severe physical pain, and that the 'trauma bonding', which the narcissist's partner will be trying to overcome, makes this pain much more acute than in a 'normal' break up. It literally hurts – and no one functions well when in agonising pain.

The separating partner of the narcissist will be suffering from:

- The acute pain of separation, intensified by 'trauma bonding' to the narcissist.

- The after effects (of possibly years) of narcissistic abuse, with the related emotional consequences.

- Cognitive dissonance (more detail follows later). Here the partner of the narcissist is holding two *opposing beliefs* relating to the narcissist, and their relationship with them, in their brain *at the same time*. Their brain is trying to marry up the notions of Dr Jekyll and Mr Hyde, or to decide on which one to believe in. This causes significant mental discomfort, and makes them vulnerable to being 'hoovered'.

- Co-dependency issues, where they are unable to recognise or stand up for their own needs.

- A propensity to being easily controlled by the narcissist.

- Emotional (and often financial) reliance on the narcissist.

- Isolation, having being alienated from friends and family.

- Episodes of 'hoovering'. If the narcissist does not want the separation they will employ the hoovering tactic; seeking to persuade the other to change their mind and continue the relationship. This is often done through love-bombing, promising to change and even threatening suicide. Often, this will lead to your client repeatedly changing their mind about whether they want to issue divorce proceedings. You may find that a petition is drafted a number of times, or even issued but not served, or withdrawn. Patience and understanding on your part as the lawyer will be vital.

- Worries about the children. Be aware that the narcissist does not want the responsibility of looking after children. They see them as pawns to be manipulated in an attempt to 'win' in the separation process. They also see their children as extensions of themselves. Like all people in the life of the narcissist, their children can only be loved conditionally, when they are of use. They must either make the narcissist look good to other people (thereby providing supply from others) or directly provide the narcissist with supply themselves (see Chapter 5).

If the children primarily reside with the narcissistic parent, there is the risk that the behaviour demonstrated will become normalised. The children may then demonstrate narcissistic traits themselves, and go on to abuse others as adults, or may attract narcissistic partners themselves in later life. The spouse/partner of a narcissist may be constantly torn between wanting to leave their narcissistic partner, yet worried about the effect the narcissist may be having on any children. They may feel that they should stay in the abusive relationship in order to protect the children, or feel extreme guilt for leaving. The potential issues here, especially in regard to with whom the children primarily live, are complex.

- New, or intensified abuse, specific to narcissistic divorces and separations. A high functioning narcissist, in particular, will stop at nothing to punish their spouse/partner, *regardless of who instigated the split*. It is not uncommon for the partners of narcissists to say that they believed the intention was to drive them to suicide. Here the family lawyer will most certainly be involved, and pre-empting such behaviour, and supporting and protecting your client from it is vital. This will be dealt with in detail below.

So, you can see why it is important to pause – to consider both how your client is feeling at this time, and what help and support may be needed to get them through the months (or sadly, even years) ahead.

One cannot emphasise enough how essential the first meeting with any new client is, especially under these circumstances. Always take the time to allow them to tell their story, and listen carefully. Providing a safe place, coupled with permission to tell their story, may be the first steps in a very important road to recovery.

If you suspect a narcissistic partner may be involved, it would be wise to consider the early introduction of a family consultant, psychotherapist or coach, with a specialist understanding of NPD, who can aid your client's return to a functioning logical state. Narcissistic abuse leads to a highly reactive state, whereby the fight, flight or freeze brainstem reflex is easily triggered by the narcissist's behaviours, shutting down the higher brain processes. These need to be restored as your client needs to be in the best possible place to give you instructions (involving life changing decisions, both for themselves and, perhaps, also their children).

As well as providing legal advice and support, you are helping your client gain their own strength to deflect damaging behaviour to which they may have been subjected for a long time. This is often in relation to how (or whether) they communicate with the narcissist in the divorce process. As narcissists seek out partners who are empathic and compliant, they will not expect this change in dynamic.

You, as the lawyer, may be blamed, criticised, or described as 'well known to be useless', as the narcissist tries to undermine the professional relationship between lawyer and client, which is causing their spouse/partner to behave unexpectedly. Whether your working relationship with your client can withstand this devaluing will depend upon the trust which has been built up between you. Much of this trust will stem from the very first meeting, when you listened so carefully to your client's story.

How the narcissist will abuse your client in the divorce or separation process

The narcissist's playbook

At this point please refer to Chapter 2 which sets out in detail the narcissist's playbook, in order to gain an understanding of the unique drivers which motivate the narcissist's behaviours towards their spouse or partner, in separation or divorce. These include:

- Sense of entitlement

- Narcissistic rage

- Need to 'win'

- Lack of empathy

- Supply gained from manipulation

- Need to have the last word

- Need to be in control

- Lack of morals or guilt

- Rule breaking

- Abandonment issues

The narcissist will employ multiple characteristic abuse tactics in divorce, and these will be hard to miss.

Financial abuse

The law is poised to change (2020) so far as that which constitutes domestic abuse is concerned, so that it will include economic abuse. Examples of economic abuse include:

- Having sole control over the family income

- Preventing a victim from claiming welfare benefits

- Interfering with a victim's education, training or employment

- Not allowing or controlling a victim's access to a mobile phone, transport, utilities or food

- Damage to a victim's property

Your client may well have been subjected to economic abuse, as above, during their relationship, but if they have not, this will almost certainly become a feature of the divorce process. Common additional examples of divorce related abuse include:

- Making false accusations against your client so they are forced to incur unnecessary legal fees defending themselves

- Refusing to provide any form of interim financial support

- Changing goalposts when agreements have almost been reached, in order to run up legal bills

- Removing and hiding all financial paperwork, including the spouse's own

- Removing or destroying items from the family home, such as jewellery, joint computers, televisions, essential furniture and vehicles

- Stopping essential payments, such as school fees, mortgage payments and utility payments, especially if the spouse has no way of paying for these, or will have to eat into limited savings to do so

- Using the children as tools of financial abuse, for example by stopping paying for their activities in order to make the other less affluent parent pay

A high earning narcissist will happily reduce their own income and assets to punish their lower earning spouse. Do not underestimate the lengths to which they will be prepared to go – at the same time to their own detriment. The narcissist may:

- Spend excessively on luxury items and socialising

- Give money away or buy unduly expensive gifts for others

- Plunge money into unsuccessful business ventures

- Sell assets, at vastly reduced prices, or give them away to friends or family

- Delay taking drawings out of their own business

- Forgo bonuses

- Reduce their income. Note that successful narcissists, due to the nature the personality disorder, are often self-employed, and so able to control their working hours and earnings

- Overpay tax in line with their previous income (if they have reduced their income) so that a smaller amount is payable in the next financial year – effectively taking money out of the financial pot in the year of the divorce, to be returned to them post financial settlement

- Claim illness and consequential inability to work

- Encourage subordinates, staff, contractors, or suppliers to make inflated financial claims, to increase their business outgoings

- Try to reduce the value of the family home by lack of upkeep or non-payment of mortgage

- Insist on selling the family home at below the market value and encourage 'low ball' offers

- Run up joint credit card debt

- Withdraw large sums from joint accounts without explanation

The lower earning narcissist may also:

- Claim illness or inability to work, possibly backing this up with unconvincing medical reports

- Threaten to adversely affect their spouse's credit rating (which is address related) by running up credit card debts

- Withdraw money from joint accounts

- Sell assets and keep the money

- Use the children as tools of financial abuse, by making inflated claims regarding their needs

- Withdraw cash in dribs and drabs, over time, to build up a secret financial pot

- Artificially inflate their 'needs' by increased spending

- Refuse to agree to matters regarding selling the family home, such as asking price, accepting offers, or being uncooperative regarding house viewings

Emotional abuse

The narcissist will also try to de-stabilise the mental health of their spouse. Tactics include:

- Stalking them both physically and online

- Making threats of or actual surveillance/bugging the home

- Enlisting 'flying monkeys' to report on activity of the spouse or to spread false rumours

- Intercepting mail or having it re-directed to themselves

- Hacking emails or mobile phones

- Removing all paperwork relating to joint finances from the family home

- Refusing to move out of the family home, whilst continuing to engage in abusive behaviours

- Openly conducting extra-marital relationships during the separation process

- Attempting to isolate their spouse by telling lies to friends and family, often alleging drug abuse/adultery/alcoholism/violence/mental health issues

- Removing sentimental items from the family home

- Threatening to move the children far away/out of the jurisdiction of the court

- Threatening to blackmail the spouse, or their friends and family, if settlement terms are not accepted

- Trying to manipulate the spouse into accepting reduced settlement/child arrangements plan through suggestions that the court will decide in their favour, perhaps claiming that their legal case is hopeless, and that they will 'lose'

- Calling the police or social services with invented claims of abuse

- Erasing or removing access to family photographs

- Claiming that others are gossiping about them, or badmouthing them behind their backs, including claims that their own legal team are badmouthing the non-narcissistic partner

- 'Hoovering' (trying to suck the partner back into a relationship with them by promising to change, threatening suicide or love-bombing)

- Threatening to destroy property, or even burn down the house

- Threatening to ruin them financially

- Threatening to badmouth them to their employers or report them to professional bodies if they do not agree to their settlement terms

Devaluing the spouse's legal team

In addition the narcissist will try to reduce your client's confidence in you as their advisor, whilst inflating the brilliance of their own legal team. They will claim to have heard bad things about:

- Your ability as a lawyer

- Your ethics (only in this for financial gain)

- Any Counsel you choose to instruct

- Counsel's performance in court

Remember that the narcissist is extremely persuasive. This is not something that they have learned; they have been hardwired into this behaviour pattern from a very early age. Your client may well believe them, as they have most likely been manipulated and gas-lighted by them for years. You will need to demonstrate consistent competency, and be 'one step' ahead of their narcissistic partner, in order to keep their trust.

Early practical steps for you to take to protect your client's position

Planning the steps which your client should take to protect themselves as early as possible into the process, alongside helping the client emotionally to deal with the narcissistic abuse, will help put your client in a better personal place to be able to deal with the provision of instructions. Overall, they will gradually become better equipped to deal with that which lies ahead of them.

They should be advised to:

- Contact all financial institutions with whom a joint account is held, and joint credit card providers, to ensure that funds cannot be withdrawn, except on joint signature

- Take copies of all relevant joint paperwork in case it might be removed from the house

- Buy a safe, or similar, to keep paperwork and documents under lock and key

- Change their Will in contemplation of divorce so that the narcissist is no longer a beneficiary

- Change all passwords for online banking etc which might be known to, or discoverable by, the narcissist

- Set up a new email account for divorce related correspondence which is kept private from the narcissist

- Download WhatsApp conversations into an archived file so that a recorded version is available should the narcissist become abusive

- Screenshot and file text messages

- Retain all emails from the narcissist

- Block the narcissist's phone numbers

- Ensure that all communication with the narcissist takes place in writing, preferably by email

- Consider changing locks where appropriate

- Consider advice regarding harassment i.e. if they have asked for no contact, but contact from the narcissist persists, two or more such incidents amount to harassment and should be reported to the police

Out of court options and likely costs

The unsuitability of out of court options, such as pure mediation or the collaborative practice, when a narcissist is involved has been demonstrated earlier (see page 111), and you must exercise caution when considering options. Supported options, such as hybrid mediation or arbitration, may be preferable. A process such as The Certainty Project, which incorporates both lawyer supported mediation and arbitration, may be ideal.

Regrettably, the court process may become an inevitability, as out of court dispute resolution options are dependent on the agreement of both parties. Your client must be warned of, and prepared for, this at the outset. A frank discussion about likely costs is essential. Be conscious that the intricacies of a case where one party is a narcissist is likely to incur costs which are beyond the usual costs estimate for the standard divorce process – not least because of goalpost shifting, delays and the requirement for more correspondence between solicitors, due to bad behaviour by the narcissist towards the spouse.

It is essential to remember that the narcissistic partner does not want a speedy resolution – they want to draw out proceedings and the consequent narcissistic supply they receive from this for as long as possible. The heightened drama, the opportunities to play act, and their need to win often make going to court the preferred option for them.

Communication through the separation process

As a consequence of their experiences in early life, it is as if the narcissist is locked into the emotional age of a young child, with all the behaviour and responses which would be expected from a child of that age. Whether or not the separation was their decision (and their behaviour will be far worse were it not), the narcissist will lash out at their spouse or partner, displaying 'toddler tantrums' and narcissistic rage. Due to the 'narcissistic injury' from which they will be suffering, they will be frantically seeking a way to punish the person who they perceive to have inflicted such pain on them. Imagine the behaviour of a wounded, but dangerous animal; even more deadly than before.

There will be nothing consistent in the communications received from the narcissist. One moment they will be raging and ranting but, in another, they may be entirely pragmatic, with previous communications ignored.

The narcissist finds it almost impossible to see the 'bigger picture', but rather, focuses on the immediate. This can give rise to major inconsistencies in their presentation of the facts. Bear in mind also that the truth is not a fixed entity to a narcissist – it is merely whatever they say it is, at the time they are saying it. Accusations against their former partner, which will come thick and fast, are likely to be fictitious, and their partner will naturally tend to want to clear their name, wasting time and money.

The communication style of a narcissist experiencing narcissistic injury and rage is surprisingly similar between different narcissists, so much so that it becomes unmistakeable, once experienced a few times. To the non-narcissist, a few steps removed from the proceedings, communications seem utterly bizarre, bordering on the nonsensical. However, to the recipient, they are deeply disturbing, as the narcissist knows exactly which buttons to press to elicit a response and to destabilise them. They often use highly emotive topics to this end. It is easy for victims to be drawn in, and to descend to the narcissist's level. And in fact, a slanging match is actually *exactly* what the narcissist wants.

Communications will usually contain all, or most of the following elements:

- Accusations (of poor character, mental instability, bad behaviour, addiction etc.)

- Threats (towards the partner themselves, or to property, friends, family or pets)

- Projections (where the narcissist accuses their partner of doing something they have done, or being something they are)

- Blameshifting (e.g. "It was your fault I took that money")

- Narcissistic pseudologic (see page 69)

- Illogical justifications

- Word salad (see page 70)

- Statements to devalue the spouse (e.g. "You never were able to parent")

- Rewriting of the past and gas-lighting (that never happened, or this happened)

- Blackmail

- Contradictions, even from paragraph to paragraph or sentence to sentence (e.g. "I could not live without us being friends" followed by "I am going to dance upon your grave")

- Hurtful personal attacks ("You are just like your awful dead father")

- Highly emotive topics (e.g. the children, pets, items of sentimental value)

There are two key reasons why the narcissist communicates in this way. The first is that they are desperate to get their spouse back firmly under their control; it gives them a sense of power. And the second is 'narcissistic supply'. Due to the separation, they have lost one of their best, and most reliable sources of supply, even if they instigated the break up, and even if they have a new partner. They need to top it up, urgently, as dwindling supply means a dwindling 'false self', the protective armour they have constructed to avoid having to face their own shame and low self-esteem. Narcissistic supply is as crucial as oxygen. As explained earlier in the book, if they can't get supply through adoration, then drama and conflict will do.

Strategies for dealing with communications from the narcissist directly to your client

It is important for the spouse or partner to have strategies in place to counter the narcissist's communications and advising your client regarding this will be essential. Reassure your client that actually, in terms of communication, *they* hold all the cards if they are willing to stick to certain recommendations.

Going 'no contact'

If at all possible, the spouse or partner of the narcissist should have no contact at all with the narcissist. However, if they share children, are still living under the same roof, or if they are involved in a joint business venture, this may not be possible. If it is possible, then they should block the narcissist from all methods of contact (including phone, email, social media, messaging apps, texts) and limit essential communication to taking place via solicitors.

If they cannot go 'no contact', the following 'limited contact' method with the narcissist should be advised. The non-narcissistic spouse should:

- Understand and agree that all divorce related correspondence should be through solicitors, and that they will not discuss legal matters with their narcissistic spouse direct, for their own protection. A narcissist will make every attempt to abuse this. As narcissists like to always be in control of the people in their lives, you will need to set clear boundaries for your client. You need to empower them to say 'no' if their spouse tries to cross the boundaries clearly imposed. You also need to be ready to step in when required to diffuse an abusive approach.

- Not speak to the narcissist on the phone, or in person, if at all possible. Insisting (to the narcissist) that if such conversations have to occur, they will be recorded using a phone app may help to keep things civil.

- Preferably agree to email as the *only* method of communication.

- Not rise to any baits, under any circumstances. Narcissists know exactly which buttons to push to elicit a response. Not only does this feed them supply and draw them into their game, they can then find their words used against them in court, making them appear unstable or unreasonable.

- Give themselves a few hours to cool down before responding to the narcissist's communications. Communication must be handled with extreme care; 'off the cuff' or 'knee jerk' replies should be avoided at all costs.

- Always decide whether there is anything to be gained by responding to the narcissist's communications *at all* – often there is not.

- Use the 'grey rock' method of communication. If they have to see the narcissist face to face (not recommended) they should limit all facial expressions, speak in a dull monotone voice, and make reduced or no eye contact with the narcissist. They should not show any emotion, say anything interesting or engage in any form of conversation. They should become unresponsive and uninteresting, using as few words as possible. Responses should be limited to short, factual replies, becoming effectively monosyllabic. In addition, they should dress down and deliberately make themselves look plain and unattractive, so the narcissist gets no supply by showing them off or being seen with them. The aim is to give the narcissist no energy and to become as boring to the narcissist as a grey rock. By becoming this boring, the narcissist will look elsewhere to have their narcissistic supply needs met.

Typical responses such as explaining, arguing or placating are entirely pointless and, in fact, counterproductive, when dealing with a narcissist. Be warned, though, that when the 'grey rock' technique is employed the narcissist will up the ante to try to elicit a response. Just like a child having a tantrum, they will believe that they have regained the upper hand if given in to and a response provided. It is important to practice detachment and to learn not to respond to outrageous criticisms and provocations. If the spouse or partner can hold firm, eventually the narcissist will tire of the lack of reaction and look elsewhere for their fix.

(Bear in mind that the focus of the narcissist's attention is likely to be another 'player' in the scenario – therefore either of the lawyers involved are a potential source of supply, as are any children, even adult children, if they have them).

It's important for the spouse to be aware that going 'grey rock' is not the same as suppressing their thoughts and feelings – it is merely not showing them to the narcissist. This is not about being submissive to the narcissist, as they may well have been in the past. Quite the reverse in fact – it is a method which puts them in control.

- Learn how to respond to a written communication. Here they should not engage in any arguing. They should not try to defend or justify themselves, or respond to or make any accusations. They should use the fewest words possible. E.g. "Yes, <u>8pm</u>", or "I do not agree to this", "Pick up will remain <u>at 5pm</u>", or "Noted." Only the absolutely essential points should be responded to. No niceties should be added (they count as giving the narcissist narcissistic supply). Not even the merest hint at dissatisfaction or passive aggression should be included. This is 'grey rock' but in the written form. Additionally, they should not respond immediately, but wait several hours or even until the next day to respond. It is important that the former partner of the narcissist is no longer at their beck and call – an important step in taking back their power.

- Be aware of what to do in situations where the narcissist sends a written communication (such as by email) falsely claiming that an agreement was reached verbally when, in reality it was not. The ex-spouse should respond in writing that no conversation ever took place, and document everything. It is common for a narcissist to try this tactic – they are highly manipulative and lie without a guilty conscience. Emails of this nature are common. E.g. "Further to our spoken conversation just now, I am writing to confirm that we agreed that I would be getting all the wedding china and the car ..."

- Set aside a short amount of time every week to ensure that all their records of communications with the narcissist are kept up to date. All written communications should be downloaded, printed and filed, and if telephone conversations do occur, they should be recorded and downloaded using a recording app on their phone. The recordings themselves may not be admissible to court but they will be useful for keeping track of what was said.

Dealing with communications received from the narcissist's lawyer

Forwarding communications to your client

Not only is your client dealing with the communications from their narcissistic spouse/partner, but they will also be the recipient of correspondence from the narcissist's lawyer (who may well just be the mouthpiece for the narcissist, in a more official guise). Always think about the effect which this correspondence will have on your client, before you send it out to them.

Do not forward correspondence from the narcissist's lawyer to the spouse without a covering letter, and do not send it out at the end of the day or, worse still, on a <u>Friday evening</u>. *Your client will need to be in touch with you on receipt of any communication.* A long period when they are unable to do so, especially if they are still living under the same roof as the narcissist, will give the narcissist the chance to work on them and to undermine them, in whatever way might be open to them. Your careful consideration of the situation can prevent this from happening and offer your client enormous protection.

Of course, if the narcissist's lawyer is aware of what they are dealing with, they will not become the mouthpiece of the narcissist. But they may not be aware. They may be glibly putting wording received from their narcissistic client straight onto their own notepaper and firing it in the direction of the spouse.

As the spouse/partner's lawyer you will know that these letters may be written on instructions rather than the product of advice. Reassure your client that the lawyer on the other side is simply doing their job. Protect your client from the belief that their husband/wife has found someone to represent them who exactly matches their behaviour patterns and is going to perpetuate the abuse. That is unlikely to be the case.

Communicating effectively with the narcissist's lawyer

As the lawyer of the spouse/partner your objective is to do everything possible to diffuse the situation and ensure that the two legal advisors are in control of the process as far as this can be achieved.

Pick up the phone to the other side. Have an 'off the record' chat if you can to try to get to the bottom of what is happening. What, if anything, does your opponent understand about the behaviour of their client and their personality disorder? Are they able to 'second guess' the demonstrable behaviour patterns and endeavour to steer the case to an outcome? Or is that simply not on their client's agenda?

Don't be afraid to draw to the attention of your opponent your understanding of the dynamic of this couple. How well this is received may depend on the professional working relationship which you have developed with the other lawyer.

Don't be afraid to draw to the attention of your opponent your understanding of the dynamic of this couple.

Pausing here for a moment, it is crucial to underscore that, in every aspect of family law work, establishing a working relationship with the lawyer on the other side is vitally important. Whilst you are each looking after and supporting the best interests of your own client, you are also working together to achieve an outcome which enables a family, often with children, to move forwards. The establishment of a working rapport will always be beneficial. This doesn't mean that somehow the two lawyers are forming some kind of liaison, behind the backs of their respective clients. They are opening and maintaining a line of constructive communication.

It is also a good idea to make it clear at an early stage to the other side that all divorce related correspondence should be through solicitors, and that your client will not discuss matters with their narcissistic spouse direct. A narcissist will make every attempt to abuse this. If the couple have children, they will use the children as a reason to have direct contact. They may be involved in a joint business venture, so this will be another route.

Deciding whether to respond

Always think about the extent to which you actually need to respond to the correspondence received from the other side – especially if it focusses on irrelevant minutiae, aimed to irritate, aggravate and cause fear, but designed to achieve little else. Your client may want you to respond to every point raised, because by not doing so they believe you are somehow acquiescing to the point made. Such an approach may needlessly increase costs and should be avoided. It is simple to say that the points raised are not accepted but you are not prepared to waste costs dealing with them in any greater detail.

This way of dealing with such correspondence will either enrage the narcissist to the extent that you receive more of the same (which should also be treated in the same way) or, disappointed not to have achieved their objective, they will try something else.

> **In every aspect of family law work, establishing a working relationship with the lawyer on the other side is vitally important.**

What you are doing, in choosing not to respond, is actually refusing to be drawn in by the narcissist's need for drama and supply. If you do respond, point by point, you are allowing the narcissist to take control of the process and increase legal fees, for no productive or beneficial reason.

Your client may be frightened or outraged by false allegations being made about them and may want to 'put the record straight'. As their lawyer you need to explain that such correspondence will not have any impact upon the outcome of the case.

Useful phrases to diffuse the situation in written correspondence are as follows:

- The allegations made by your client are denied, but we do not consider it beneficial to go through the points made in turn. We prefer to focus on the future and a settlement rather than dwell on past issues which are not relevant to the key issues between our clients.

- We do not propose to argue a different perspective of past events in correspondence. Our client does not accept your client's version of events, but we would encourage both to move forwards and put the past behind them.

- Reference to the issues raised does not serve any useful purpose and, save to confirm that your client's position is not accepted, we are not instructed to comment further.

- If there are matters which do require discussion, we believe the most cost effective route would be to engage in hybrid mediation, with lawyers present. Our three suggested hybrid trained mediators are X, Y and Z. Please take urgent instructions.

Do always bear in mind that imposing a time deadline on a narcissist is entirely futile. They will *never* adhere to it and therefore once that deadline has passed you are left with the invidious task of deciding what to do next having effectively boxed yourself into a corner. Proposals therefore should remain open ended or be withdrawn if there are good reasons no longer to leave an offer on the table.

Does your client realise that their spouse/partner may suffer from NPD?

Not all those who are married to (or in a relationship with) a narcissist, are aware of the personality traits which are driving the behaviour of their partner, or why. This can be particularly true when the couple have been together for a long time.

The 'silver separators' – couples who separate in later life, after a very long time together – may be particularly at risk of this, and narcissism may well be involved. It is worth being especially attuned to this possibility in this group, not least because they are probably the largest age group currently divorcing.

This is as a consequence of:

- Younger couples often choosing not to marry, so reducing relative divorce numbers in this demographic

- The couple, having married at a young age in the 1970's, or earlier, having now grown in different directions

- People living longer and seeing retirement age as a new life chapter, rather than as the approach of the end of the story

- Pension sharing meaning that retirement income can be divided

- The, now real, possibility of working past retirement age

- Unhappiness no longer being tolerated in today's culture

As the lawyer involved with their divorce or separation, you may well be the very first person they come across with an understanding of their spouse's behaviour and personality type. The onus will therefore be on you to manage this tricky terrain, competently and compassionately.

During your first meeting with your client, using the knowledge which you have of narcissistic behaviours, listen carefully for the signs.

Try to decide whether your client knows what they have been subjected to, and what you will both be dealing with.

If they come to you openly suggesting that their partner has NPD, first and foremost, *tell them that you believe them.* These people have been invalidated and have had their version of reality questioned, often for years. Next, explain what you know about the condition. Demonstrate that you have an understanding of the way their life has been, and why. They will be looking for a lawyer with a specialist understanding of NPD, and demonstrating your competence in this area will help create the level of trust which needs to be in place. (Be aware, however, that there is a very small possibility that they are themselves the narcissist, and are projecting this label on to their spouse).

Provide them with a copy of the partner book to this, '*Divorcing A Narcissist: The Lure, The Loss And The Law*', to provide them with cost effective support and essential information. You may also wish to have an information sheet readily available, perhaps downloadable from your website, with reading recommendations and information as to what to do if they realise that their partner is demonstrating narcissistic behaviour. Signposting your client to online resources may also be valuable.

Consider whether a specialist narcissistic divorce and recovery consultant, a family consultant or a psychotherapist may be valuable. It is likely that you will be inviting your client to behave uncharacteristically, and will be taking them out of their comfort zone, as you represent them on a long and difficult journey to the next stage in their life. Third party support is very likely to be helpful.

If they are not aware of NPD as a possibility, don't be afraid to make suggestions about the personality of their life partner.

Be prepared to accept that your client may not believe you or may not be ready to accept that their spouse/partner has a personality disorder. Don't force the issue with them. They do not have to accept the label in order for you to be able to predict the behaviour of the narcissist.

It may be more appropriate to explain that particular patterns of behaviour in divorce are common or typical when those involved have a certain type of personality, such as NPD. Explain that it is useful to be able to predict these behaviours and to respond in a particular way. Encourage the client to watch out for certain things. Don't forget that they may have been brainwashed and conditioned for many years. Stepping out of the control of the narcissist can be a difficult and even physically painful process. It is not something your client can achieve except over time and with support. When they begin to see that your predictions are correct you can start to explain that these patterns of behaviour are present in their case and suggest strategies to deal with them.

Perhaps make it clear that those who suffer from NPD do not do so out of choice, and therefore their behaviour is inherent – it is an inevitability, not a reaction to their partner's behaviour during the relationship. This may help your client understand that what they have experienced, and what they will now be subjected to, is not their fault. Such a realisation can make the situation more understandable, more tolerable, and consequently easier to combat.

Be aware that your client, when trying to come to terms with what has happened to them in their relationship, will be suffering from the psychological phenomenon of 'cognitive dissonance'. Essentially, this occurs when a person is holding two or more contradictory thoughts or beliefs in their minds at the same time. This creates a sense of unreality, confusion and a mind-set of not trusting their own perception of a situation. Leon Festinger (1957) was one researcher who studied the theory of cognitive dissonance – a deeply uncomfortable psychological state which the brain needs to resolve in some way. Cognitive dissonance can appear where someone's beliefs about a relationship or person conflicts with how that person behaves.

Let's put this into simple terms.

Jo meets Alex on a date and they get on well. They eventually move in together and Jo thinks Alex is the perfect partner. The relationship seems great and they both feel very happy.

Then one night they have a row and Alex lashes out, hitting Jo on the cheek. It doesn't leave a mark but the whole event is very painful and distressing for Jo, who is hurt both physically and emotionally.

Why did Alex do this? Jo doesn't understand. Jo has a cognitive dilemma. She loves Alex and believes that Alex loves her.

On the other hand, though, Alex's behaviour was horrible and not what one would expect from someone who loves you. Jo experiences cognitive dissonance.

Jo believes Alex loves her (Belief A).

Jo believes that Alex's behaviour is not consistent with Alex loving her (Belief B).

The cognitive dissonance which Jo experiences makes her feel uncomfortable. One of the attitudes needs to change. In order to solve the dissonance the mind has to cause the two attitudes (or beliefs) to be consistent.

Jo must either:

- accept the behaviour that she doesn't like, and the belief (Belief B) that Alex doesn't love her, and rationalise why she is staying in the relationship in spite of this behaviour (often for the sake of the children or financial security).

- accept the behaviour but make an excuse for it (Alex was stressed/drunk/not thinking what he was doing/didn't mean to do what he did, and he does love her). Here Belief A has won.

- end the relationship. If Alex is capable of this behaviour then he doesn't love her and she certainly doesn't love him. Again, here Belief B has won.

Someone who is in a relationship with a narcissistic individual is likely to have faced cognitive dissonance often, and have historically selected either the first or second option. Here, they have justified some example of behaviour to themselves, so that they are able to find it acceptable, so losing the feeling of discomfort which it creates. They may have arranged to have an appointment with you because, this time, they are driven to the third option. This will be a very big step.

If the decision to end the relationship is not theirs, they are likely to still be suffering from cognitive dissonance, and therefore be emotionally troubled and uncomfortable. They will have justified unacceptable behaviour in their own mind in order to perpetuate the relationship, and if the relationship has come to an end regardless, this will now be difficult to bear.

Note that even if they have chosen to end the relationship themselves, they may still be suffering from cognitive dissonance, wavering between images and beliefs of their partner as a loving individual and then as an abuser. Cognitive dissonance, like grief, can take months or even years to resolve, especially as, in a narcissistic relationship, they will have experienced the cycle of idealisation (love-bombing), devaluing and near discard many times. It is perfectly normal that, one day, they are convinced that their partner is a narcissist and, the next, they are unsure.

You will need to explain to your client that the narcissistic rage they will trigger if they raise their suspicions with their partner of them having NPD will be entirely counterproductive. The narcissist will either seek to then undermine them, or will employ projection, claiming that it is your client who is in fact narcissistic or personality disordered. No matter how tempting it may be, they should not discuss this with their partner.

It is practically inevitable that the non-narcissistic partner will, at some stage, question whether *they* are, in fact, the narcissist. You may wish to reassure them that this is a normal phenomenon, and that the very fact that they are questioning it, and care about the issue, means that they are most likely not.

It is also important to explain to the client that, as things stand in the UK at the moment, openly bringing up their suspicions of the personality disorder in court will also, sadly, be counterproductive, and that trying to obtain a formal diagnosis of NPD will also reflect badly on them rather than on the narcissist. At the moment, the best that can be hoped for is that the narcissistic individual's bad behaviour in court, and beforehand, may work slightly against them.

Managing your client's expectations within the divorce process

Once you have a fair understanding of the make-up of your client's spouse, the next step is, from the outset, to seek to manage your own client's expectations. This falls into two categories.

The narcissist's behaviour in the legal process

The first is what to expect from the process and how their spouse is likely to behave within it. We have dealt with the behaviours and tactics that the narcissist will employ through the divorce process in detail earlier in the chapter, in the section entitled '*How the narcissist will abuse your client in the divorce or separation process*.' Your client will need to be warned to expect these behaviours.

If the narcissist has discarded their spouse they will not look back. In a narcissist, the developmental stage of empathy has never been reached. Whilst they may have learned how to feign empathy for the purpose of securing supply, they have no ability to empathise in the true sense. This means that the narcissist cannot care about how their former spouse might feel, or about their future. It is helpful here to pause on the word 'cannot'. It may be helpful to your client for them to understand that a narcissist does not choose to be unempathic; they simply can't help it. This is not an invitation to put up with more abuse, however.

If the spouse has decided that 'enough is enough' you, as their lawyer, will need to recognise and communicate the enormity of the reaction which it will inspire within the narcissist. Narcissistic injury and narcissistic rage – a deadly combination – will both be at play. In addition to injury and rage, there will be the loss of control which may be almost more than the narcissist can bear. They will not bow out gracefully, but will either want to regain control or punish their spouse in the most extreme way they can.

The inability to care or be empathic also extends to any children who will quickly become pawns in the game against their spouse; the children's other parent. Chapter 5 deals specifically with issues regarding the children.

There is no way that a narcissist is going to let their partner 'win', even if it means severely damaging themselves at the same time. Narcissists are driven

> **There is no way that a narcissist is going to let their partner 'win', even if it means severely damaging themselves at the same time.**

by the need to be seen by everyone around them to have 'won'. The definition of 'winning' may, however, be determined by their own skewed view of their world. They must be seen as 'special' and 'perfect'. Therefore, necessarily, their spouse must be the 'loser'; the 'bad guy' in the relationship. Rules do not apply to a narcissist. They do not subscribe to a moral code. Bad behaviour will be blatant and unrelenting.

The spouse of the narcissist will need to accept that the court process is far too slow and inefficient to properly regulate those who refuse to play by the book. If one does not understand what one is dealing with (and, sadly, even if one does) the narcissist will likely get away with the tactics described earlier. Damage limitation and preservation of sanity are wins here.

The narcissist will behave unreasonably, refuse to disclose, produce everything at the very last minute, move the goalposts, refuse to negotiate etc. You may reach a point where you have made a sensible proposal and the other side, instead of negotiating, are diverting the focus of the process to irrelevant issues.

You may decide that it is in the best interests of your client to temporarily go off court record. You can still provide advice from 'in the wings' but the narcissist is prevented from running up exorbitant legal fees for your client while you are simply waiting for the next stage in the court process. This can be a surprisingly powerful tactic – the fact that the non-narcissistic spouse no longer officially has the benefit of legal representation limits the ability of the other side to bully them, or to act solely as the narcissist's mouthpiece.

Expectations regarding final outcome

The second is what to expect in relation to 'outcome'.

Your client needs to understand at the outset that the judge is likely to simply divide the resources available at the time of adjudication. 'Add back' arguments are notoriously difficult to win unless the assets are sizeable. The key is to preserve the available resources throughout the process as far as possible.

Money may be taken, hidden and excessively spent, but unless the resources are vast a forensic accounting report is unlikely to be seen by the court as cost effective. A judge at the First Directions Appointment will not be keen to allow what they perceive to be a fishing expedition, and will be concerned to ensure that costs remain proportionate. Your client may well lose out financially, but part of the overall assessment is the value of being free from ongoing manipulation, control and rage.

In a situation where the narcissist did not want the relationship to be over, you will need to evaluate the benefit of a spousal maintenance order in favour of your client. Is it likely to be paid? Does it provide a route for further manipulation and control and prevent the spouse from going 'no contact'? Where possible, a clean break will always be desirable – even if it comes at a price.

The lawyer's job is to ensure that any settlement falls within the bracket of what a court will deem as 'fair', but the negotiation must have built into it the opportunity for the *narcissist to believe they have won.*

Your client will, once they realise what they have got into, want to be extricated from the ghastliness of the situation at as early a stage as can be achieved. The narcissist will be keen to punish through prolonged and expensive proceedings. Without underselling your client's claims, you need to balance the need for an exit against a fair and reasonable outcome. Settling closer to the bottom end of the bracket may still be a triumph.

How to prepare your client for an FDRA appointment

As First Directions Appointments become more procedural, and likely to be resolved via agreed directions, the first opportunity for the narcissist to use the court process against your client is the FDRA. Even when you are certain that an FDRA appointment will not result in a settlement, the court is unlikely to allow you to skip this stage of the process and go straight to Final Hearing.

If you want to go immediately to adjudication, arbitration is the process for you – but this can only take place with the agreement of both sides.

Make it clear to your client, well in advance, that the FDRA judge can only give an indication of what he/she might do at a Final Hearing. Stress that they will underline the fact that this is a discretionary jurisdiction, and that a different judge may hold a different view, especially if submissions have been tested through oral evidence and cross examination.

The FDRA is a wonderful event for the narcissist. It will usually involve the instruction of Counsel – someone new to idolise or blame as the fancy takes them. Another player to add to the dynamic. And of course, the judge. An opportunity to be charming, to make their spouse feel uncomfortable. To belittle and criticise them through the authenticity of the narcissist's legal team. And to get the judge on board.

The narcissist can't lose. If the judge is against them it is all too easy to blame the system; they didn't read the papers properly; at least it will be a different judge for the Final Hearing. Or perhaps Counsel was not up to scratch – an opportunity for an argument over fees. And throughout the hearing they can change the goalposts in a constant attempt to undermine the negotiating position of the other side.

As lawyer for the narcissist's spouse you will want to consider a number of things:

- Never send Counsel to court without someone to take a note.

- If you think the case won't settle, consider doing the hearing yourself instead of instructing Counsel, in order to keep costs to a minimum. In exceptional cases the client can even go to the hearing in person, if they feel up to it.

- The pace of negotiation may be fast and offers made which will subsequently be withdrawn before they can be properly considered. Plan in advance with your client where their bottom line might lie so that if an offer comes close – even if it is not in line with what your client wants, or your advice – you can quickly evaluate whether the benefits of acceptance are too great for the offer, albeit financially low, to be ignored.

- If you are agreeing directions for trial, make sure that the time estimate is realistic. Ensure that section 25 statements are limited in length (no more than 10 sides of A4), and also in the number of exhibits.

- The day will be gruelling. Make sure your client has some support when it is over, particularly if they are still living with their narcissistic spouse. Warn them that the narcissist will be critical of the judge and their representation, and will do everything possible to undermine your client's confidence both in the process and their legal team.

- If the case doesn't settle at the FDRA make a written offer as soon as possible after the hearing – and consider whether it should be open. You want to place the other side under as much pressure as you can. Then stand back. Don't allow yourself to be lured into increasing costs, if it can be avoided, until the time comes for preparation for trial.

Preparing for Final Hearing

The Final Hearing will be an event which the narcissist will look forward to. An opportunity to charm the judge and get them on side. They will see the role of their Counsel to be to tear their spouse apart in the witness box. They may tell Counsel how much they are looking forward to seeing their skills in action, thereby setting expectations. If their Counsel does not understand the nature of their client, their desire to do a good job might cause them to take over the role of abuser. Your client will need to be prepared for this when being cross examined in the witness box.

- Explain to your client very carefully, in advance, what to expect from the Final Hearing; from what to wear, to where everyone will sit, and the actual format for the day.

- Make sure they have seen and read the hearing bundle and are very familiar with their own documents (Form E, Replies to Questionnaire and s25 statement). Encourage them to practice finding their way around the witness bundle.

- Ensure that they bring with them something to eat and drink, especially if they are giving evidence in

The 3 Golden Rules For Giving Evidence

▶ **Answer the question**

▶ **Tell the truth**

▶ **Don't get emotional**

the afternoon.

- Ensure that your client understands that being in the witness box should not be seen by them as an opportunity to tell their story. Just answering the question directly, in as few words as possible will stand them in much better stead.

- Explain the golden rules of giving evidence (answer the question, tell the truth and don't get emotional) and encourage them to practice in advance, listening to questions posed to them in everyday life, and giving a short succinct and accurate answer.

- Stress that whatever outrageous things their spouse might say in the witness box, they must not react in any way, save to write a short note to you if necessary. Short essays should be avoided, along with gasps, sighs, shrieks and, especially, tears. The narcissist will see their time on the stand as their chance to play to the audience of the courtroom, and to berate their spouse out loud, for all to hear. Any reaction to such behaviour should be stifled, at all costs.

- Explain to your client that the judge is human, and acknowledge the possibility that they may be swayed by the charm and tactics of the narcissist. At least the hearing will bring matters to an end, which is often a favourable result in itself.

- Explain, in advance, that even if the outcome feels unpalatable, an appeal would only be viable in the most exceptional of circumstances.

Most of the above are really the things you would be thinking about for any Final Hearing. When you are acting for the spouse of a narcissist it all becomes doubly important.

When the hearing is over – what now?

The narcissist may not like the imposed outcome occasioned by judicial intervention. The opportunity to take control and cause distress is, however, not yet over.

The drafting of any order, whether by consent or following adjudication, must be done with extreme care. This is something which must be impressed upon Counsel. All too often we are so relieved to have achieved a concluded agreement, or received the judgment in a case, that the job of drafting the document, which will implement that outcome, is not given sufficient care and attention.

The narcissist will do everything possible to hinder and thwart the implementation of the order. Each provision must be considered in isolation, and enforcement considered at every stage. What are the 'sticks or carrots' in the order which will compel the narcissist to comply with their obligations? What are the interim arrangements pending sale of the house and how can they be enforced?

Providing for the financial shortfall created by non-compliance to be deducted from the narcissist's share of the net proceeds of sale of the house can be a good safety net.

Stipulating levels of offer price for the family home which will be seen as acceptable can avoid a subsequent return to court and the associated delay and cost.

If child support will terminate at the end of secondary or tertiary education include the actual month when this will end (June? July? August?). Also deal explicitly with what will happen if a gap year is taken (paid or unpaid). Be clear on any roofing allowance agreement.

> **Put yourself into the place of the narcissist; look for the loopholes and make sure that the order blocks them.**

Put yourself into the place of the narcissist; look for the loopholes and make sure that the order blocks them.

When you are preparing your Final Hearing costs estimate in Form H1, bear in mind that the work involved in implementation may be greater than usual, and ensure this is reflected in the relevant section.

Expected issues post-divorce

Where there are children, some form of ongoing working arrangement with the narcissistic former partner is unavoidable. It needs to be as good as it can be for the sake of the children. The introduction of a specialist co-parenting app, such as 'OurFamilyWizard' or similar, as a safe means of communication, can help maintain boundaries, while at the same time creating a channel for child focused dialogue. The narcissistic former partner is unlikely to agree to this, so it is worth considering how to frame such an app as a suggestion to them which would work in their favour.

Child arrangements are likely to be littered with unreasonable demands and last minute changes. Your client needs to work on having a strategy in place, in advance, to deal with this when it arises. They should aim to avoid conflict (which will have an adverse effect on the children) where possible, while ensuring that they are not simply complying with demands and allowing themselves to be controlled. Even if their decision is to 'give in', they should make sure that is their conscious choice, for validated reasons. Chapter 5 deals with parenting issues, post-divorce or separation, in more detail.

It is likely that the financial fortunes of the narcissistic spouse will improve post settlement. This is something to be prepared for. If the change is immediate and significant, consider whether there is the option to return to the process and raise material non-disclosure. The non-narcissistic former partner needs to give careful consideration as to whether this is another battle they wish to face, analysing the costs, risks and likelihood of success, and at the same time evaluating the potential effect upon their own well-being.

> **It is likely that the financial fortunes of the narcissistic spouse will improve post settlement. This is something to be prepared for.**

If they have the benefit of an ongoing maintenance provision, expect payments to be irregular or changed unilaterally. The Court Order must have provision for payments to be made by standing order into a designated account. They should try to make sure that they have a contingency in place, if possible, to provide short term cover if support is withheld. If there is provision for an annual uplift in line with RPI or CPI, they should be advised to stay on top of this, to ensure the change is implemented annually at the appropriate time. Arrears which are more than 12 months old cannot be enforced without leave of the court, and 'de minimis' sums can often be overlooked and then be difficult to reinstate.

Case History

Solicitor – Emma

Client – Naomi

Emma is consulted by Naomi on the recommendation of a friend. Naomi telephones Emma's PA in order to make the appointment. Naomi presents as very anxious and rather teary. Clearly this is an enormous step for her. She asks if her friend can accompany her to her appointment with Emma. Emma's PA reassures her that this will not be a problem and is something which happens quite regularly.

Naomi and her friend, Jessica, attend a meeting at Emma's office. Emma immediately recognises how anxious Naomi appears to be. Without asking, it was apparent to her which was the client and which the friend. Jessica is an enormous help and, alongside Naomi who is clearly very distressed, explains to Emma the life which Naomi has been compelled to lead at the hands of her husband. They have been married for 34 years. Naomi has not worked since the birth of their eldest daughter, Sophie. They have three children. Naomi explains that she has derived significant support from their eldest daughter, Sophie. She had thought about asking Sophie to accompany her to the meeting with Emma but felt that this was not fair to involve her at that level.

Jessica explains that Mike has pretty much done what he likes during the marriage. She feels that Mike has behaved in a very controlling way towards Naomi. Naomi believes that Mike has had a number of affairs during the course of their marriage. When their youngest daughter, Olivia, went travelling to Asia recently with a group of friends, Sophie showed Naomi how to check whether Olivia had been 'online' via WhatsApp so that she could see that she was 'alive' even if not directly contacting her mother. This gave Naomi considerable reassurance.

Emma & Naomi

Naomi then began to look at when Mike was online and, through this, discovered a regularity of conversation with the woman with whom she believes Mike to be having an affair. Mike denied this vehemently, telling Naomi that all he had ever done was work hard to support his family, and that he found her accusations really quite abhorrent. He had accused her of being menopausal and 'crazy'.

Emma provided Naomi with plenty of time to 'tell her story'. From the description which Naomi provided of Mike's behaviour she began to form a view that Naomi may have been subjected to long term narcissistic abuse. Naomi clearly presented as someone who lacked in confidence. The presence of her friend, Jessica, was an enormous support to her.

Emma explained to Naomi that, as she and Mike are still living together, if she wanted to bring the marriage to an end she would need to petition on the basis either of Mike's adultery with an unnamed person, or alternatively on the basis of what is described as 'unreasonable behaviour'. Naomi was clearly very nervous of Mike's reaction to this step, and explained that she would want to give it some further thought.

Emma reassured Naomi that no steps would be taken without her specific instructions to do so and suggested that she prepare a draft letter to Mike for Naomi's consideration and approval. Emma said that at this stage she could simply set out in the letter that Naomi wanted to separate. Emma confirmed to Naomi that she would set out all of her advice in writing. Emma informed Naomi that she did think that Mike may suffer from a personality disorder which would dictate the way in which he behaved. Emma explained that she could of course not make any 'diagnosis' in relation to Mike whom she had not met and, in any event, she was not qualified to so, but wondered whether it might be of benefit to Naomi if she provided her with some reading material which would describe the personality disorder, and Naomi could form her own judgement as to whether she believed Emma's suspicions to be correct. Jessica confirmed that she too had reservations about the way in which Mike behaved. Emma explained that were she to be correct, Mike would be 'hard wired' into a manner of behaviour which he would be unable to help. She explained that it would, however, be very important that she and Naomi were able to predict this behaviour as it would hugely assist Emma in her role as Naomi's lawyer and would cause her to provide advice to Naomi in a slightly different way. Emma explained that it would be necessary to take account of the way in which Mike would be likely to react during the course of the process.

Naomi welcomed the opportunity for further information. She did, however, ask that anything be sent to Jessica's postal or email address as she was very nervous of Mike finding anything at home. Emma confirmed that this could of course be facilitated.

Emma provides a draft letter to Naomi which she approves shortly afterwards. This is sent to Mike at his home address.

A phone call is received at Emma's office from Mike. Emma is engaged. Mike is extremely rude to Emma's PA, informing her that he has received a letter that he is extremely annoyed about and will be taking legal advice. He informs Emma's PA that his wife is having some kind of breakdown.

When the conversation is relayed to Emma, she sends a short email to Mike thanking him for making contact and suggesting that he seek independent legal advice. She hears nothing further from him directly. Emma informs Naomi that Mike has been in touch but does not refer to the content of the conversation. She says that she is hopeful that he will take independent legal advice.

Emma then receives correspondence from Kate who is instructed by Mike. Emma knows of Kate professionally; she has a reputation for being quite adversarial and having a tendency to issue court proceedings in most of her cases. Emma is not surprised that Mike has chosen to instruct a more litigious family lawyer. She informs Naomi that Mike has taken independent advice which should be seen as a positive step. At least Emma now has someone with whom to correspond, and Mike will have the benefit of independent advice. Unfortunately, however, the letter from Kate suggests that Mike does not consider the marriage to have broken down irretrievably, and invites Naomi to consider reconciliation. Emma discusses this with Naomi. She invites Naomi to come back to the office for a further appointment and for Jessica to accompany her again. Naomi explains to Emma that she has now engaged a counsellor and is finding this extremely supportive. She says that she is certain that she wishes to proceed with the divorce. She believes that Mike will deny adultery and therefore asks Emma to prepare a draft divorce petition on the basis of Mike's unreasonable behaviour. Emma discusses with Naomi the fact that she could claim costs in the petition for the costs of the divorce proceedings. Naomi has no wish to antagonise Mike. She has some savings and her parents are prepared to help her a little. Also Sophie's husband, Tom, who is in well paid employment has offered to help her with legal fees. Sophie and Tom have been extremely supportive. Naomi has discussed with Sophie the possibility of Mike suffering from some kind of personality disorder. Sophie has asked to read the literature which Emma supplied to Naomi and is convinced that her father does indeed fall into this category. She has sought to persuade Naomi that she must now bring the marriage to an end so that she can get on with her life away from the control of her father. Naomi is concerned about Sophie's approach to her dad, but welcomes her support, and does now want to adopt this course of action. She confirms to Emma that she would only wish to claim costs if the petition were to be defended.

Emma explains to Naomi that it will be necessary for there to be financial disclosure. Emma writes to Kate providing a draft petition for divorce and inviting Kate to prepare voluntary financial disclosure on Mike's behalf in Form E, confirming that she will do likewise on behalf of Naomi. In her letter she states that as the children are all independent her client hopes that matters can be resolved swiftly and cost effectively. Emma proposes mediation as a process for resolving matters if an agreement cannot be readily achieved. It is Emma's 'default' position to recommend the process of mediation to clients. She does not think that mediation in its "classic" format would work for a couple such as Mike and Naomi but recognises that they need to find some process through which matters can be resolved without increasing acrimony or cost.

Emma senses that Mike may prefer the 'court room battle' which she knows Naomi would find extremely difficult. She hopes to suggest hybrid mediation which is lawyer led, as a means of resolving the issues through discussion and communication with Naomi, at the same time having the essential legal support which she requires.

Emma has recognised that Mike may suffer from NPD. She realises that Naomi may be unaware of this. She has tried to provide Naomi with information to assist her in dealing with the issues ahead of her. Emma is pleased that Naomi has been to see a counsellor and that she has the support of her friend Jessica. She is a little wary of the support which comes from her oldest daughter, Sophie, but notes that Sophie seems aware of the difficulties experienced by her father and may provide Naomi with some insight into this. She is also pleased to see that Naomi has access to some financial support in terms of meeting legal fees via Sophie's husband, Tom.

Emma hopes that she can persuade Kate to engage in the process of hybrid mediation as a way of resolving issues, with Mike and Naomi both having the support from their lawyers which they would undoubtedly need. Emma is concerned that were the couple to engage in mediation simply with a mediator, Mike would seek to manipulate that process, and Naomi would find herself unable to cope. The mediator may also be in some difficulty managing the process unless they have a clear understanding of the personalities with which they are dealing. Emma does have a list of mediators who would be able to be instructed, but prefers the hybrid mediation approach.

Emma's next contact with this matter is when she is telephoned by Naomi in floods of tears. Naomi has received a divorce petition, sent to her at home, issued by Kate on behalf of Mike, on the basis of Naomi's alleged unreasonable behaviour. Naomi is uncertain how this could have happened. Emma explains that she had received no draft and that Kate ought to have informed her, in advance, that Mike was considering the issue of proceedings. Also, Kate was aware that Emma was acting on Naomi's behalf and, therefore, she ought to have queried whether Emma was instructed to accept service of proceedings. Emma explained to Naomi that this behaviour was reinforcing her concern that Mike may suffer from NPD. Naomi explained that the situation at home was intolerable.

Emma & Naomi

Emma & Naomi

She had been at home on her own when the letter was received by her from the court, and she immediately spoke to her friend, Jessica, who told her to phone Emma straight away. Mike is constantly rude to Naomi and nothing that she does in the house is right. He is constantly criticising even her ability to undertake housework. Naomi feels that she is treading on eggshells. Emma informs Naomi that she will write to Kate expressing concern about the issue of a petition in this way, and also explaining that the situation at home is intolerable. She will invite Mike to move out while matters are being resolved. Naomi tells her that Mike is away a lot for work purposes and, therefore, this should not be too inconvenient for him.

The response from Kate is unhelpful and acrimonious. Kate states by email that Mike believes that Naomi should find some form of gainful employment. Mike will pay the bills on the house and provide Naomi with £500 per month to meet all of her other expenditure which he believes should be sufficient. Naomi appears to have paid Emma's first invoice from the joint account, which Mike has now seen.

Emma prepares an immediate response, advising that this approach on behalf of Mike will leave her with no alternative other than to apply for interim financial support for her client. She sends Kate's original email and the draft response to Naomi for her consideration. Naomi contacts her by telephone almost immediately upon receipt. She is extremely distressed. She realises that she has much more limited access to funds than she realised. She has, however, spoken to their eldest daughter. It transpires that in fact her husband, Tom, recently received an inheritance from his late father, and that the relationship between Mike and Tom has always been poor. Tom appears more than happy to provide Naomi with financial help to bring her marriage to an end, and has agreed to loan Naomi the sum of £10,000. Emma prepares a loan agreement between Naomi and Tom confirming that this sum will have to be repaid.

Naomi informs Emma that Mike will be very angry if Sophie is helping her. Sophie was always Mike's favourite child, but when she decided to marry Tom, that changed. Naomi believes that it was because Tom seemed to stand up to Mike that Mike did not like him. Since Sophie's marriage, their middle daughter, Nathalie, has become Mike's favourite. It seems that Mike has now offered Nathalie the money that she needed to purchase a new car when her existing vehicle failed its MOT. Naomi is concerned that this approach is going to cause a rift between her daughters. Emma recommends that this is something which Naomi should discuss with her counsellor. Naomi is clearly struggling to deal with the situation. Emma is conscious that Naomi is contacting her quite regularly, and wants to divert that contact to the counsellor who is more able to deal with the emotional problems from which Naomi is suffering and, also, will be a cheaper alternative. Whilst it is very generous for Tom to provide the sum of £10,000 to meet legal fees, Emma is acutely aware that this is insufficient to deal with contested proceedings and could leave Naomi in a very invidious position, running out of funds to meet legal costs at a crucial stage in the process, if Emma is not careful to manage expenditure at an early stage.

Emma has recognised that Mike's approach to the process will be adversarial. She senses that Naomi requires a huge amount of emotional support. Mike is clearly going to cut off financial support for Naomi and Emma is concerned about how Naomi may meet ongoing legal fees. Sophie's husband, Tom, has offered to provide a loan. This is helpful for Naomi but Emma recognises that costs could escalate and she needs to do everything possible to prevent this, at an early stage. She therefore recommends that Naomi speak to her counsellor except when she needs legal advice. Emma has explained to Naomi that this is to ensure that the right person is dealing with issues for her at the right level of cost.

Emma prepares Naomi's Form E, which is relatively straightforward. Sophie helps Naomi collate the necessary bank statements etc. Emma then contacts Kate to agree a timetable within which Forms E can be exchanged. She informs Kate that Naomi's form is ready. Kate informs Emma that she is waiting for documents from Mike.

Feeling stronger with the support of her friends, family and counsellor, Naomi asks Mike when he is at home why he is holding things up. Mike flies into rage. He tells Naomi that his Form E is being prepared by Kate's assistant in order to keep legal fees to a minimum. He informs her that her lawyer is useless and just taking her for a ride ensuring that costs increase unnecessarily. He says that any lawyer "worth their salt" at Emma's level of qualification would be asking a junior assistant to do this basic work. He tells Naomi that he has provided all of the documents required and will speak to his solicitor in the morning to see what has happened.

Naomi relays this information to Emma who in turn contacts Kate. Kate, after speaking to Amelia, her assistant, who is helping with the preparation of Form E, advises Emma that Mike has not sent all of the necessary information but reassures her that she will deal with the completion of Form E as soon as possible.

Emma reassures Naomi that Mike's lawyer is perfectly competent. She informs Naomi that the production of her Form E has indeed been handled by the appropriate member of her team. She explains that in Naomi's case, Naomi should retain direct contact with herself as they have built a solicitor/client relationship, and she feels that Naomi needs the support which she can better provide than someone who is more inexperienced. Naomi is reassured by this.

Weeks pass and no progress is made. Emma writes, again, to Kate about the interim financial position. Emma receives an unhelpful response suggesting that Naomi should find a job and criticising the fact that she is being "bank rolled" by the parties' eldest daughter, Sophie. Emma would prefer to discuss the content of this correspondence face to face and invites Naomi to a meeting at the office. During the course of their conversation, Naomi expresses some surprise at Mike's stance as she informs Emma that he has told her that he has done everything necessary to progress the case. He appears to be blaming his lawyer.

Emma explains to Naomi that she is concerned that she may run out of funds to deal with the resolution of issues between herself and Mike. She informs Naomi that whilst her preference would be to direct Naomi and Mike towards hybrid mediation, she fears that Mike will just use this to stall and waste

Naomi's limited funds to meet legal fees. She therefore recommends (unusually for her) that financial remedy proceedings should be issued in Form A. Naomi is comfortable with the advice which Emma has provided for her to date, and she does feel stronger than she did when she first instructed Emma. She is finding her counsellor very helpful and supportive, and is also benefiting from the support she receives from Jessica and Sophie. Her relationship with her daughter Nathalie has deteriorated but she hopes that this will turn around when Nathalie becomes more aware of the situation which her father is creating.

Emma explains to Naomi the need to understand the value of Mike's business interest and also for there to be a pension sharing report, so that an actuary can properly advise Naomi and Mike on how the pension resources should be shared to achieve a fair outcome.

Naomi feels that she understands everything which Emma is explaining to her, and agrees that this course of action should be adopted. Form A is therefore issued.

When the date for First Directions Appointment is received, Emma explains to Naomi that it will be more cost effective if Naomi is represented at court by a barrister. Emma says that a representative from her firm would also attend, but it would be a more junior solicitor as it does not warrant Emma's charge out rate. Naomi is nervous about the court hearing and says that she would prefer Emma to be there with her, especially if she may not have met the barrister before the hearing. Emma suggests that perhaps a saving could be made by not having a conference with Counsel in advance, as the issues are relatively straightforward. Naomi confirms that her preference would be for Emma to be there with her and for the barrister of Emma's choice to represent her at the hearing. This is the course of action which they decide to adopt.

Emma is endeavouring to manage the support which Naomi requires against the need to minimise legal costs. Her worry is that Mike may do everything possible to absorb Naomi's limited resources, thereby rendering her unable to take legal advice at a crucial point in the process. She gives consideration to whether

Emma & Naomi

she should deal with the First Directions Appointment herself but feels that on balance Naomi needs her devoted attention and support, and Counsel can then deal with the hearing. Emma feels that she would perhaps be "juggling too many plates" if she resolved to deal with both, albeit that this could give a slight cost saving for Naomi. She decides to actually charge a fixed cost for her attendance at court to keep costs to a minimum for Naomi. This is another example of the narcissistic behaviour of one of the couple having an effect on the solicitor's approach to billing to their own detriment, as a consequence of the nature of the case.

Eventually First Directions Appointment documents are exchanged. This is later than the 14 days prior to the First Directions Appointment date required by the timetable, but Emma has sufficient time to send the paperwork to Counsel. The questionnaire provided on behalf of Mike is full of questions which have undoubtedly been raised by him as opposed to Kate. Emma is not surprised. She informs Naomi that this is the case and reassures her that a number of the questions are likely to be deleted by the judge at the court hearing. She provides Naomi with details of the barrister who will represent her at the First Directions Appointment and the agreed brief fee. She tells Naomi that she will limit her own charges for attendance at court, irrespective of how long the hearing lasts. Naomi is extremely grateful for this. Emma explains that Mike is resisting a pension sharing report and a company valuation. She tells Naomi that the judge will have to make a decision over this.

Emma writes to Kate expressing some surprise and concern about the content of her draft questionnaire. She does not receive a response.

The First Directions Appointment proceeds. Emma introduces Naomi to Counsel when they arrive at court. Naomi is entirely happy to leave Counsel to deal with the hearing, having been fully briefed by Emma. She is pleased to have Emma present for support. Naomi finds it difficult being in the court room with Mike and is pleased that she opted for Emma to be present with her. As Emma advised, the judge deletes some of the questions in the questionnaire submitted on behalf of

Mike. An order is made for there to be a pension sharing report on joint instruction, and also a value of Mike's business. Naomi finds the process more bearable than she had expected, notwithstanding the fact that at home prior to their departure, Mike did his best to undermine Naomi's confidence in her legal team.

After the hearing Naomi has an opportunity to speak with Emma and Counsel jointly. Emma explains Naomi's need to resolve matters as expeditiously as possible as she has limited funds. Naomi wants to be away from Mike as soon as is achievable. She has discussed, with her counsellor, the need for her to embark on a new life away from Mike, and recognises that this may mean taking a settlement which is below that which she might be able to fight for at court. Emma advised Naomi about weighing up the cost of achieving an uncertain outcome through a litigious process, and the reduced cost of settling for something which falls within the bracket of that which a court would consider to be fair, but perhaps nearer the lower end of that bracket from Naomi's perspective, which may be attractive to Mike and bring matters to a conclusion relatively early.

During the course of the hearing it had become clear that the judge had had limited time to read all of the paperwork. This made Naomi feel nervous of the court process and she preferred to place her trust in Emma to negotiate a settlement instead.

Naomi needs some sort of financial support from Mike in the short term, but is confident that she would be able to find some sort of work which, although relatively lowly paid, would assist with meeting her expenditure. She is happy to look at shop work or a receptionist position. She has made enquiries in relation to both and believes that she may be able to achieve some form of employment of this nature.

With the assistance of Counsel, Emma discusses possible proposals with Naomi. As all three girls are now independent Naomi is happy to set her accommodation costs at a modest level. She asks that a proposal is put to Mike as soon as possible. A purchaser has been found for the family home which

Emma & Naomi

Naomi has already discussed with Emma. Emma advised Naomi that she is entitled to a pension sharing order which would provide her with an equal division of the pension assets. Naomi believes that she could rehouse herself with 70% of the net proceeds of sale of the family home and would be prepared to take a little less. She agrees that it would be reasonable for Mike to provide her with some financial support for a period of three years, which would be capable of extension.

Emma prepares a draft letter when she returns to the office. Naomi discusses the content briefly with her counsellor and then instructs Emma to put forward the proposal.

A response is received relatively quickly, offering Naomi 60% of the net proceeds of sale of the house, but agreeing to the maintenance proposal and the pension share. Emma advised Naomi that the capital division is perhaps on the low side but as Mike has agreed to the maintenance provision it may not be unreasonable. Naomi is at the stage where she wants to exit the marriage as soon as possible and move quickly into alternative accommodation. She has seen a house which she likes and could afford. She has a small sum left from the £10,000 loan to her by Tom and she would be prepared to use this for her conveyancing costs and moving expenses. She instructs Emma to confirm that the proposal is acceptable.

Emma prepares a draft application for Order by Consent. Mike is very slow to respond and Naomi's anxiety increases. She is again grateful for the support of her counsellor and also of Emma. There is a possibility that the purchaser for the family home might be lost due to the delays. Naomi raises this with Mike, who characteristically blames both his legal team and Emma's. He says that he fails to understand why these professional people cannot just get on with their job, and warns Naomi that, were the sale to be lost, it would be entirely the fault of the lawyers involved.

The matter is resolved within sufficient time for the sale to proceed. Naomi leaves Emma to deal with all of the paperwork and is delighted to move to her new home. She continues with the assistance of her counsellor to look at rebuilding her relationship with Nathalie.

As soon as the Court Order is sealed Emma receives a letter from Mike advising that his financial position has changed significantly. Company profits have fallen and it looks as though his employment position is unsustainable. He states that he is not in a position to continue to pay the maintenance at the agreed level and defaults on the next monthly payment.

Naomi is not in a financial position to meet costs which she might incur with regard to enforcement. Emma advises her that she has an enforceable Court Order. Naomi is so relieved to have extricated herself from her situation with Mike that she decides to leave this temporarily on the 'back burner', and see if she can manage or not. She has no stomach for expensive litigation with Mike which might actually prove fruitless. She decides to retain her order and see what happens.

Mike has successfully encouraged Naomi to take a lower capital settlement because of her desire to not lose the purchaser for the family home and to extricate herself from the relationship as soon as possible. Emma needs to be sure that she covered this off very carefully with Naomi in correspondence, warning her of the risks that Mike may not honour the maintenance element of the order. Naomi needs to evaluate whether the sanctuary of her own home away from Mike and the fact that she has been able to achieve modest gainful employment means that she does not need to resurrect litigation with Mike at this stage. Her counsellor has warned her that this is probably what he wants. Emma feels sorry for Naomi but acknowledges that the incurrence of further legal fees may not be to her overall benefit, in a situation where funds are as limited as they are. Mike has shown ruthlessness, lack of empathy and narcissistic rage. He has shown a blatant disregard for the rules regarding the Court Order, and, having played on Naomi's fears throughout the process, has worn her down so that she feels she is not strong enough to fight him through the courts any more.

Issues regarding children

5

T hose with narcissistic personality disorder view others *not as people*, with hopes, dreams, desires, wants and needs of their own, but more as *objects* to be used for their own benefit. The lack of empathy which is fundamental to this disorder is the reason for this; a narcissist has a very limited ability to step into another's shoes and view the world from their perspective. Although it may not superficially appear to be so, they cannot deeply feel another's pain or joy, or anything in between, although they may be able to cognitively understand it, and so use it to their own advantage. Team this with a tendency to exploit others and a sense of entitlement, and you have a recipe for unsatisfactory relationships.

People are simply a means of securing narcissistic supply, directly (from their adoration of the narcissist) or indirectly (by making the narcissist look good to others). The children of a person with a narcissistic personality adaptation are, sadly, also viewed in this way, and are treated accordingly.

Narcissists rarely look like the Childcatcher from Chitty Chitty Bang Bang or the Wicked Witch of the East. They can appear to the outside world (and sometimes to their own children) to be caring parents. But underneath this veneer, damaging behaviours will be playing out as a result of the narcissist's mis-wired brain.

Narcissists view children as extensions of themselves

With children, however, the matter becomes a little more complicated. Not only are they used as mere objects or accessories to the narcissist, the narcissist also has trouble separating their own sense of self from the child; they view their children not as individuals but as *extensions of themselves*.

This makes boundary violations with children particularly common, as the narcissist does not see themselves as separate. What the narcissistic parent wants, the child should also want and, if they assert their boundaries, they will cause narcissistic injury and rage and find themselves at the mercy of their narcissistic parent's wrath.

These boundary violations can take various forms. They may constantly demand to know exactly where their children are, what they are doing and whom they are seeing. They may walk into rooms without knocking, read diaries and look through their devices. They may feel threatened by the idea of the developing child separating from themselves and may try to stop them from becoming independent by not letting them leave home or making them financially dependent on them in adulthood, perhaps even insisting that they work for their own firm where they can be kept under the thumb.

Issues also frequently arise in relation to the new partner/partners of the narcissist. As we have established, narcissists find it difficult to be on their own, and therefore, without the insight required to heal from the loss of a significant relationship, tend to quickly jump into a new relationship. Very often, they do not consider the feelings of their children when introducing them to their new partner, again as a result of their lack of empathy and inability to see the children as separate from themselves. (What is fine with them should be fine by their children too.) The children can be forced into spending time with the new partner when they feel uncomfortable about it, or find themselves thrown in at the deep end, being introduced without warning. They may even be subjected to exhibitionist public displays of affection, perhaps when they are still getting used to the fact that their parents are no longer together.

If they try to avoid such situations, perhaps by refusing to visit the narcissistic parent if their partner is present, they will be turned upon, or the former spouse will receive accusations of alienating the narcissist from their child. Narcissists do not accept blame for their actions. They are unable to see themselves as anything other than special or perfect; if they did, they'd risk puncturing the false image they need to have of themselves, to avoid feeling their underlying feelings of shame and worthlessness. As the lawyer representing the narcissist's spouse, you may find yourself in correspondence of this nature. As the lawyer representing the narcissist, you may find yourself, once again, having to deny, minimise, invalidate or justify these issues to the other side, whilst failing to convince your client to see the sense in changing their behaviour.

This view that children are extensions of themselves can also lead to other issues. Remember Susan, our Closet Narcissist? She was unable to tolerate the suggestion that her son, Sebastian, had dyslexia, and refused to get him tested for this, in spite of the school suggesting it. Sebastian struggled throughout his school years as a result, and long term his confidence in his own ability became severely eroded. This is very common indeed. Narcissists need to believe that they are perfect and special. It is often the case that this need for perfection is extended to their children. In the case above, Susan refused to take on the belief that their child could have learning difficulties, even at her child's expense.

As a lawyer, you may find yourself in the midst of cases such as these where one party, the narcissist, is attempting to block diagnosis and treatment. It is also common, should a diagnosis be obtained, that the narcissist refuses to accept it as true and may refuse to administer prescribed medication whilst the child is with them as a result, even for potentially serious illnesses such as asthma. Where a child needs counselling or psychotherapy, a narcissist may also step in and prevent this, deeply uncomfortable with the child revealing anything they cannot control to a third party.

Narcissists are often risk-takers, and, again as a result of seeing their children as their own extensions, they may not consider that the risks they are taking are inappropriate with children in tow. Bad driving at high speeds, taking the children on the back of motorbikes without the other parent's consent and leaving young children unattended near swimming pools, are just some of the many safety issues you may find yourself writing about to the narcissist when acting for their spouse.

Conditional love

A narcissist will generally purport to adore and love their children, but, as with their other relationships, love is merely conditional and transactional. As with all matters of the heart with a narcissist, they themselves truly believe that what they are feeling is love, but once again it is merely a reflection of the amount of adoration or supply they are receiving from the child. It is a *sort* of love in a way, but a shallowly felt, easy to break kind. And, of course, a narcissist does not know any different. And nor do their young children.

> **A narcissist will generally purport to adore and love their children, but, as with their other relationships, love is merely conditional and transactional.**

This brings us on to the topics of 'whole object relations' and 'object constancy'; psychological attributes which develop in healthy individuals, as described in Chapter 2. Narcissists have not developed these, and so have a tendency to see others (and themselves) as being either 'all good' or 'all bad'. They therefore swing between the two extremes in their view of others, behaving accordingly.

They are also unable to maintain positive feelings to someone who has hurt or disappointed them, making their feelings towards others highly unstable. Narcissists are unable to accept or like people as they truly are – imperfect beings with a blend of good and bad traits. A narcissist therefore idealises their children in their own minds, and when they fall off their pedestals due to their imperfections, they vilify them. Needless to say, this is a cycle that is confusing and damaging to children.

Consider the toddler who is beaming sweetly at their parent and tottering around dressed as a bear. The narcissistic parent, most likely, will feel positively disposed to this child, and may pick them up and toss them playfully into the air, especially if they have an audience. The child might chuckle and squeal in delight. All is well. The narcissistic parent is happy and feels their version of love for the child; the child is responding just as the narcissist wants them to, affirming their own abilities as a parent. But just a few moments later, the child is suddenly hungry and becomes grouchy. Within moments this good-natured child has started to cry and is on the way to a full blown tantrum. The narcissistic parent, unable to coax the child back into their former state of happiness, becomes angry. This is not what they wanted. Suddenly the child is a monster, and their feelings of love vanish. It's not just irritation, but with love still running underneath. It's a disappearance of the feelings of love. The child is now 'all bad', and the narcissistic parent has stormed off, hurriedly withdrawn, or is shouting at the child, having lost their all-important control of the situation.

Narcissists have a sense of entitlement

A narcissist's sense of entitlement can also play out in the parenting arena. Often narcissists do not want to engage in menial jobs that do not give them the gratification of narcissistic supply. As any parent knows, parenting, especially of younger children, involves a never ending loop of thankless tasks, from nappy changing, to meal preparation, to refusal of the child to eat the carefully prepared meal, to tantrum throwing in public etc. Unless the narcissist is receiving supply from these tasks (perhaps by developing the outward persona of 'perfect parent' when in public), they may simply refuse to do them. This is all well and good when another parent can step in, but in separation and divorce, the parenting deficiencies of the narcissistic parent can quickly become an issue.

Narcissistic parents, for example, can forget to feed their children altogether until they themselves feel hungry. Children, even young ones, may end up cooking un-nutritious meals for themselves when staying with a narcissistic parent. If a child is ill, the narcissistic parent's intrinsic lack of empathy can mean that symptoms are ignored, or no sympathy or care is forthcoming. I have heard of narcissistic parents who have failed to seek medical attention for suspected broken bones for their children whilst in their care. They can forget to ensure their children are bathed, and may fail to even think about providing their child with a toothbrush or toothpaste when they are staying with them, teeth going un-brushed for days as a result.

Emails from the school may be deemed as unimportant and not looked at. They are unlikely to ensure that homework is completed, and may not even consider doing their children's laundry or ensuring that they have clothes, or even made up beds at their house. Parent's evenings and sports days are often not attended (unless there is an opportunity to gain admiration and supply in attending, or if they are helicopter parenting, gaining supply from controlling their children's lives and achievements). Routine appointments, such as for opticians and dentists, will usually fall upon the non-narcissistic spouse, regardless of who the children primarily live with.

The narcissist's sense of entitlement over their ex-spouse does not end with a decree absolute. They will simply expect them to continue to follow orders, pick up the pieces or take up the slack when their own parenting falls short. We recall the tale of a narcissist who was financially abusing his ex-spouse by refusing to pay child maintenance. When his father died after a long illness, he refused to contribute to suitable clothes for the children to wear to the funeral, but criticised his ex-wife heavily for not having bought the children new outfits for the occasion. Due to limited funds, she had borrowed clothes from friends instead, which he found unacceptable. He simply could not see that this was now his responsibility, not hers.

Lateness is another typical behaviour that will be seen with narcissistic parents, as a result of their sense of entitlement. They can be hours late picking up their children for visits, with no prior warning, but if made to wait on *their* arrival, can fly off the handle. They will often change arrangements and visitation days without notice, or cancel altogether. Lateness can also be used against the non-narcissistic parent in other ways: for example, if their ex-spouse has somewhere important to be (for example they have a flight to catch, or a function to attend), and the narcissist gets wind of this, the narcissist will very often attempt to sabotage the other's plans, using lateness in picking up the children or sudden cancellation as their excuse. This can be wearying and stressful for the other parent who will eventually learn to make contingency plans for situations such as these. Also, getting children to school or to out of school activities in a timely fashion seems difficult for many narcissistic parents, as these are not areas of high priority for them, and it is common for children to miss out here.

How the narcissist uses their children as weapons

One of the most shocking behaviours is the way that narcissist will punish their children in order to get back at their spouse. Narcissists do not feel remorse or guilt – they cannot, because those feelings threaten the existence of their false selves, which they have worked so hard to establish and maintain. Moral standards, in reality, apply only to others. They show no mercy when dealing with their ex-spouse, and using the children is a perfect way to punish that spouse; one of the best tools in the narcissist's war chest, in fact.

Children are *objects* to be used in whatever way is in the narcissist's interests. They are pawns in the narcissist's game of needing to win, of needing to crush their 'opposition' (the former spouse).

Financial abuse is such an area, ripe for exploitation.

A narcissist may deliberately reduce their earnings in order to reduce their child maintenance payments. An affluent narcissist whose children are in private education will commonly stop paying school fees so that the children may be forced to leave their schools, in order to burden the other parent with the guilt.

When they have the children with them, they may refuse to take them out for food or to events, or to buy them birthday presents, claiming that the other spouse has all the money and they cannot afford it. They may refuse to continue to contribute to much loved hobbies, activities or school trips, in order to guilt trip the other, less affluent parent into paying. They will often have inappropriate discussions with the children about the finances relating to a divorce.

If the narcissist is not the main earner, they can also try to exploit the children for financial gain, and may take the other parent back to court repeatedly to this end. It is not uncommon for this behaviour to go on for years until the child has reached their 18th birthday. Consider the case of a narcissistic mother, 15 years post-divorce, who took her high earning husband back to court in order to claim child maintenance. This narcissist lied to the court that the child, who was 17, was in full time education, even though he had left school and had a full time paid apprenticeship. After two years of fighting, the court finally asked the narcissistic parent for evidence of the full time education. The case collapsed at this point, but significant anguish and pain had been caused to both the father and the child. The child, although he knew what was happening, did not dare stand up to the wrath of his mother and, despite pleas from his father to write to the court explaining the truth of the matter, felt unable to do so. Narcissists are masters of guilt tripping, and have an enormous hold over their children, who have been worn down through abuse which has lasted their entire lifetimes. It is interesting to note that, even though this narcissist had already been given a jail sentence for child benefit fraud some years previously, she was still able to wreak havoc in the legal system, using it to perpetuate abuse of her ex-husband.

Less extreme narcissists will do all manner of things to control their ex-spouse's finances, pettiness featuring highly here. One narcissist we heard of took both TVs from the family home in an attempt to force their spouse to buy another, purely to run down funds. And another, who did not live with the children, insisted upon taking the Christmas tree and all the Christmas decorations from the family home just a few days before the big day. We have even heard of narcissists removing their children from their film and music streaming accounts, even though they had spare accounts available, just in order to get their spouse to buy accounts for the children. Threatening to remove beloved pets from the home in which the children live is another real life example of just how far a narcissist will go to seek revenge, even at the emotional expense of the children they believe they love.

Children may even be enlisted to remove things from the other parent's house, either on the grounds that they are merely 'borrowing' them, or that they are the narcissist's to take. Of course, for children whose parents have relatively recently split, this is confusing as they were used to things being shared and also don't understand why their parents shouldn't be friendly towards one another. If the non-narcissistic parents tries to resist having items taken from their home, the narcissist will inevitably turn it on them, suggesting to the children that they are being unreasonable, and mean spirited. In fact, by trying to maintain a friendly relationship with the narcissist, the ex-spouse is opening themselves up to more abuse and boundary violations themselves, as they will eventually come to realise.

Some narcissists may seek to highlight the difference between their life and the non-narcissistic spouse's life to their children. We recall the story of the very wealthy narcissist who failed to pay interim maintenance pending suit to his spouse with whom the children lived so that even buying food became an issue. When the children visited him, he would alternate between telling them that he had no money and could only afford to feed them beans on toast, to offering them fillet steaks and high end mouthwatering treats. He would confuse them further by taking them away to 5 star luxury resorts to show the wife what she was missing out on as a result of her desire to divorce, all the while purporting to the children to be poor.

Narcissists will also use their children to de-stabilise their spouse. They may use the children to give them information about the spouse such as regarding a new partner or a new job. We know of one narcissist who used her son to obtain the spare key to her ex-husbands flat which she then had copied. She would regularly visit the flat, go through the paperwork on his desk, look at pictures on his mantelpiece and rifle through drawers, looking for his new partner's underwear.

Badmouthing

Narcissists will always carry out a smear campaign, telling frank lies about their spouse to others so that they are seen as the long-suffering injured party. They will also enlist others (their 'flying monkeys') to badmouth their former spouse.

Narcissistic injury leads to narcissistic rage as we have already ascertained. Narcissists need to hurt their spouse, to punish them, regardless of who instigated the split. What better way than by attempting to alienate the children from the other parent?

Unfortunately, it is absolutely typical for the narcissist to badmouth their ex-spouse to their children and blame them for their new, less salubrious, living situation. They often lie to them in order to confuse them and turn them away from their other parent. Projection is often employed here, by telling the children that their other parent is guilty of things that *they themselves* have actually done. Narcissists may tell the children that the other parent has mental health issues, has had affairs, is lazy, is a drug addict; whatever works to undermine them in the eyes of their children. The children may know in their hearts that these accusations are not true, but begin to believe them anyway. Of course, they do not know that this is gas-lighting, a hallmark of narcissistic abuse.

Badmouthing the other parent to both sets of grandparents and to the children's aunts and uncles is another common tactic. Of course, this has knock on effects for the children, affecting their relationships with cousins and other important extended family members. This is very wearing indeed, eating away at the resilience of the non-narcissistic spouse, and affecting their own ability to parent optimally.

Child arrangements issues

It is extremely common for narcissists to demand that the children live with them, regardless of what would be in the best interests of the children. A narcissist experiencing narcissistic injury needs others to see them as special, perfect, a nice person, the 'good' parent. They need topping up with narcissistic supply urgently. They need others to see them as 'all good' so that *they* can see *themselves* in this way. They need to discredit and devalue the other parent to others so that they are viewed by others as *they* see them; as 'all bad'. This pushes the narcissist's sense of superiority up further, and validates them even more.

The narcissist may insist that their spouse attends mediation regarding child arrangements issues, particularly the issue over with which parent the children might primarily reside. This is commonly employed as a scare tactic and as a method to reduce the spouse's funds further. As explained in Chapter 2, mediation is usually not an effective method for tackling issues involving a narcissist, and the process is highly likely to break down. The narcissist merely uses the mediation process as a way to create drama, fear and conflict, whilst attempting to feel superior by running rings around all parties involved with constantly shifting goalposts and attempts to undermine the impartiality of the mediator.

If the narcissist is particularly aggrieved, the matter may reach court where they will relish the adversarial environment, where they can prove their superiority and cleverness. The worry here is that the narcissist may well have the advantage. They seem initially plausible and charming. If very high up on the spectrum (tending towards psychopathy) they are often able to behave in a fearless manner, coming across as the calm, rational parent.

They can play the quiet victim with aplomb, and as lying is second nature to a narcissist, they are able to make realistic sounding arguments explaining why the other parent is unfit for parental duties. The frightened parent on the other side, whose fight, flight or freeze response has been activated and whose stress hormones are flooding their system, diverting blood away from the logic and thinking areas of their brain, may not come across as quite so rational. This may well come at the cost of their children if they and their legal team are unprepared.

Another common ploy, designed to punish the non-narcissistic parent, is to threaten to move to another part of the country, or indeed to another country altogether, taking the children with them. This may also be used as leverage in order to procure a better financial settlement, where the narcissist will attempt to blackmail the other parent into agreeing to give a greater proportion of the assets to them so that they do not move to a part of the country which they claim is more affordable. Again, the children are weaponised here.

The golden child, the scapegoat and the invisible child

When there is more than one child, other patterns of behaviour often manifest.

The narcissist enjoys drama and will usually favour one child over another. This is whichever child is the most effective at securing the most narcissistic supply for the parent. The child may be the one who is most adoring of the parent, the one who subjugates their needs most, or the one whose achievements bring the narcissist attention and praise. It may even be the child who most closely physically resembles the narcissist. Whichever child is living up to the expectations and demands of the narcissist the most is the 'golden child,' and is treated differently to the others. They will be spoiled with gifts and praise but, like all children of narcissists, will eventually come to know that being loved by that parent is conditional on them being who the narcissist wants them to be, rather than who they actually are. They are likely to carry this pattern into their adult lives, either becoming narcissistic themselves or attracting a narcissistic partner.

Where there is a golden child, there is often also a 'scapegoat'. The child who stands up for themselves, with healthy, non-porous boundaries may find themselves in this position, or perhaps the child who may be unfortunate enough to physically resemble the non-narcissistic parent, the now reviled former spouse of the narcissist. They will be subjected to all the normal narcissistic abuse tactics – devaluation, projection of the narcissist's own actions on to them, gas-lighting, passive aggression, name calling, triangulation with others. They will watch the other child receiving no-expense spared gifts, whilst they are left out. They will be forced to always eat what the other child wants, watch the movies they want, and they will be subjected to silent treatments when they are visiting their narcissistic parent. If they decide not to visit, they will receive a tirade of abuse, by text, and multiple phone calls. They will be drawn into arguments involving the other parent. They will experience the narcissist's pseudologic and word salad. In some cases, the narcissist will enlist the whole family in scapegoating this child.

We recall a parent describing this dynamic to us. The narcissistic parent would be sending loving texts full of pet names to one child, whilst *simultaneously* demeaning and criticising the other child in short sharp sentences, also by text. The two children, who were teenagers sitting on the sofa next to each other, would incredulously compare the messages they were receiving, in real time, shocked at how their mother could be so cutting to one of them at the same time as being so warm to the other. Manipulation came absolutely naturally to her.

The golden child/scapegoat dynamic may not be a stable one, however. It may take months or even years, but at some point, the roles may well be switched. This could be as a result of external circumstances, or if the golden child learns to assert their own autonomy. At this point, the golden child moves out of the idealisation phase into the devalue phase (becoming the scapegoat), and the former scapegoat may then enter the idealisation phase, grateful at last to be the golden child.

Another child in the dynamic may be forced into the role of the 'invisible child'; this is the child who simply is not seen. They jump through hoops to try to get noticed, and is usually the affable, compliant child who was always ignored and overlooked.

The invisible child learns that they do not matter. They grow up without the concept of having rights, wants or needs, and this plays out in their adult relationships, where they either develop their own narcissistic defences in order to feel special or they become echoists, with a revulsion to feeling special, thus becoming magnets for narcissists and other psychologically unhealthy types.

Narcissistic mothers

Interestingly, although narcissistic fathers are more common (there is a gender bias of around a 3:1 male to female ratio in narcissism), it seems to be the narcissistic *mothers* who cause a disproportionate amount of damage to their children as they are more likely, due to societal norms, to be the primary caregivers in the early life of the children, and also, post-divorce, to be the parent with whom the children spend more time.

Narcissistic mothers have an even more complicated dynamic with their daughters in that not only do they see their daughters as extensions of themselves, they also see them as threats, and may be envious of their youth, looks, achievements and even boyfriends. They may, in public, flaunt their daughter but, in private, criticise and demean them for not being good enough. They see them as frank competition and may even flirt with their boyfriends to assert their own superiority, put down their daughter and gain narcissistic supply. Far from preparing their daughters for the world of adulthood and independence, they place the focus on themselves.

Harmful behaviours of narcissistic mothers are not just limited to daughters, however. With sons, a narcissistic mother may compete with, and be jealous of, his girlfriends or wife. Criticism and devaluation will take place as she fails to live up to her mother-in-law's exacting standards. A narcissistic mother needs to be her son's number one, and if he is used to tiptoeing around his mother's needs above all else, he may fail to set appropriate boundaries with her, and, caught between a rock and a hard place, lose his significant other altogether.

A narcissistic mother may also use her son as a confidant or companion, enlisting him to support her emotionally, to glorify her and to attend to her physical comfort; his needs, on the other hand, will be seen as irrelevant and he may well be told to 'man up' if he expresses them or his own emotions. Narcissistic sons are often forced to become enmeshed and over-involved with their mothers, and they may be parentified, finding themselves taking over the role of their father. Adult sons may be relied upon to make decisions and manage the narcissistic mother's finances, with guilt and a sense of misplaced duty running the show.

The long-term effects of narcissistic parenting

Symptoms of narcissism inevitably affect the narcissist's ability to parent, as behind the scenes, they subject their children to the same abuse as everyone else. The children of narcissists may go on to:

- become narcissists themselves

- become narcissist 'magnets', due to becoming co-dependents or echoists

- develop insecure attachment styles with others, leading to difficulties in adult relationships

Narcissists will shame and devalue their children about anything they can; the way they look, their weight, their lack of achievements, their friends. This is not always done with overt cruelty; subtle put downs or disguising criticism as 'jokes' is common too. Narcissists will use their children for narcissistic supply, expecting adoration. They will be highly controlling, expecting them to do exactly what they want them to do, so that they reflect well on themselves, in all areas of their lives. They may demand perfection, but never be satisfied by the child (unless they happen to be the golden child).

They triangulate their children with each other ("why can't you be more like your brother?"), their peers, cousins, or anyone else they can. They use the children's friends as sources of supply in whatever way they can, sometimes even in highly inappropriate sexual ways; a narcissistic mother we knew of once sent topless selfies to her 13 year old son's friends as a way of securing adoration and attention, with no empathy or regard for her son. By the time he was an adult, sadly, he was highly narcissistic himself.

Narcissists can be highly manipulative and interpersonally exploitative. They can be quick to anger and may be prone to physical violence, passive aggression and giving silent treatments. They will invalidate (and may even ridicule) their child's emotions, thoughts, wants and needs. They will prioritise their own needs and expect their children to do the same so that life becomes about tiptoeing around their egos to keep them happy, at the same time avoiding incurring narcissistic rage. They are devoid of true empathy and unable to care when the child needs their support most.

You could be forgiven for thinking that such behaviour would simply result in turning the children away from the narcissistic parent but it is not quite that simple. Don't forget that Exhibitionist Narcissists can be charming and great fun; when they are receiving enough narcissistic supply, they can be the 'coolest' parent, the magnanimous parent; they can shine brilliantly, and the child will love being the apple of their eye, feeling special by association and worshipping their greatness. They can be amazing and awful, in equal measure. This is confusing enough for adults who know about NPD, so what chance does a child have in making sense of it? It's easy to see how they come to accept things as they are, taking the rough with the smooth.

Exhibitionist Narcissists can be charming and great fun; when they are receiving enough narcissistic supply, they can be the 'coolest' parent, the magnanimous parent; they can shine brilliantly, and the child will love being the apple of their eye, feeling special by association and worshipping their greatness.

The emotional consequences on the child

Children want to be loved by their parents. They believe that their caregivers know best. When the narcissist is behaving badly, the children may make excuses for them, blaming themselves for it and internalising these feelings.

They can believe that if they tried harder, or did better, that they could make things better. They learn to ignore their gut instincts about what behaviours are right and wrong, and suppress and invalidate their own negative feelings. They may feel extreme guilt if they dislike the narcissistic parent and so try to overcompensate for it.

They may come to feel that they are 'not enough'. They may learn the psychological phenomenon of 'learned helplessness', where they just accept that they cannot make anything any better, and they should just accept things as they are. This can be a lifelong affliction, affecting all future relationships, careers etc. Children may learn to subjugate their needs, prioritising the needs of their narcissistic parent instead, simply to keep the peace.

Becoming a narcissist magnet

This subjugation of needs is *co-dependency in the making*, and may lead to similarly unhealthy future relationships with narcissists, alcoholics or substance addicts. The child of a narcissist accepts their parent's behaviour as *normal*. It is little wonder that, as an adult, they then accept such behaviours from others in their adult lives. In romantic relationships, they may feel intensely drawn to narcissists due to the subconscious pull of the *familiar*, mistaking it for 'chemistry'. This can perpetuate a lifetime of abuse. The adult children of narcissists should be very wary indeed of 'instant chemistry' when dating – for them, what most people hail as an essential component in a new relationship is actually a recipe for disaster. Their new partner, to whom they are so powerfully drawn, may be the polar opposite of their narcissistic parent on the surface but *underneath* the similarities may be striking, as they will likely discover with the passing of time.

Becoming a narcissist

Narcissistic parenting can also, of course, lead to the development of narcissism in the child, and can they go on to become the abuser themselves. These children adapt to their deficient upbringing by developing their *own* false self, in order to feel special. These children are bound by (and find themselves perpetuating) the generational chains of NPD.

Alternatively, it may be that a child 'gets away with it', and neither of the two scenarios above unfold. What determines whether a child raised by narcissists becomes a narcissist is determined by a complex interplay of factors.

Some children have a stronger, more resilient inborn temperament than others. Others may be from households where perhaps gender differences and expectations played a role in how they were treated, with a daughter being treated differently to a son, thereby reinforcing narcissistic behaviours more in one gender than another. And some may have had other, more healthy relationships modelled to them by grandparents, friends or teachers which negated some of the adverse effects of the narcissist's parenting.

Forming insecure attachment styles

A child's development, ability to regulate their emotions and ability to form secure healthy attachments to others is largely determined by their mother. If she validates their pain and meets their needs effectively, and is empathic and securely attached to them, then they will be positively impacted by this.[1]

So, even if a child does not become narcissistic nor attract other narcissistic relationships into their lives, they may still be emotionally damaged to some extent by a narcissistic parent, especially a mother, who simply cannot give them what they need emotionally.

So called 'attachment styles' with significant others will likely be affected, with the child of a narcissist either having a 'dismissive avoidant', 'fearful avoidant' or 'anxious preoccupied' attachment style, leading to difficulties forming close, stable, secure bonds with a partner. Briefly, in spite of craving closeness, they may avoid or drive others away through fear of abandonment, a feeling of not needing anyone, or by an anxious neediness. (The good news with these is that, with awareness, they can be overcome, and secure attachments formed).

What can the non-narcissistic parent do to limit the damage to the children by the narcissist?

Modelling good behaviour is key to making up for the parenting deficiencies of the narcissistic parent. The children will eventually come to see the contrast between the two parents. The non-narcissistic parent has to be consistent,

---

[1] Brumariu LE, Kerns KA. Parent-child attachment and internalizing symptoms in childhood and adolescence: a review of empirical findings and future directions. Dev Psychopathol. 2010 Winter; 22(1): 177-203.

establish clear boundaries and rules and be emotionally available for the children. They should listen to them, hear their fears and be interested in who they are as people. Supporting their wants and needs, celebrating their successes, and commiserating and encouraging when they fail will also be essential. The non-narcissistic parent will need to be on time for the child, and will need to make it clear that they are *unconditionally loved*; that they are *more than enough, exactly as they are*. Of course, none of this is rocket science, just good parenting, and that is all that is needed.

Modelling good behaviour is key to making up for the parenting deficiencies of the narcissistic parent.

A really important part of this is modelling and encouraging the development of *empathy* in the child. Talking about empathy and discussing how people in real life or characters in books or movies must be feeling are all helpful. If a child can develop true emotional empathy, developing narcissism is unlikely.

Trying to explain the behaviours of the other parent to the child is a tricky issue, and one that can lead to claims from the narcissist of parental alienation, so it is best avoided. Expressing empathy for the child when they tell the non-narcissistic parent about things they have experienced, and explaining that those behaviours are not desirable or how most people relate to others, is the best one can do here. Encouraging the child to set boundaries and stand up for themselves with the narcissist and others is also important. Also, passing on communication tips when the narcissist is sending threatening, ranting, guilt-tripping, accusatory messages to the child will help them enormously; explaining to them how to disengage for a while when "daddy goes off on one" in order to let things cool down. Of course, stepping in immediately if the child is in physical danger is essential.

In no longer being in a relationship with a narcissist, one finally has the ability to step away from being the narcissist's enabler. Whilst many unhappy non-narcissistic couples *stay together* for the 'sake of the children', it is not surprising that many former spouses of a narcissist report having found the strength to *leave* them for the very same reason.

Parenting with a narcissistic parent after divorce or separation – the case for parallel parenting

If the non-narcissistic parent doesn't understand the complexities of NPD they may believe that healthy, co-operative, empathetic co-parenting with their former partner may be possible, once the dust of their separation has settled. They may believe, even though it is extremely unlikely that the narcissist ever co-parented with them *during their relationship*, that they will become motivated to learn the skills required and, in time, overcome their negative feelings towards them, 'for the sake of the children'.

The uninformed non-narcissistic parent may well have expectations of being able to invite the narcissistic parent in for a cup of tea when they come to collect the children to take them to an after school activity, perhaps. They may expect to be able to discuss how their child is doing at school and to sit down together to discuss choice of secondary schools and GCSE or A level subject options. Attending parents' evenings and sports days together may be an expectation, or sharing university open day visits. Fairly splitting extra child costs, and flexibility on helping each other out regarding childcare if work or other commitments arise may be hoped for. Perhaps even being at the child's birthday party together or jointly contributing to a present. They almost certainly may hope to see eye-to-eye on safety issues for the child, such as wearing helmets and protective pads during certain sports. And surely some compromise regarding Christmas arrangements, Mother's and Father's day and holiday time will be a given?

Sadly, this is highly unlikely to ever be the case, and not only should this be understood by them, but it should be understood by their lawyer. *Projecting expected qualities of a good, cooperative, loving, giving parent on to a narcissist by the lawyer is simply not helpful if you are representing the spouse of a narcissist.* Realism would serve all concerned much better instead. The narcissist is wired to be selfish and unempathic, and this will not change, even if they are able, on the surface, to play act the role of 'perfect mum', or 'fun dad'. At the very least, they will continue to wish to manipulate and control and upset the other parent, using the children, as previously discussed, for as long as they have to be in each other's lives.

Moreover, the only way the former partner of a narcissist can heal from narcissist abuse is to, first and foremost, disengage from them. The ideal here is to go 'no contact'; to cut all ties and communication of any sort completely. However, this is simply not possible when joint children are involved and so other measures have to be employed to ensure the well-being of that parent and, by extension, the children.

This is where 'parallel parenting' comes in.

Here contact between the parents is very limited indeed, allowing them to disengage from each other as much as possible whilst remaining connected to their children. The aim is also to shield the children from being placed in the middle of parental conflict. Communication between parents only occurs when absolutely necessary.

In parallel parenting, everything is separate – extracurricular activities, school meetings and doctor's appointments are not attended together. Generally speaking, unless otherwise agreed, the rules of whichever household the child is staying in at the time are followed.

Absolutely key to establishing parallel parenting is to create, with your clients, a child arrangements plan. Where one parent is a narcissist, the child arrangements plan must be as detailed as possible; no stone must be left unturned, and no potential eventuality left unconsidered. This will be dealt with in detail later in this section.

Communication tips for parents

It is also very important indeed to advise your client (whether the narcissist or not) to agree on a *single method of communication* between themselves.

For the non-narcissist, being bombarded with multiple ranting phone calls, texts, WhatsApps and emails may be the result of not establishing such communication rules with a narcissist. *It is generally better for parents to communicate only by email*, where both parties can be more considered in their reply than by more intrusive methods such as text, which can be instantly received and responded to in the heat of the moment, inflaming tensions further.

It may be beneficial for the couple to communicate only using a specialised parenting app, such as OurFamilyWizard or similar. These apps enable all necessary child related communication, including schedules and calendars and appointments, and communication cannot be retrospectively edited. There is even a 'tonemeter' which encourages less inflammatory communication. Narcissists don't generally like such apps as they find them to be controlling, but if they can be persuaded to agree (perhaps by being persuaded by their own lawyer, or by being made to think that it was their own idea) they can be very effective all round. Notably, these records are admissible as evidence to the court.

The non-narcissistic parent must be very careful how they communicate with the narcissist. As the lawyer it would be useful if you were able to advise them to:

- Refrain from rising to any baits, under any circumstances. Narcissists know exactly which buttons to push to elicit a response, which the ex-spouse can then find used against them in court, making them appear unstable or unreasonable.

- Agree, preferably to email, as the only method of communication.

- Refrain from speaking to them on the phone or in person if at all possible. Insisting (to the narcissist) that, if such conversations have to occur, they will be recorded using a phone app may help to keep things civil.

- Give themselves a few hours to cool down before responding to the narcissist's communications.

- Decide whether there is anything to be gained by responding to the narcissist's communications *at all*.

- Use the 'grey rock' method of communication. If they have to see the narcissist face to face (not recommended) they should limit all facial expressions, speak in a dull monotone voice, and make reduced or no eye contact with the narcissist. They should use as few words as possible, and give the narcissist no energy, moving away as soon as they can. This is in order to ensure that they are not a source of narcissistic supply, and are as boring to the narcissist as a grey rock. It may feel rude to a non-narcissist, but they will soon see how effective it is at forcing the narcissist to move on to more rewarding climes, narcissistic supply-wise.

- Know how to respond to a written communication. Here they should not engage in any arguing. They should not try to defend or justify themselves, or respond to or make any accusations. They should use the fewest words possible. For example, "Yes, 8pm", or "I do not agree to this", "Pick up will remain at 5pm", or "Noted." Only the absolutely essential points regarding child related arrangements should be responded to. No niceties should be added (they count as giving the narcissist narcissistic supply). This is 'grey rock' but in the written form.

- Be aware of what to do in situations where the narcissistic parent sends a written communication (such as by email) falsely claiming that an agreement was reached verbally, when it wasn't. The former spouse should respond in writing that no conversation ever took place, and document everything. It is common for a narcissist to try this tactic – they are highly manipulative and lie without a guilty conscience. Emails of this nature are common, e.g. "Further to our spoken conversation just now, I am writing to confirm that we agreed that I could have the children for the entire Christmas holiday this year..."

- Refrain from having an unflattering name for the narcissistic parent in their phone/email contacts. Whilst this may help take the sting out of any communications received from the narcissist in the heat of the moment, it's likely that the children will stumble upon it, and worse, tell the narcissistic parent, leading to potential difficulties and even claims of parental alienation.

Documentation

You should also advise your client to set aside a short amount of time every week to ensure that all their records of communications with the narcissist are kept up to date.

All communications should be downloaded, printed and filed.

If telephone conversations do occur, they should be recorded and downloaded using a recording app on their phone. The recordings themselves may not be admissible to court but they will be useful for keeping track of what was said.

Keeping a dedicated log detailing late pick-ups, cancellations, injuries sustained by the child etc should also be encouraged in the non-narcissistic parent.

Parental responsibility

Parents should also be told their rights – all too often in these cases involving narcissists an assumption is made, post-divorce, that the parents will get over their differences and be able to calmly and rationally share information and make joint decisions about the children. As we have established, this is not the case where a narcissist is involved. As the lawyer, providing information, perhaps in a handout, about parental responsibility would be very useful post-divorce, as narcissists thrive in exploiting any grey areas or areas of uncertainty. Note that GP surgeries and hospitals should be made aware of both parent's names and addresses, so that they are able to send information to both parents.

Your client (narcissistic or otherwise) should be clear that those with parental responsibility have rights to:

- access children's medical records

- be involved with the choice of the child's school

- be involved in decisions regarding medical treatment

- be involved with the religious upbringing of the child

- be involved when it comes to naming a child or changing their name

- be involved in decisions regarding holidays abroad and trips away with non-family members

- know where their children are living unless there are safeguarding reasons which means that an address must be withheld

Parental alienation

The term 'parental alienation' describes a process through which a child becomes estranged from a parent as a result of the psychological manipulation of the other parent. The child's estrangement may manifest itself as fear, disrespect or sometimes even hostility towards the distant parent.

There is a fear that, in the context of family separation, one parent may seek to suggest that it is not in the interests of the child to spend time with the other parent who may then allege 'parental alienation'. All too often there are simply unresolved emotional issues between the parents in which the child becomes inappropriately entwined.

Unfortunately, this can be an approach taken by one parent in an attempt to punish the other for issues relating to the breakdown of their own relationship. They do not give due consideration to the adverse effect such an approach can have on their child.

In a situation where one parent suffers from NPD, however, it is not unusual for that parent to accuse the other of 'parental alienation' as part of their 'smear campaign' or attempt to undermine or devalue the non-narcissistic parent. This could be in a situation where child arrangements are entirely child focused but either not liked by the parent suffering from NPD or they are simply intent on causing mischief and upset.

Communication tips for the non-narcissist parent

►   Use a single method of communication

►   Communicate only by email or a specialised parenting app if possible

►   Refrain from rising to any baits, under any circumstances

►   Refrain from speaking to your ex-partner on the phone or in person if at all possible

►   Give yourself a few hours to cool down before responding to the narcissist's communications

►   Decide whether there is anything to be gained by responding to the narcissist's communications *at all*

►   Use the 'grey rock' method of communication

►   Try not to defend or justify yourself, or respond to or make any accusations

►   Document everything

This needs to be identified at an early stage by both solicitors involved, who should be carefully considering the motives behind any accusations made, focusing firmly on the welfare of the child. This might be a situation where you would seek to jointly instruct an Independent Social Worker at a very early stage, before the situation escalates to something which may be damaging for the child.

In accordance with the Welfare Checklist set out in Section 1 of the Children Act 1989, the welfare of any child is of paramount importance to the court. In the event that one parent has genuine concerns about the adverse influence which the other may have on minor children, these should be clearly documented.

Overriding everything else it may still be best for the child to have ongoing contact with both parents, notwithstanding any personality disorder or other issues which either parent might have. An understanding of NPD and the effect that this may have on the children of the family is vitally important so that the other parent can carefully monitor any adverse effects of behaviour upon the child. It may be appropriate for them to work ongoing with a family consultant/coach who may be able to provide guidance as to when behaviour is such that contact should be limited or brought to a conclusion. Expert evidence will always be extremely important if, in the interests of the child, contact should be limited or terminated.

A balance must always be achieved between the interests of the child and the benefits of an ongoing relationship with both parents, considered against the damage which such an ongoing relationship may have on a long term basis.

It is important that there is a clear understanding of the behaviour to which the child is being subjected at the hands of the narcissistic parent as clear and cohesive evidence will need to be presented to the court if any application to limit or suspend/terminate contact is to be successful. The needs of the child would have to be very carefully considered and additional professional support involved to assess the situation would be vital.

The child arrangements plan

Whether you are representing a client suffering from NPD or their spouse, when dealing with child arrangements it is vitally important that any child arrangements plan is almost 'overdetailed' to endeavour to have a 'road map' for every conceivable eventuality in order to avoid the need for recourse to the court system.

If you are negotiating an agreed child arrangements plan at court the euphoria of achieving an outcome which is negotiated can sometimes lead to rushed drafting of the detail of that arrangement. Particularly where Counsel is instructed who may not fully understand the requirements of the couple involved, it is vitally important for the solicitor in attendance to stress the need for detailed consideration when drafting such a document. This is another reason why a junior solicitor should not be the person attending court with Counsel in this sort of case.

If you are fortunate enough to be drafting such a document in an office environment rather than at court, again crucial attention must be paid to the detail. Either of the couple may query the cost of such dedication, but do not be nervous to reassure them that this detailed consideration at an early stage will avoid unnecessary litigation or disputed issues in the future.

It is important to remember that an individual suffering from NPD can have the emotional response of a small child. Someone with this emotional impediment may respond well to a clear set of guidelines which are indisputable.

These are some of the topics which you should not be afraid to include in a child arrangements plan.

General parenting guidelines

a) The importance of providing a united front for the children. How will the parents behave in front of the children? Is it important for the children to see that decisions are made collectively?

b) Might it be important to have meetings in a neutral place to discuss parenting issues? How regular should this be? Or should these conversations only take place by email, given the difficulties faced by the couple?

c) How do the parents ensure that the children have a voice within the process? Might it be appropriate to arrange for them to speak with a grandparent or other relative?

d) How will the parents communicate to the children the arrangements which they have made?

e) How will the parents make sure that the children stay in contact with supportive relatives from the other side of the family, or friends?

f) Are there any important rules that the parents consider essential for the children (for example bedtimes, when homework is done, computer games or films, staying out late)? Is it agreed between the parents that 'house rules' should be imposed in both homes? If not, why not and how will this be explained to the children?

g) How do the parents work together to make significant decisions (for example school, course selection and careers advice)?

Communication

a)   Deciding on one form of communication. Perhaps the use of OurFamilyWizard.

b)   What is a reasonable time frame for responding to emails (for example 72 hours maximum)?

c)   What communication with the children is acceptable between the child and other parent when they are not staying at their home? Should specific times be agreed or a level of frequency during a period of time?

d)   Should the children have a mobile phone? If so, who should pay for the contract? Who pays for the new phone if lost/damaged?

Education

a)   What are the arrangements for 'pick up' and 'drop off' at school? How might these be altered in exceptional circumstances?

b)   Who will attend parents' evenings? Will the parents attend together or separately?

c)   How is information from the school shared between the parents? Is the school happy to accept an email address from each parent or does some mechanism need to be in place?

d)   How are agreements to be achieved regarding extracurricular activities? Who will ensure that the children attend?

e)   Are any other third parties allowed to collect the children without a parent from school or any other activity? If so, who and in what circumstances?

f)   How does the school/parent portal for the child get set up so both parents have access to read school reports, activities etc.? Should there be one account with a shared password or is it possible for the school to set up two linked accounts, one for each parent?

g)   Who pays for each extracurricular activity?

h)   What extracurricular activities are acceptable and how is this agreed?

i) Who should attend school events (sports days, plays, concerts etc.)? Are the parents happy to sit together or should there be an agreement that they sit separately? Is the child permitted to speak to both parents on these occasions if the parents attend separately and how is this managed to ensure minimum embarrassment and awkwardness for the child?

j) How should information regarding with whom the children are friends be shared i.e. possible friends who may be a bad influence etc.?

k) Who pays for school trips and how are these agreed?

l) Who pays for instrumental lessons and examinations or similar?

Medical issues

a) Which parent attends medical appointments? Is one parent responsible even if an appointment falls in the other's parenting time or is this responsibility shared?

b) Who is responsible for taking the child to the opticians? Who pays? Who holds any prescriptions? How is information about this shared?

c) Who is responsible for dental appointments and treatment? Or the orthodontist? Who arranges and takes the child to appointments and who should pay?

d) How is medical information shared?

e) Should medication be held at both homes or taken between the two? Where inhalers are required, how should it be ensured that they are retained at both homes, and are up to date? Can the parents agree how and when medication is administered?

f) Agreements regarding diet such as vegetarian or vegan in each home, food intolerances, allergies etc. Where a particular diet is required to support treatment for other conditions, how can it be ensured that this is uniform in both homes?

Holidays

a) Who should hold the children's passports? Will the other parent always retain a copy? Who has the obligation to renew (and pay for) passports? If this is shared how are funds reimbursed in a timely fashion?

b) Who holds EHIC/GHIC cards for European travel? A time frame for these to pass from one parent to the other ahead of trips needs to be agreed.

c) In advance, each parent should inform the other of the location of any holiday including flight details, destination address and a contact telephone number for the duration of the trip.

d) A framework needs to be agreed for permission to take the children abroad.

e) Agreement to organise and take the children for travel immunisation in good time if you are the parent taking them abroad.

Introduction of a new partner

a) Agreement as to how and when new partners should be introduced.

General contact arrangements

a) How will the parents inform the child about arrangements that have been made?

b) What will be done in the case of an emergency?

c) What happens if one parent is going to be late either collecting or returning the children? What is an acceptable period of time to wait and what might mean that the visit should be cancelled? What is the agreement as to how and when the late party will communicate this to the other parent?

d) Where should 'pick up/drop off' take place? Can this involve the home of each parent or does it need to be a neutral place? If so, where? Can the children walk up the path to their parent's home unaccompanied? Must the other parent stay away from the property?

e) What is the arrangement if one parent has consumed alcohol and is unable to drive? Should a taxi be involved? If so, which company and who should pay? Can a third party collect and return the children without the parent?

f) What activities are deemed unacceptable at the other parent's house? For example, cycling without head protection etc. Can these guidelines be agreed?

g) Should clothes/toothbrushes etc. be kept at both homes or packed and taken from home to home?

h) Who provides and launders school uniform/games kit if contact takes place over a weekend and into the school week? Should there be two sets of school uniform/games kit and does each parent pay for one set?

i) Do the parents have uniform guidelines for discipline? What discipline is deemed acceptable?

j) What happens on the other parent's birthday/Mother's day/Father's day? Do the parents agree that they will each enable the child to get a present for the other or agree not to do so?

k) If forms need to be signed by both parents how will they be returned to the other parent? What is the time frame for this?

l) If a weekend needs to be swapped, is the main schedule retained or does that parent then have two weekends in a row?

It is so important to have a clear and complete understanding of the requirements of your client. There may be other points which need to be added to this (non-exhaustive) list.

If there are very specific issues for the couple with whom you are working, do not be afraid to address these in detail.

A judge may consider such level of detail to be unnecessary. If you believe it to be important for your client do not hesitate to seek to include a level of detail which you believe will avoid problems in the future. If the other side is resistant to a detailed child arrangements plan be sure that you have the information to hand to support this requirement.

Conversely, do not allow a child arrangements plan to become over-detailed where it is clearly unnecessary. This is where the judgement of the lawyer involved is so crucial. You need to know the people you are dealing with.

Well-being   **6**

Being a practitioner of family law is inherently stressful. The work, particularly for Counsel who will regularly receive papers only days or even hours before they are to represent their client, requires a high level of intense concentration. This is often coupled with sleep deprivation, as the high volume of work needs to be completed over a short period of time with absolute deadlines.

Divorce is adversarial by its very nature – it starts out as an adverse environment in which to work. The competitive nature of your work, where you are pitted against the lawyer on the other side, makes 'winning' an important outcome, and a run of 'losing' can feel like failures which may be difficult to swallow. The very fact that you are compared to your peers and ranked against them in publications such as The Legal 500 can further isolate you from them. And the burden of confidentiality can add to that isolation. Often lawyers feel they cannot discuss cases with their colleagues, and have no outlet to express their concerns with fellow professionals. Add to that high workloads and a common belief that one must put one's own emotional reactions to one side in favour of objectivity for the sake of the case, and you have all the ingredients for an assault on your well-being. Now let's add a narcissist to the mix, either as your own client or as the spouse of your client, and look at what this could mean for you.

If you are representing a narcissist, at first the narcissistic client is likely to present very few challenges, as they are probably going to be charming, extremely likeable and possibly, in the initial stages, respectful of your boundaries.

However, over time, communication will deteriorate. It will become apparent that the narcissist is not listening to your advice, and is completely inflexible in their position, unable to compromise. You will come to realise that the narcissist believes themselves to be more knowledgeable than you, even in legal matters.

You will be enlisted to write letters which perpetuate the narcissist's abusive treatment of their spouse. You will find yourself justifying or denying abuse tactics, such as harassment, that have come to light through letters you have received from the other side. You will be aware of the narcissist's heartless use of their children as pawns in the game that they are playing to win, and feel powerless to speak out. You will find yourself trying to gloss over why your narcissistic client has not complied with court orders.

You will be forced to submit late or incomplete documentation to the court. You will start to appear incompetent to others, and your reputation amongst your peers and in your wider community may suffer. You will be made to re-draft letters repeatedly and be made to feel guilty for charging for the time you have spent on this.

You will find yourself becoming a mere mouthpiece for your narcissistic client, copying and pasting their unreasonable and continually shifting demands onto your own letter headed notepaper, feeling that you have no choice. You may find yourself confused as goalposts change, just as agreements look like they have been reached. Unless you have bent completely to the narcissist's will, you will be badmouthed by the narcissist, and also by the narcissist's spouse, for what looks like your own 'narcissism by proxy'.

You will become, as all people who have become entangled with those with narcissistic adaptations do, another of their puppets on a string. Your bills will be challenged and left unpaid, your professionalism will be questioned and you may well end up facing a formal complaint.

Your heart will sink every time you receive a call, email or visit from your client, and you will dread working on their case. You may start to wake in the night, feeling like you are stuck in what seems like a drawn out process which your client does not appear to want to bring to a conclusion. You may be shouted at and bullied by your client one day, coldly demeaned the next, and then apologised to and sweet-talked to hours later. You may well start to question your own competency and choice of career. It is not hard to see why, if unprepared, working with a client with NPD can adversely affect your well-being.

If you are representing the spouse of a narcissist, a different set of challenges to your well-being may emerge. You will find yourself in a battle which the other side seems to wish to prolong. Negotiations will fall apart, compromises will never be reached, and just when you think you are getting somewhere with the other side, the rug will be pulled out from beneath you. You may be having lengthy conversations with the spouse of the narcissist who is paralysed by indecision and fear, who is often changing their instructions, and who is highly emotionally reactive to the narcissist's behaviour towards them. You may feel their pain yourself due to your empathic nature, and find yourself burdened by it. You may not be able to manage the hysteria, anger and panic of your client, and may try to avoid speaking with them. You may feel guilty about this, and try to palm them off on a junior colleague who will be even more ill-equipped to deal with them and may suffer themselves as a result.

You will find your costs racking up quickly. You will be trying to respond to written accusations about your client and attempting unsuccessfully to agree on interim maintenance pending suit. You will be writing letters requesting that the narcissist on the other side desist from abusive behaviours towards your client. You will be attempting to do things by the book, and will be shocked by how the narcissist refuses to play by the rules, simply refusing to provide financial disclosure for example. You may be stonewalled by the narcissist's solicitor and badmouthed to your client by the narcissist, who may well believe what they are told as they have learned to put faith in what the narcissist tells them.

Whilst you will be submitting your client's information in a timely fashion, in doing so you will be placing all the cards in the hands of the narcissistic spouse, who will be able to use the information against your client without providing truthful information themselves.

You may lose faith in your abilities as you fail to protect your client. You may, in answering every accusation and point in letters from the other side, be an un-witting pawn in the narcissist's game, running down your client's funds through your bills and actually enabling the narcissist's financial abuse through you. You may find yourself not being paid as a result. Your own competence may well be questioned, with complaints being made against you by your own client.

You may even begin to start losing faith in your own abilities as a lawyer and question your own negotiating skills.

Compassion fatigue

Practically by definition, as a family lawyer, you are likely to be an empathic individual. The fact that you reading this book shows that you are someone who wants to understand new things and develop new perspectives; a person with an open mind. Only you know what drew you into this area of law in the first place, but it's likely, in spite of the stress and the hard work, that you know your work has meaning and purpose. You know you are needed and that you have a significant role to play in taking people out of the dissatisfaction and pain of

> **You may, in answering every accusation and point in letters from the other side, be an unwitting pawn in the narcissist's game, running down your client's funds through your bills and actually enabling the narcissist's financial abuse through you.**

their old lives, into the new. Your job involves not just a thorough knowledge of the law, but an understanding of people, and of the vicissitudes of the human condition. You care, and you can take great pride in that.

The flip side of being this way, of being this sort of person, is that compassion fatigue can lurk in the shadows, just around the corner, and can either creep up on you little by little, or can steam roll right over you without warning. The very nature of your job puts you at higher risk of this, as well as burnout (see below), than other professionals and research shows that lawyers actually suffer from both burnout and compassion fatigue more than doctors, mental health professionals, police and first responders. It stands to reason that the risk of tipping into compassion fatigue when one is working for the spouse of a narcissist is even higher than usual. Protecting yourself from it is of paramount importance.

What is compassion fatigue?

Dr Charles Figley, renowned expert in the field of compassion fatigue, burnout, traumatic stress and resilience says of compassion fatigue:

> *"There is a cost to caring. Professionals who listen to clients' stories of fear, pain and suffering may feel similar fear, pain and suffering because they care. Sometimes we feel we are losing our sense of self to the clients we serve. Those who have enormous capacity for feeling and expressing empathy tend to be more at risk of compassion stress".*

Compassion fatigue results from an accumulation of exposure to your clients' pain, distress and injustice, which, as we have already ascertained, are particularly pronounced in the spouse of a narcissist. You are particularly at risk if you are conscientious, a perfectionist and self-giving, if you are in an environment with low social support and are under high personal stress.

The effects on you can be emotional, physical and cognitive.

Emotional symptoms of compassion fatigue include:

- Chronic fear and anxiety

- Guilt and shame

- Self doubt

- Social withdrawal and isolation

- Feeling overwhelmed

- Irritability

- Anger

- Powerlessness

- Numbness

- Lack of engagement and connection with people and areas of life not connected to work

- Intrusive thoughts and concerns about work cases

Physical symptoms of compassion fatigue are largely as a result of the chronic over-stimulation of the sympathetic nervous system, resulting in a prolonged fight or flight response. Symptoms include:

- Shortness of breath

- Hyperventilation

- Fast heart rate or palpitations

- Chest pain

- Sleep problems

- Decreased appetite

- Headaches

- Decreased libido

- Musculoskeletal aches and pains, such as back pain

- Decreased immunity to bugs such as bacteria and viruses

- Allergies

Cognitive effects of compassion fatigue include:

- Black and white thinking

- Poor concentration

- Memory loss

- Confusion

- Loss of sense of direction and purpose

- Minimising problems

- Rumination about current stressors

Burnout

Burnout occurs when one believes that the needs of a task are exceeded by the resources available for that task, or that there is a discrepancy between expectations and outcomes.

Those who are particularly idealistic, who have poor professional and personal boundaries, who define themselves by their work and who find themselves in jobs that do not match their skills and interests are more prone to eventual burnout.

It's not hard to see how an unremittingly demanding narcissistic client who is constantly violating your boundaries and shifting the goalposts could edge you in the direction of burnout. Similarly, representing the spouse of a narcissist could do the same – their needs may be so great that you could find yourself acting as a therapist, marriage guidance counsellor, social worker, confidante and friend, none of which you are qualified to carry out. This can leave you feeling unable to perform the roles that you are being asked to perform in the time available, leading to untenable working hours, all in a misguided attempt to meet your client's infinite needs.

Symptoms of burnout include:

- Loss of hope

- Avoidance of clients and colleagues

- Agitation

- Irritability

- Self doubt

- Loss of confidence

- Cynicism

- Apathy

- Poor problem solving skills

Burnout can co-exist with compassion fatigue. Both can lead to chronic health problems, relationship problems, addictions and poor job performance.[1]

How to take care of yourself

Of course, your role as a family practitioner is to represent the best interests of your client diligently, and with the utmost skill and care. First and foremost, however, you have a responsibility to take proper care of yourself if you are to do

---

[1] *Lee Norton, Jennifer Johnson, and George Woods, "Burnout and Compassion Fatigue: What Lawyers Need to Know" University of Missouri-Kansas Law Review 84:4 (2016): 977-1002.*

your job well and live a healthy, happy, balanced life. We have split what follows into two main categories to consider when dealing with narcissistic individuals: practical steps to take at work to protect your well-being, and building general day-to-day resilience.

Practical steps to take at work to protect your well-being

Decide whether to take the case on

Of course, first of all, you need to train yourself as far as possible to identify when you are dealing with a case where one of the parties may suffer from NPD. You should not be afraid to refuse to act right at the outset if you feel:

- your current levels of work are such that you simply do not have the extra time which will be needed to devote to this case

- you do not feel sufficiently resilient to take this case on either at this particular time or at all

None of us like to turn work away, but some cases can become unreasonably demanding and far less remunerative than they might initially appear, not least because fees may have to be reduced, or a high level of non-chargeable work undertaken, simply as a consequence of the nature of the case. If you don't want to take on the case, don't, no matter how pressurised you may feel by the client. Narcissists can be very persuasive. If something feels 'off', go with your gut instinct.

Have a mechanism in place for terminating your retainer

If you do take on the case but discover at a later stage that you do not wish to continue, have in place your mechanism for terminating your retainer.

You will have to get your ducks in a row before you do so, especially in terms of payment of outstanding fees.

The reason you give to your client may be simply as a result of a breakdown in the trust and confidence of the solicitor/client relationship, but if there are other, more specific, reasons do not be afraid to set these out. Be clear on what you are prepared to tolerate from your client, and if those are overstepped, do not give second and third chances. The narcissist will be adept at drawing you back in time and time again (hoovering), often by apologising and playing on your sympathy. Be aware of this, and do not fall for it. Understand that once you have terminated your retainer with a narcissistic client, you will invoke narcissistic injury and rage in the narcissist leading, at the very least, to refusal or delay in paying fees, and a potential complaint against you. It's worth remembering that these would probably have been on the cards anyway, further down the line, even if you had continued to represent the narcissist.

Make sure you have enough time available to represent a narcissistic client

If you have decided to take on a narcissistic client be aware that, even if the bare bones of the case might seem relatively straightforward, the case itself will be anything but. The narcissistic client will be doubly demanding. Letters will have to be drafted and re-drafted until the client is happy with the final version and meetings and telephone calls will be longer. Make sure that you have the time available to deal with the case properly. You will need to know how to handle your narcissistic client to ensure that you can represent them in a manner which will achieve a time efficient, cost effective outcome.

Set immovable boundaries with your narcissistic client

Narcissists push boundaries and expect to receive special treatment above and beyond other clients. Do not allow them to extend your working day beyond that which you would deem acceptable. Do not blur the edges between your personal and professional life no matter how much they may encourage you to do so – this is all part of their charm offensive designed to leave you feeling indebted to them, so that you 'go the extra mile' for them. Do not give them your personal mobile phone number, nor allow them to drop by the office to see you without an appointment. Stress your requirement for punctuality, and for deadlines to be met on time when it comes to court paperwork. Have specific rules regarding payment of fees. Set these guidelines at an early stage and perhaps even incorporate them in your terms and conditions so that you have a document to which you can refer the client if they endeavour to 'overstep the mark'. Be aware that the narcissistic client's need for attention will be immediate, and they will expect replies to emails within minutes of you receiving them, even if out of hours. Practice good email hygiene and do not even check emails from the narcissistic client outside of your working day.

Be prepared to be badmouthed, blamed and scapegoated by the narcissist

Regardless of whether you are representing the narcissist or their non-narcissistic spouse, the narcissistic party will 'badmouth' you to their spouse, the other side's representative, friends and family and anyone else who may be prepared to listen, at some point. None of us respond well to criticism or blame, and the impact which either can have on our well-being can be significant. Nothing is ever the fault of the narcissist and therefore your professional judgement and abilities are likely to be called into question, both to your face and behind your back. Think about how this will make you feel, and whether it might impact on your ability to carry out your work generally for other clients, and build resilience against it. Again, if your narcissistic client causes something unacceptable or intolerable to happen, do not be hesitant in concluding your retainer with appropriate reasons.

Do not take *anything* personally

Recognise which phase the narcissist is drawing you into in their cycle of idealisation, devaluation and discard, and have strategies in place to deal with it. Notice which role you are playing as you are moved around the drama triangle – the victim, perpetrator or rescuer. It can help just knowing that nothing, positive or negative, in the way they behave towards you nor that which they say about you is personal. You are, quite literally, irrelevant to them. Like all people, your only purpose is to be of use to them in securing narcissistic supply, be that from an adversarial court process, as the co-creator of drama and conflict, or as their legal gladiator, enabling the punishment of their former spouse. They will forget you much quicker than you forget them, so try to remain detached.

Ensure that the other legal professionals working with you on the case have an understanding of NPD

If you are a solicitor instructing Counsel and know that the client either suffers from NPD or is the spouse of a narcissist, pick up the phone to Counsel before they commence work to discuss whether they have a good understanding of how to act in this circumstance and what assistance you might be able to provide. Counsel will need, for example, to understand how to over-detail consent orders so that loopholes and grey areas are removed, and the reasons why this will be so important where a narcissist is involved. Working as a team will be helpful in reducing your stress levels.

Be aware of becoming preoccupied with the case at the expense of other things

It is easy to allow a case involving a narcissist to play on your mind if you are being required to act unorthodoxly or unreasonably, but this can have many knock-on effects. A preoccupation of the case of the narcissist could encourage you not to properly prioritise other work which can lead to dis-instruction through failure to provide proper client care, for example. When one of your clients is a narcissist it's even more crucial to ensure that all clients take their turn to be dealt with. As far as possible, try to ensure that you do not allow the narcissistic client to infiltrate your thought process beyond the appropriate time allocated to carrying out their work – often harder said than done.

It can be particularly challenging trying not to 'take work home' when representing a narcissist, but this is key to maintaining a proper work/life balance and your all-important home relationships. Notice what you find yourself thinking about, and if a case keeps intruding on your mind, try counting the number of times you find yourself thinking about it. Just becoming aware of the scale of the problem in this way can help you to put it in perspective. If you regularly find yourself thinking about a particular client late at night or in the early hours of the morning, ask yourself why, and consider whether this is a client for whom you wish to continue to act.

Prioritise your work and recognise procrastination

Do not put off work which you find difficult – deal with everything in order of priority. If you are avoiding dealing with a matter, ask yourself why, and consider whether it is right for you to continue to deal with this case.

Be aware of your own limitations when representing the spouse of a narcissist

Those who work in the area of family breakdown are regularly dealing with the most distressing, disturbing and often quite toxic forms of human behaviour. The five stages of grief are denial, anger, bargaining, depression and acceptance. Most individuals experiencing the breakdown of their relationship with their significant life partner will go through most, if not all, the stages, although not necessarily in the order shown. But the spouse of a narcissist is likely to be experiencing a much stronger grief reaction than in an 'ordinary' divorce, complicated by fear of the future, increased abuse, and attempted financial, emotional and psychological annihilation by their narcissistic spouse. Be aware of your own limitations when it comes to dealing with the complex emotions of your client, and refer them to other specialists such as narcissistic divorce consultants and coaches or therapists who specialise in narcissistic abuse. This is not your burden to bear if you are to do your job effectively for your client and if you are to look after yourself in the process.

Plan so that you can work effectively

Plan your working day, at least a week in advance if you can, and if you have complicated documents to consider or draft, make time in your diary just like a client appointment during which you will not be disturbed. Perhaps consider moving to a space which is away from your desk and therefore your other work when dealing with complex matters, so that you are not distracted from the task in hand.

Take regular breaks from a computer screen and from sitting down

People who sit for long uninterrupted periods of time have an increased likelihood of dying prematurely than those who sit for shorter periods.[2] Specifically, people who sit for more than 12.5 hours per day, with uninterrupted bouts of 30 minutes or more have the highest risk of death, even when other risks such as smoking and alcohol have been adjusted for. Getting up from your desk at least every half an hour and having a short walk, even if it is just to the kitchen, reduces your risk. Setting a discreet alarm at work to remind you to stretch your legs may be beneficial for you, or even changing your workstation to an adjustable 'sit stand' desk.

Equally, taking regular lunch breaks, during which you detach from work, increases your energy levels at work and decreases exhaustion, and raises vigour and energy levels long-term.[3] Social breaks, such as chatting to colleagues during a break, are also beneficial, the sense of relatedness leading to a feeling of recovery after the break.[4]

Prepare adequately so that you can take a holiday without worrying

Make clear holiday notes and apprise your covering colleague of the idiosyncrasies of the client. Take care not to note anything on the file which you would not want the client to see. As narcissists tend to change solicitor regularly, do not add to your concerns by leaving something on a file which passes to another firm.

---

[2] *Patterns of Sedentary Behavior and Mortality in U.S. Middle-Aged and Older Adults: A National Cohort Study; Keith M. Diaz, PhD, Virginia J. Howard, PhD, Brent Hutto, MSPH, Natalie Colabianchi, PhD. Annals of Internal Medicine, October 3, 2017, Volume 167, Issue 7 Page: 465-475.*

[3] *Korpela K, Kinnunen U, Geurts S, de Bloom J, Sianoja M. Recovery during Lunch Breaks: Testing Long-Term Relations with Energy Levels at Work. Scand J Work Organ Psychol. 2016.*

[4] *Waber BN, Olguin Olguin D, Kim T, Pentland A. Productivity Through Coffee Breaks: Changing Social Networks by Changing Break Structure. SSRN Electron J. 2012 Jan 5.*

Build reflection time into your schedule

Set time aside each week to consider the nature of cases contained within your workload and the effect which they might have upon you as an individual. Revisit your working practices regularly to ensure that you are recognising and dealing with the challenges presented by your caseload. Encourage your junior colleagues to do likewise.

Protect your firm as well as yourself

Update the office manual regularly and make sure that all practice procedures are adopted, especially by more junior staff. Make sure that your terms and conditions are signed by the client and that they properly protect you and your firm.

Ask for help

Do not be afraid to ask for help. Resolution and The Law Society have mentoring schemes. Try to ensure that your firm has its own structure for the provision of support for practitioners. If appropriate, consider seeing a therapist or coach skilled in the area of narcissistic abuse.

Building general day-to-day resilience

The basics

Some elements of personal day-to-day care are self-evident but are worth repeating, as many of those engaged in family practice will not follow such simple guidelines, giving 'the pressure of work' as the reason for not doing so. So, if this sounds like you, remember to prioritise the basics:

- Drink plenty of fluids, especially water

- Eat well and regularly

- Exercise daily

Get away from it all, regularly

It may sound crass, but a change really is as good as a rest. Have regular holidays when you switch off from work to the greatest extent that you can – if not completely. Do not allow your 'holiday boundaries' to be breached by any client except in what you know to be a clear emergency. This should only be if someone else in the office is unable to deal with this emergency in your absence.

Changing the sensory stimuli around us leads to different neural networks than the ones we are used to becoming stimulated. This, in turn, allows the over stimulated areas in our brains (the ones that are constantly turned on due to work) to rest and reset. Going somewhere completely different, where you are surrounded by different people, cultures, nature, music and where you can do different activities, is actually highly restorative and can have almost instant benefits, especially if you've been ruminating about your work difficulties. It allows you to gain a sense of perspective. Try to build adequate holiday and travel time into your life, as far as you are able.

Build a diverse and strong social network

The longest ongoing study of adult life, the Harvard Study of Adult Development, has shown that the major factor in determining human happiness is as a result of the quality of the relationships that people have with family, friends and community. And in fostering relationships with those who think differently than we do, we build yet more new neural pathways which allow us to think in new ways, gaining a broader world view and changing our perceptions and perspectives. Finding your tribe of people who are empathic and understanding will stimulate your joy and your creativity. It is known that strong relationships protect people from life's discontents, thereby building resilience. Lifespan and health is also affected by the quality of peoples' relationships; it has been shown that people in unhappy marriages feel more emotional and physical pain than those in happy ones.

Prioritise sleep

This is not always easy, but it is more important than you might realise.

A lack of sleep makes you more prone to mental heath issues such as depression, anxiety and thoughts of suicide. Brain scans of poor sleepers show an amplification in the reactivity of the amygdala, the area of the brain responsible for throwing the body into a stress response, leading to the production of the stress hormones cortisol and adrenaline. This over-activity of the amygdala leads to people being on a shorter fuse than usual with increased anger and rage. Not only this, but the chronically raised blood pressure and heart rate that results from these stress hormones leads to damage to blood vessel walls in the brain and heart causing, in turn, heart attacks and strokes. Science tells us, categorically, that a good night's sleep down-regulates the reactivity of the fight or flight system, and decreases these associated health risks accordingly.

Sleep is also important for decision making, creativity and forming new memories. But not only do we sleep to remember *we also sleep to forget*, with dreaming, which takes place in deep sleep, being a factor in helping us to deal with emotionally charged experiences, making them easier to tolerate – a valuable resource when dealing with the stress of a case involving a narcissist. Sleep has too many physical effects to describe here (such as producing chemicals that break down toxins, reducing the risk of cancer, heart attacks, strokes, Alzheimer's disease and diabetes) and sleep scientists are only just beginning to get these messages heard by the world.

Sleep also has an effect on two hormones, ghrelin and leptin, which affect your appetite. Too little sleep results in the level of these hormones being skewed so that you crave large amounts of unhealthy food, leading to a poor, unnourishing diet, with all the physical knock-on effects of that. On the plus side, a good night's sleep actually makes it easier to lose weight if you are dieting by changing the ratio of these two hormones so that you feel appropriately satiated.

In order to cycle through the different phases of sleep, you need to be actually asleep for at least 7 to 8 hours a day, preferably in an unbroken stint. Only then can the essential processes (that are the very purpose of sleep) be effectively carried out. Even losing an hour of sleep a night has adverse effects. There are decades of data proving that when the clocks go forward every year, admissions to hospital for heart attacks rocket over the subsequent days. The reverse is true when they go back, due to the associated extra hour in bed.

Be aware that prescription sleeping tablets don't actually give you true sleep. Odd though it may seem, they don't give you the crucial restorative phases of sleep that you need, although they do knock you out. The same is true for alcohol – the sleep you get if you've been drinking is short on the type of sleep you actually need. The only type of sleeping tablet that leads you into true sleep is melatonin which is the naturally occurring chemical that the body already produces, rising at night and telling your brain and body that you are ready for sleep, lulling you into it. Melatonin tablets will get you to sleep, and the type of sleep you will have is proper sleep, but it may not keep you there. Although melatonin is available on prescription in the UK, it is rarely prescribed. In the USA and many other countries it is available over the counter.

Don't underestimate the power of this one simple, free and natural resource – sleep could make all the difference to you. So, reduce alcohol and caffeine, have a hot bath or shower so that you can cool down afterwards once in bed (the cooling off being a signal for the brain for sleep), and try to develop a sleep routine which your brain will eventually associate with shutting down for the night. When you bath a baby, lower the lights and read a soothing bedtime story to them you are establishing a bedtime ritual to signal to their brain that it is time to increase their own natural melatonin so that sleep can begin. Consider nurturing yourself as if you are that baby.

> **Don't underestimate the power of this one simple, free and natural resource – sleep could make all the difference to you.**

Of course, anxiety will often affect your sleep, and you may find yourself waking in the small hours of the night, consumed by a feeling of fear and dread, particularly if you are stuck in a case involving a narcissist. The main thing here, rather than tossing and turning and just hoping that you will be able to get back to sleep, is to have a plan.

Consider:

- Having a hypnosis mp3 or mediation mp3 downloaded on your phone ready to listen to as soon as you wake up. Keep headphones by your bed. You may wish to try an app such as Calm for this.

- Using a mental technique such as building a house from the foundations up in your mind, or cooking a meal in your mind from the beginning.

- Taking a hot bath or shower when you wake in the night, to signal to the pineal gland in the brain to produce melatonin, the body's naturally occurring sleep hormone.

- Using lavender oil. Have some ready, either to put in your middle of the night bath, on your pillow, in an aromatherapy diffuser, or on your wrists and temples. Several studies confirm the effectiveness of lavender as a natural sleep remedy.

Re-set your amygdala

Just as getting adequate sleep will re-set your amygdala, other measures can also be taken to calm the over-active stress system which is stuck on 'on'. If you are dealing with a case involving a narcissist, whether you are representing the narcissist and their abuse has been directly turned on to you, or whether you are representing their spouse but being bullied by the narcissist via their own solicitor, you will be in a highly reactive state, easily triggered by the narcissist's bad behaviour. You may find yourself flying off the handle, short tempered and angry, or frozen with indecision.

As mentioned above, feeling this way is as a result of activation of the part of your brain called the amygdala – the part responsible for your fear and survival reflexes of fight, flight or freeze. Your brain is on high alert for threats at this time and often overreacts to situations, and once activated it results in the production of the stress hormones cortisol and adrenalin. These quickly flood the system and crucially, divert blood flow away from your brain towards your muscles, so you can escape the threat. (This part of the brain is, from an evolutionary perspective, an old structure – it still perceives threat as if you are a caveman being attacked by a bear, and responds accordingly).

But the important point here is that blood is being diverted away from the logical, thinking part of your brain – making logic and thinking difficult. Of course, you will need your mental faculties when you have a narcissist manipulating you and, even if you are not representing the narcissist themselves but their spouse, constant bullying from the other side can compromise your ability to advise your client regarding vital decisions about their finances, future and children. It's not hard to see how poor advice from you can lead to formal complaints being made about you further down the line, further affecting your career and your well-being.

So, if you find yourself in a heightened state of anxiety, your amygdala needs a system re-set – the threshold at which it fires needs to be lowered. Now bear with us on this next bit, especially if you are sceptic. It has been shown again and again that meditation and mindfulness are practices which reduce this activation threshold, as well as having numerous other benefits. We strongly recommend that you develop a daily practice of meditation and mindfulness. Consider attending a course in Mindfulness Based Cognitive Therapy (MBCT) or Mindfulness Based Stress Reduction (MBSR) – these courses are recommended by NICE (the National Institute for Clinical Excellence) and they run for a couple of hours every week over eight weeks, with some daily meditation based homework. They have been shown on brain scans to increase the density of grey matter in the prefrontal cortex area of the brain, after just eight weeks. There are also a number of meditation apps available that you may wish to start off with instead, such as Headspace and Calm.

There are a whole host of additional benefits that result from just 20 minutes a day of mindfulness and meditation practice which (since the scientific breakthrough of functional MRI brain scans) have

> **You are not your thoughts. You are the one having the thoughts, and you get to choose which ones to engage with, listen to and believe.**

been validated by science. They range from better memory, greater empathy, a more active immune system, increased happiness and less physical pain all the way to the slowing of aging at a cellular level.

Silence the negative self-talk

Do you recognise the critical little voice in your head telling you that you are not good enough? Perhaps it tells you that you are unattractive when you look in the mirror. Perhaps it calls you stupid when you make a mistake, or when things don't go well. Maybe it tells you that you are ridiculous. This voice is 'the narcissist in your head', and you may have got used to allowing it to devalue you without realising it was even there, so constant its commentary might have been.

The good news is that this is one narcissist you *can* control. These negative thoughts have become wired into the brain through repetition, and have become ingrained as habits. Key to breaking these neural pathways is simply *noticing* these thoughts when they occur and, instead of taking them to heart, immediately denouncing them as you would if someone had criticised your friend in such a way. After all, you would never let your friend be spoken to so harshly, so why would you allow yourself to be? It is therefore time to stand up for yourself, and become your own advocate. Slay 'the narcissist in your head' to boost your self-esteem and increase your overall sense of well-being.

Schedule nourishing activities

In stressful situations, we humans have a tendency to cut down on the activities that nourish and energise us, eventually leaving us carrying out only the bare essentials. Unfortunately, most of these seem to be activities that deplete us of energy and dampen our mood. Of course, at times of stress you aren't going to feel motivated to do the things that you enjoy, but it is important to do them anyway, *regardless of whether you feel like it*, as this is an essential component of taking care of yourself to prevent a further decline in mood, and a potential descent into full scale depression. In other words, don't wait to feel like doing something you enjoy – do it even if you don't feel like it. But first, we need to work out what those nourishing activities actually are.

So, write a detailed list of all the things that you do on a typical working day over a 24 hour period, breaking the activities down into small parts. For example, get out of bed, have a cup of coffee, shower, get dressed, make the children breakfast, drive to work, talk to colleagues, answer emails and so on.

Once you have this list, consider each item, and how it makes you feel. If it raises your energy and mood, mark it with an N, as a nourishing activity, and if it does the opposite, mark it with a D for depleting activity.

Now list the nourishing activities separately, and you will notice that there are two groups. Some activities may give you a direct sense of pleasure (for example phoning a friend, having a hot bath, getting eight hours sleep) and others may not be pleasurable in themselves, but give a sense of accomplishment once achieved, such as perhaps tidying a drawer, completing a tax return or working out at the gym.

The next step is to consider what other nourishing activities you could add to the list to carry out when you are feeling down.

If you get stuck, try asking yourself the following question: "If it were possible to be living five completely different other lives, what would they be?" This can give powerful insights into what you might enjoy, and reawaken passions which you may have let slide. Now, where possible, take elements from those other lives and incorporate them into this life. For a simple example, if you put down singer, perhaps commit to learning how to sing just one of your favourite songs.

It is also important to look at the depleting activities, to see if you could find a way to convert any of them into nourishing activities. For example, an unpleasant rush hour drive to work might be made more nourishing by downloading an interesting podcast to listen to. Cleaning the house may be made more pleasurable by dancing to music at the same time, or promising to reward yourself with a coffee or treat afterwards.

Once you've done this, create a 'playlist' that you can refer to when you need an activity to boost your mood, and make a commitment to schedule as many nourishing activities into your day as practically possible.

Stimulate your brain through hobbies

Neuroplasticity is the brain's ability to form new neural networks when new activities are practised. It has been known for some time that you can, in fact, teach an old dog (well, a human) new tricks. By limiting yourself to what you know, you are staying in your comfort zone and avoiding growth – both brain growth and growth as a person. Accomplishing a personal goal within a hobby, no matter how small, is a sure-fire way to build new neural networks and build resilience, and will once again give a sense of perspective to life which will be invaluable in helping you to combat stress.

De-program your negativity bias using gratitude

As humans, we are wired to focus on the negatives in life. This 'negativity bias' is a somewhat outmoded evolutionary survival tactic – a relic of days of old. Back then, focusing on the negatives – on what could go wrong – was essential to the survival of the species. But we are no longer hunting or foraging for food whilst trying to avoid becoming prey ourselves.

It has been proved that it is much harder to get rid of a negative thought than a positive one – negative thoughts are 'sticky', like Velcro, and positive thoughts are not, like Teflon. It has also been shown that negative thoughts are harder to change into positive thoughts than the other way around.

Think back to a recent day which you felt was completely spoiled by just one bad event, which really got under your skin and you couldn't shake off. If you delve a little deeper you might remember that, actually, five good things also happened that day, but the day was completely ruined by the one bad event. That was the negativity bias at work.

Thankfully, you don't have to be at the mercy of the negativity bias, once you are aware of it. The practice of daily gratitude has been proven to be one of the most powerful coping techniques there is, one that has the power to change your experience of life for the better. It literally rewires your brain to see things as they really are, and not through the lens of doom.

There are various ways to incorporate gratitude into your daily routine, but a great start is to commit to simply becoming aware of all the little things that you are grateful for through the day, in real time, as they are happening – and the smaller they are, the better. Feel grateful that when you open the tap to wash your hands you are met with lovely warm water which feels good on your fingers. Feel grateful for that first sip of tea in the morning. Feel grateful for the birds singing as you make your way to the car. For the dog greeting you with enthusiastic wagging upon your return. For the fact that you have a working oven in which to cook your dinner. For the nice conversation you had with the shop assistant. For the warmth of your winter coat. For the children you saw giggling together as they got off the bus. For the smell of that scented candle you lit.

Then, last thing at night, think back over your day and find ten things to count, on your fingers, that you were grateful for that day. As you think of them, remember the feeling of them, and actually engage with the feeling of gratitude you had for them at the time.

The practice of gratitude, carried out every single day in the way described above, has the power to turn your thinking around within just a few days. Many people report that once they start it, they don't want to stop.

Savour your achievements

If you are involved in a case involving a narcissist, you may feel professionally out of control and may well question your own competency. It is likely that your self-belief and self-confidence will need a supercharge at this time in your life. This method below could help you to widen your perspective on your own life, and remind you of who you actually are as an individual and what great things you are capable of.

To do this, take yourself right back to your earliest memory and make a list of every little thing you feel you have achieved all the way up to the present. As long as the achievements meant something to you at the time, they still count – even things from childhood that you may not consider to be big now, such as a piece of work done in primary school, or the achievement of being Joseph in the school nativity play. Include all aspects of things you are proud of – having made lifelong friends, coming out of a traumatic experience with greater strength, not being put off by failure. These would all be very appropriate.

Once the list is complete, enjoy connecting emotionally with the memory of each achievement, and basking in them. This is a wonderfully life affirming exercise, and well worth the time spent on it. It may also be worth keeping the list, and forcing yourself to look at it when a low mood or low confidence strikes, as it may when you are being devalued by a narcissistic client. Perhaps glancing at this list of achievements could be added to your playlist of nourishing activities. You might even find yourself doing the wholly un-British thing of finally putting your certificates up on the wall as a result. And why not?

Become aware of who you are

Increasing your awareness of who you are, and delving into understanding your own personality is a key part of self-care. Taking the time to identify your core values and your strengths can be enlightening, and can help you to work out how you can better slot into your own life, and what matters to you. Research has shown that knowing what your character strengths are *and then actively using them* helps you increase happiness and well-being, find meaning and purpose, boost your relationships, manage stress and health and accomplish goals. The VIA Institute On Character has a highly regarded online survey that ranks your own individual character strengths in order.

Even just pausing to consider whether you are an introvert or an extrovert, whether you are a 'big picture person' or a 'detail person' or whether you are more person-orientated or task focused can be interesting. Or you may wish to try the "Big Five Model of Personality", which boils down personality traits into 5 factors (OCEAN) existing on a spectrum – openness to experience, conscientiousness, extraversion, agreeableness and neuroticism. Other well known personality tests include the four quadrant tests such as DISC and the four colour personality quiz. The Myers Briggs test and the Enneagram personality test are also popular.

If you are aware of who you are and what matters to you, you can begin to live your life in accordance with those traits and values, and may gain an understanding of why you feel and behave in certain ways in different circumstances. You may begin to see why what might be a particular challenge to you might flow off another like water off a duck's back, and vice versa. Understanding who you are is fundamental to self-acceptance and self-compassion, and these are two of the basic building blocks of well-being.

Conclusion

We believe that in reading this book you have demonstrated your desire for broadening your understanding and knowledge of the narcissistic personality type, and we thank you for that. For too long, those with narcissistic personalities have wreaked havoc on the mental well-being of those closest to them, as well as on whole societies, with little general understanding of the forces at play. Their unhealthy personality adaptations, which have occurred as a survival tactic in response to their own suboptimal upbringings, have had profoundly negative impacts on those around them since time began – but arguably nowhere can this be more clearly seen than in the arena of family law.

We hope that this book has been an enlightening journey for you, and that it will prepare you for the rocky road that lies ahead when you next find yourself in a case involving a narcissist, with all the emotional complexities and challenges that will inevitably result.

We particularly hope that you are able to see that, in spite of the abuse of others that results from such personalities, for the developing narcissist as a child, NPD was never a choice. Whether continuing toxic behaviour in *adulthood* is a choice, however, remains a hotly debated question. On that, as they say, the jury is still out.

The Last Word

When dealing with a narcissist, whether your own client or the spouse or partner of your client, one thing is always to be remembered, particularly in negotiations. Those with NPD need to feel they have won. And if they can't win, at the very least, they *need to have the last word*.

In line with that, we have given the last word of this book to the narcissist, in the form of A Narcissist's Prayer – an excellent summary of narcissistic behaviour and a final reminder that a narcissist, in some regards, has not developed emotionally past a certain stage, through no fault of their own. We hope this book has been of use to you, and that you will recommend our companion book, *Divorcing A Narcissist: The Lure, The Loss And The Law* to any of your clients leaving a relationship of this nature.

A Narcissist's Prayer

That didn't happen.

And if it did, it wasn't that bad.

And if it was, that's not

a big deal.

And if it is, it's not my fault.

And if it was, I didn't mean it.

And if I did,

You deserved it.

Anonymous

Glossary

Term	Definition
Altruistic Narcissist	Another name for a Communal Narcissist.
Attachment styles	The child of a narcissist could have a 'dismissive avoidant', 'fearful avoidant' or 'anxious preoccupied' attachment style, leading to difficulties forming close, stable, secure bonds with a partner.
Blameshifting	Those with narcissistic adaptations do not take the blame (except in the rare instances when doing so will give them narcissistic supply) and will pass the blame on to others with lightning speed.
Closet Narcissist	This type of narcissist (also called the Vulnerable, Introverted or Covert Narcissist) tries to feel special by association, by attaching themselves to a person, cause or object that they hold up as being special. Then, rather than asking people to admire them directly, they divert attention away to this third party, asking people to admire it instead, whilst basking in the reflected glory, soaking up its perfection, wonderfulness, uniqueness and entitlement to special treatment. They often consider themselves as 'the wind beneath the wings' of another.

Term	Definition
Co-dependents	Co-dependency is a specific relationship addiction characterised by preoccupation and extreme dependence – emotional, social and sometimes physical – on another person. Co-dependents feel extreme amounts of dependence on loved ones in their lives and they feel responsible for the feelings and actions of those loved ones. The partners of narcissists, alcoholics, substance abusers and those with chronic illnesses are often co-dependents. They characteristically put the other's needs ahead of their own.
Cognitive dissonance	Essentially, this occurs when a person is holding two or more contradictory thoughts or beliefs in their minds at the same time. This creates an uncomfortable sense of unreality and confusion, which the brain resolves by choosing one of the thoughts to believe, discarding the other as unimportant through denial, minimisation or justification.
Communal Narcissist	Also called the Altruistic Narcissist. These are the narcissists who prop up their self-esteem and sense of specialness by giving to others. They obtain admiration, attention and a sense of specialness ('narcissistic supply') from good works and deeds, (seeing themselves as the *most* generous, the *most* caring, the *most* kind).They may start off in this vein with their significant others, but eventually their narcissism comes at the expense of those closest to them. They pride themselves on being 'nice', but quite often they give themselves away by becoming overly territorial in whatever arena they are practising their altruism.
Covert Narcissist	Another name for a Closet, Vulnerable or Introverted Narcissist.

Term	Definition
Cycle of 'idealise' and 'devalue'	The initial stage of a relationship with a narcissist is the 'idealisation' phase, also known as the 'love-bombing' phase, in romantic relationships. The next stage, the devalue stage, follows love-bombing/idealisation. It occurs as the narcissist realises that their target is not the perfect human that they had idealised and put on a pedestal during the initial phase.
Deletions	Pieces of information that the brain filters out that are not in line with your beliefs or your view of the world and those around you.
Devalue stage	The second stage of the cycle of idealise and devalue. This stage follows love-bombing/idealisation. It occurs as the narcissist realises that their target is not the perfect human that they had idealised and put on a pedestal during the initial phase. It is usually not an abrupt change, but a gradual turning up of the heat, so slowly that you may not notice. The victim becomes the proverbial frog in boiling water, and does not jump out.
Devaluing Narcissist	Also called the Toxic or Malignant Narcissist. These narcissists turn on others to bring them down. They exhibit many of the other more general narcissistic behaviours too, but what is more prominent in this type of narcissist is that they devalue, criticise, and demean others in order to inflate themselves.
Distortions	The brain distorts how we view reality, in line with our own personal prejudices due to former experiences, magnifying or diminishing our perceptions of things. Our perceptions of reality are therefore distorted, producing distortions.

Term	Definition
Drama triangle	Karpman's drama triangle was first described in the 1960s as a description of conflict in social interactions. There are three roles within the triangle – victim, rescuer and perpetrator. In high conflict relationships people tend to move around the triangle taking up the different roles at different times, perpetuating the drama, so that it continues on and on.
Echoists	Echoists are essentially the polar opposites of narcissists, on the opposite end of the spectrum. They have poor interpersonal boundaries, and do not like asking for or accepting help or gifts. They feel uncomfortable having needs at all, and prefer to focus on fulfilling other's needs and wishes. They have an aversion to feeling special.
Exhibitionist Narcissist	Also known as Grandiose or Overt Narcissist. They are typically the extroverted type. They are superficially charming in whatever way works best for them, and on the surface there are unlimited different outward appearances. They may present themselves as the affable buffoon, or the magnanimous entrepreneur. The altruistic pastor, with a dedicated following. The hardworking doctor, the dentist, or the strong, powerful CEO. The housewife, with over-achieving children and the perfect home. The childless housewife engaging in Twitter rants. The failed actress, or the famous actor. Many are financially successful in their chosen fields, but many are not, preferring instead to exploit others financially, as a result of the sense of entitlement which is part and parcel of the disorder.
Exploitation	One of the triple Es of pathological narcissism, the others being empathy and entitlement.

Term	Definition
False self or false persona	Narcissists outwardly project a 'false self', which they cannot maintain without attention from others (which comes in the form of drama, conflict and adoration). This false self often appears grandiose or self-assured, and is so convincing and so at odds with the underlying emptiness that a casual onlooker would find it difficult to see what lies beneath. Many refer to this outward image as a 'mask', which can temporarily drop when the narcissist feels threatened or abandoned.
Fight, flight or freeze response	When a human brain sees a threat, which it perceives as a threat to life, the old brain gets activated first, and without even thinking, the person is thrown into an instinctive fight, flight or freeze response, with the release of various stress hormones, such as cortisol and adrenaline. Blood is diverted away from the cortex (the thinking part of the brain) to other areas of the body, such as muscles, so that they can fight harder or run faster.
Financial abuse	A type of domestic abuse, commonly employed by narcissists. Other types include emotional, physical and legal abuse.
Flying monkey	One of the narcissist's fan club. Named after the flying monkeys in the Wizard of Oz who do the evil bidding of the wicked witch, they abuse the narcissist's victim on their behalf, spying on them and spreading lies about them to curry favour with the narcissist.
Fogging technique	A communication technique where the non-narcissist acknowledges the literal truth in what the narcissist is saying, but doesn't react to any implicit suggestions they are making, and doesn't agree to do things they may want them to do.
Gas-lighting	The act of undermining another person's reality by denying facts, the environment around them or their feelings.

Term	Definition
Generalisations	Another way in which the human brain filters out incoming information (others include deletions and distortions), by making automatic assumptions based on the person's past experiences, ignoring any exceptions that may be present.
Golden child	The child who is being idealised by the narcissist and is treated differently to the others, as if they can do no wrong.
Grandiose Narcissist	Another name for an Exhibitionist or Overt Narcissist.
Grey rock technique	A communication technique to minimise the amount of narcissistic supply one gives to a narcissist, by giving no emotional response at all – not even the merest hint. The ways in which this can be done include reducing eye contact (possibly to no eye contact at all), making the voice flat and boring, speaking slowly, ignoring completely inflammatory statements and immobilising all facial expressions.
Hoovering	The term given to the narcissist's tactic to suck the target back into the relationship, so that the narcissist can continue to use them as a source of narcissistic supply. It is another form of idealisation but specific to imminent abandonment.
Idealisation phase	Also called the love-bombing phase. The idealisation phase is the initial stage of a relationship with a narcissist, during which the narcissist puts their victim on a pedestal.
Intermittent reinforcement	Technique used by narcissists to keep their victims hooked to them by giving them unpredictable, varying wins.
Introverted Narcissist	Also called a Closet, Covert or Vulnerable Narcissist.

Term	Definition
Invisible child	The child who is not seen or heard by the narcissist, whose siblings may be cast in the roles of golden child or scapegoat by the narcissistic parent.
Kubler-Ross model	A 5 stage grief process model consisting of denial, anger, bargaining, depression and finally, acceptance relevant in the loss of a relationship.
Love-bombing	Also called the 'idealisation' phase. The initial stage of a relationship with a narcissist.
Malignant Narcissist	Another name for a Devaluing or Toxic Narcissist.
Mask	The mask is the outward projection of the narcissist's false self. But when the narcissist does not get enough narcissistic supply or enough of what he or she wants from their target, the mask will drop, to reveal their true nature. See also false persona.
Narcissistic abuse	This is mostly covert emotional abuse but physical abuse can also be a feature of narcissistic behaviour.
Narcissistic injury	This occurs when the narcissist's outer bubble is punctured; when the protective suit of armour is penetrated by some external event. It could be a perceived personal slight which brings on the injury, or any situation in which things do not go the narcissist's way. It leads to narcissistic rage.
Narcissistic Personality Disorder	Personality disorder characterised by a pattern of exaggerated feelings of self-importance, an excessive craving for admiration and low levels of empathy.
Narcissistic pseudologic	A typical narcissist's communication style which includes multiple contradictions, irrational conclusions, and loose associations between ideas.
Narcissistic rage	Intense fury as a consequence of narcissistic injury.

Term	Definition
Narcissistic supply	Narcissists need 'feeding' attention, in some form or other, to maintain the fragile image that they present to the world. This external validation is what is termed 'narcissistic supply'. Without narcissistic supply those with NPD are forced to feel their own sense of unworthiness and shame. Almost everything a narcissist does is with the aim of securing narcissistic supply through attention, adoration, drama or conflict.
'No contact'	If at all possible, the spouse or partner of the narcissist should have no contact at all with the narcissist. However, if they share children, are still living under the same roof, or if they are involved in a joint business venture, this may not be possible. If it is possible, however, then they should block the narcissist from all methods of contact (including phone, email, social media, messaging apps, texts) and limit essential communication to taking place via solicitors. 'No contact' is the most effective way to remove narcissistic supply from a narcissist.
Object constancy	The ability to believe that a relationship is stable and intact, despite the presence of setbacks, conflict, or disagreements. Narcissists have not developed this ability, so they cannot see you as somebody they love, and someone who has angered them at the same time.
Overt Narcissist	Another name for an Exhibitionist or Grandiose Narcissist.
Passive aggression	Examples are silent treatment, lateness, procrastinating on jobs, sabotaging other's work and name calling and insults re-framed as jokes.

Term	Definition
Projection	A psychological defence mechanism unconsciously used by many people, but by all narcissists. Anyone who finds it difficult to accept their failures, weaknesses, poor behaviours and own less flattering traits may unwittingly use projection as a way of feeling better about themselves, by accusing another person of exhibiting those traits or carrying out those behaviours. Essentially they are assigning those imperfect or flawed parts of themselves to other people.
Projective identification	If a victim has been gas-lit for years, it is quite common for them to take on, believe and identify with whatever it is that the narcissist is projecting on to them. This is called 'projective identification'. They come to believe what the narcissist is telling them about themselves.
Rescuers	Rescuers need to rescue others to feel needed and to matter, and although they may think their rescuing tendencies are generous in nature, in fact, even with non-narcissists, they are dis-empowering to the recipient. A narcissist will exploit this trait time and time again, pulling the target into the drama triangle and keeping them there by playing the victim.
Scapegoat	The child of a narcissist who is blamed, shamed and can do nothing right – the golden child's opposite number.
Shamedumping	Giving away ('dumping') feelings of deep shame to others, so that they do not have to feel the shame themselves – characteristic of narcissists.
Spectrum of narcissism	Narcissism exists on a spectrum. Those at the lowest end of the spectrum, who do not feel special, are the echoists. Those at the opposite end of the spectrum are the narcissists who are blind to the needs and feelings of others, concerned only with meeting their own needs to feel special.

Term	Definition
Toxic Narcissist	Another name for a Devaluing or Malignant Narcissist.
Trauma bonding	The neurochemical addiction of a victim to the narcissist, as a result of their intermittent reinforcement schedule of rewards.
Triangulation	Where the narcissist brings a third person into the equation, playing them off the others in the triangle. That person will often be another unwitting victim of the narcissist, who is being groomed by the narcissist as another source of narcissistic supply.
Vulnerable Narcissist	Another name for a Closet, Covert or Introverted Narcissist.
Whole object relations	This is the capacity to integrate the liked and disliked parts of a person into a single, realistic, stable picture – as opposed to alternating between seeing the person as either all-good or all-bad, as narcissists do. The ability to see people as being a mix of good and bad traits.
Word salad	The nonsensical style of communication from a narcissist after they have descended into narcissistic rage – illogical and ranting in nature, with very loose associations between ideas.

Further reading

Rethinking Narcissism: The Secret to Recognizing and Coping with Narcissists by Dr Craig Malkin

Co-dependency for dummies by Darlene Lancer

The Narcissism Epidemic: Living in the Age of Entitlement by Jean M. Twenge and W. Keith Campbell

Disarming the Narcissist by Wendy T Behari

Why We Sleep: The New Science of Sleep and Dreams by Matthew Walker

Divorcing A Narcissist: The Lure, The Loss & The Law by Dr Supriya McKenna and Karin Walker

Narcissism as addiction to esteem by Baumeister and Vohs

The American Psychiatric Publishing Textbook of Personality Disorders by Torgersen, S. Epidemiology. Oldham JM, Skodol AE, Bender DS

Prevalence, correlates, disability, and comorbidity of DSM-IV narcissistic personality disorder: Results from the Wave 2 National Epidemiologic Survey on Alcohol and Related Conditions by Stinson F, Dawson D, Goldstein R, et al

The bright side of dark: Exploring the positive effect of narcissism on perceived stress through mental toughness. Personality and Individual Differences by Kostas A. Papageorgiou, Foteini-Maria Gianniou, Paul Wilson, Giovanni B. Moneta, Delfina Bilello, Peter J. Clough

The positive effect of narcissism on depressive symptoms through mental toughness: Narcissism may be a dark trait but it does help with seeing the world less grey by Kostas A. Papageorgiou, Andrew Denovan, Neil Dagnall

Understanding the better than average effect: Motives (still) matter. Personality and social psychology bulletin 2012 by Brown JD

Burnout and Compassion Fatigue: What Lawyers Need to Know by Lee Norton, Jennifer Johnson, and George Woods

Patterns of Sedentary Behavior and Mortality in U.S. Middle-Aged and Older Adults: A National Cohort Study by Keith M. Diaz, PhD, Virginia J. Howard, PhD, Brent Hutto, MSPH, Natalie Colabianchi, PhD

Recovery during Lunch Breaks: Testing Long-Term Relations with Energy Levels at Work by Korpela K, Kinnunen U, Geurts S, de Bloom J, Sianoja M

Productivity Through Coffee Breaks: Changing Social Networks by Changing Break Structure by Waber BN, Olguin Olguin D, Kim T, Pentland A

The Emerging Self (1993) by James F Masterson

Parent-child attachment and internalizing symptoms in childhood and adolescence: a review of empirical findings and future directions, Dev Psychopathol. 2010 Winter; 22(1): 177-203 by Brumariu LE and Kerns KA

Index